D1571946

SOCIETY FOR NEW TESTAMENT STUDIES
MONOGRAPH SERIES

GENERAL EDITOR
MATTHEW BLACK, D.D., F.B.A.

ASSOCIATE EDITOR
R. McL. WILSON

31

THE NEW TESTAMENT CONCEPT OF WITNESS

THE NEW TESTAMENT
CONCEPT OF
WITNESS

ALLISON A. TRITES

Associate Professor of Biblical Studies
Acadia Divinity College, Acadia University, Wolfville, Nova Scotia

CAMBRIDGE UNIVERSITY PRESS

CAMBRIDGE

LONDON · NEW YORK · MELBOURNE

Published by the Syndics of the Cambridge University Press
The Pitt Building, Trumpington Street, Cambridge CB2 1RP
Bentley House, 200 Euston Road, London NW1 2DB
32 East 57th Street, New York, NY 10022, USA
296 Beaconsfield Parade, Middle Park, Melbourne 3206, Australia

First published 1977

Printed in Great Britain
at the
University Printing House, Cambridge

Library of Congress cataloguing in publication data

Trites, Allison A.   1936–
The New Testament concept of witness.

(Monograph series – Society for New Testament studies; 31)
Bibliography: p.
Includes index.
1. Witness bearing (Christianity) – Biblical teaching.
2. Witnesses – Biblical teaching.   I. Title.   II. Series: Studiorum
Novi Testamenti Societas.
Monograph series; 31.

BS2545.W54T74   268'.5   76–11067
ISBN 0 521 21015 1

CONTENTS

v

PREFACE

I wish to take this opportunity of expressing my thanks to the Beaverbrook Foundation, the American Philosophical Society and the Canada Council for their financial support of this research; to Principal G. H. Davies and Dr G. Pearce of Regent's Park College for their guidance during the early stages of the investigation; to Professor G. D. Kilpatrick, the Rev. D. E. Whiteley and Professor A. R. C. Leaney for their comments on an earlier draft (my thesis); to Professor C. F. D. Moule and Dr Colin Hemer for their helpful advice in preparing the manuscript for publication; to Dr M. R. Cherry and Dr A. J. Langley of Acadia Divinity College for their encouragement and to the college itself for granting me a sabbatical to complete my revision and prepare the manuscript for publication; and to St Deiniol's Library, Hawarden and Tyndale House, Cambridge for the use of their research facilities. I cannot sufficiently express my gratitude to Dr G. B. Caird, Principal of Mansfield College, Oxford, whose acute and constructive criticism of my work was invaluable; I am also grateful for the editorial suggestions of Professors Matthew Black and Robert Wilson of St Andrews University, Scotland. Above all I owe a debt of gratitude to my family, both English and Canadian, for their interest and concern and to Eugenie my wife, whose love and patience have sustained me throughout the preparation of this book.

Acadia University, Wolfville, N.S.   ALLISON A. TRITES

ABBREVIATIONS

ABR	*Australian Biblical Review*
Aeg	*Aegyptus*

Arndt & Gingrich   W. F. Arndt and F. W. Gingrich, *A Greek–English Lexicon of the New Testament*, Cambridge, 1957.

ASTI	*Annual of the Swedish Theological Institute*
ATR	*Anglican Theological Review*
AUSS	*Andrews University Seminary Studies*
BC	*The Beginnings of Christianity* (ed. F. J. Foakes Jackson, K. Lake and H. J. Cadbury), 5 vols., London, 1920–33.
BETS	*Bulletin of the Evangelical Theological Society*
Bib	*Biblica*
BJRL	*Bulletin of the John Rylands Library*

Blass & Debrunner   F. Blass and A. Debrunner, *A Greek Grammar of the New Testament and Other Early Christian Literature* (tr. and ed. F. W. Funk), Cambridge, 1961

BR	*Biblical Research*
BS	*Bibliotheca Sacra*
BZ	*Biblische Zeitschrift*
BZAW	Beihefte zur *Zeitschrift für die alttestamentliche Wissenschaft*
CBQ	*Catholic Biblical Quarterly*
CBSC	Cambridge Bible for Schools and Colleges
CGT	Cambridge Greek Testament
CIG	*Corpus Inscriptionum Graecarum* (ed. A. Boeckh *et al.*), Berlin, 1828–77
CJT	*Canadian Journal of Theology*
CN	*Coniectanea Neotestamentica*
EeT	*Église et Théologie*
EQ	*Evangelical Quarterly*
ETL	*Ephemerides Theologicae Lovanienses*
EvTh	*Evangelische Theologie*
ExpT	*Expository Times*
GR	*Gordon Review*
HJ	*Hibbert Journal*
HTR	*Harvard Theological Review*
IB	*The Interpreter's Bible* (ed. G. A. Buttrick), 12 vols., New York, 1952–7
ICC	The International Critical Commentary
IDB	*The Interpreter's Dictionary of the Bible* (ed. G. A. Buttrick), 4 vols., New York, 1962.

Int	*Interpretation*
ITQ	*Irish Theological Quarterly*
JBL	*Journal of Biblical Literature*
JES	*Journal of Ecumenical Studies*
JTS	*Journal of Theological Studies*
LCL	Loeb Classical Library

Liddell & Scott H. G. Liddell and R. Scott, *A Greek–English Lexicon* (revised by H. S. Jones), Oxford, 1940

MNTC The Moffatt New Testament Commentary

Moulton & Milligan J. H. Moulton and G. Milligan, *The Vocabulary of the Greek Testament*, London, 1930

MTB	*McMaster Theological Bulletin*
NovT	*Novum Testamentum*
NRT	*Nouvelle Revue Théologique*
NTA	*New Testament Abstracts*
NTS	*New Testament Studies*

Peake *Peake's Commentary on the Bible*[2] (ed. M. Black and H. H. Rowley), London, 1962

PEQ	*Palestine Exploration Quarterly*
RB	*Revue Biblique*
RE	*Review and Expositor*
RHPR	*Revue d'histoire et de philosophie religieuses*
RQ	*Restoration Quarterly*
RSPT	*Revue des Sciences Philosophique et Théologique*
RTA	*Religious and Theological Abstracts*
RTP	*Revue de Théologie et de Philosophie*
RTR	*Reformed Theological Review*
SBT	Studies in Biblical Theology
Sc	*Scripture*
SEA	*Svensk Exegetisk Årsbok*
SJT	*Scottish Journal of Theology*

Strack–Billerbeck H. L. Strack and P. Billerbeck, *Kommentar zum Neuen Testament aus Talmud und Midrasch*, 5 vols., Munich, 1922

STRT Studia Theologica Rheno-Traiectina (ed. H. W. Obbink, A. A. van Ruler and W. C. van Unnik).

StudEv	*Studia Evangelica*
TaL	*Theology and Life*
TB	*The Tyndale Bulletin*
TDNT	*Theological Dictionary of the New Testament* (ET of *TWNT*, tr. and ed. G. W. Bromiley), Grand Rapids, 1964ff.
TF	*Theological Forum*
Them	*Themelios*
TT	*Theology Today*

TU   *Texte und Untersuchungen zur Geschichte der altchristlichen Literatur*

TWNT   *Theologisches Wörterbuch zum Neuen Testament* (ed. G. Kittel; now G. Friedrich), Stuttgart, 1933ff.

VE   *Vox Evangelica*

VT   *Vetus Testamentum*

WTJ   *Westminster Theological Journal*

ZNW   *Zeitschrift für die neutestamentliche Wissenschaft*

CHAPTER I

INTRODUCTION

In 1936 C. H. Dodd wrote his famous book on the preaching of the apostolic church.[1] In it he argued that there was a definite pattern to the preaching of the apostles, which he sought to explain in terms of the kerygma. Dodd's book was widely acclaimed and exercised an immense influence on New Testament scholarship. However, it had the unfortunate effect of magnifying the term kerygma at the expense of other equally important words which the New Testament uses to describe the Christian message. It is this danger to which E. G. Selwyn points in the *Festschrift* for C. H. Dodd:

I sometimes wonder whether the term κήρυγμα has not been worked too hard, and whether the word μαρτυρία and its cognates would not better describe the primitive and indispensable core of the Christian message. At any rate, if we examine the comparative occurrences in the New Testament of the two sets of terms, we find that the occurrences of the verbs alone which speak of 'witness' considerably outnumber the occurrences of κηρύσσειν, while the occurrences of the noun μαρτυρία outnumber those of the noun κήρυγμα by more than six to one. There is nothing here which will make C. H. Dodd's *The Apostolic Preaching and Its Developments* less important than it was when it first appeared. But there is room for another monograph on the Apostolic testimony.[2]

In fact, F. L. Fisher thinks that 'a thorough study of witnessing would necessitate a study of the whole Bible'.[3] The present work is an attempt to fill this need.

To begin this study, however, is to confront a fundamental difference in scholarly opinion about the development and use of the idea of witness in the New Testament. On the one hand, there are some writers who believe that the idea of witness is by

---

[1] C. H. Dodd, *The Apostolic Preaching and Its Developments* (London, 1936).

[2] E. G. Selwyn, 'Eschatology in I Peter', *The Background of the New Testament and Its Eschatology*, eds. W. D. Davies and D. Daube (Cambridge, 1956), p. 395.

[3] F. L. Fisher, 'Witness, Testimony', *Baker's Dictionary of Theology*, ed. E. F. Harrison (Grand Rapids, 1960), p. 555. On the whole range of problems connected with testimony see E. Castelli *et al.*, *La Testimonianza* (Padua: CEDAM- Casa Editrice Dott., 1972).

no means a dead metaphor in the New Testament. 'The term "witness" expresses somewhat more strongly [than κηρύσσειν] the opposition to the foolishness, the obstinacy, and unbelief of a world that will not put its trust in Christ. The term "witness" suggests something of the atmosphere of a trial, a lawsuit between Christ and the world, in which the apostles are witnesses.'[1] The same general position is held by Robert V. Moss, Jr:

Like other terms as 'judge' and 'justification' in biblical language, the term 'witness' has been borrowed from the language of the law-court by the teachers and writers of ancient Israel and the early church. The term of course appears in its legal sense in both the Old Testament and the New Testament, where witnesses are called to appear for testimony in a court of law, but its most significant use is to be found in its metaphorical extension to the calling of Israel and the church to serve as 'witnesses' for God in the world...the term 'witness' retains something of its original juridical meaning and Israel and the church are regarded as God's witnesses.[2]

On the other hand, there are exegetes who have held that witnessing was inseparably related to suffering for the Christian *martys*.[3]

This latter approach has arisen partly from the fact that the English word 'martyr' comes from the Greek word *martys*, and partly from the close relation that developed in the early church between the two ideas.[4] Here some remarks of R. P. Casey are pertinent:

[1] J. H. Bavinck, *An Introduction to the Science of Missions* (Philadelphia, 1961), p. 66. Cf. T. Preiss, *Life in Christ* (London, 1954), pp. 9–34.

[2] R. V. Moss, Jr, 'The witnessing church in the New Testament', *TaL*, 3 (1960), 262. Cf. S. de Dietrich, '"You are my witnesses"', *Int*, 8 (1954), 273–9. D. Dunn Wilson, 'The biblical background of *martys* and its derivatives with special reference to the New Testament', M.A. thesis, University of Birmingham, England, 1958.

[3] Cf. H.-W. Surkau, *Martyrien in jüdischer und frühchristlicher Zeit* (Göttingen, 1938), H. von Campenhausen, *Die Idee des Martyriums in der alten Kirche* (Göttingen, 1936), and literature cited in Arndt-Gingrich, p. 495. J. M. Boice, *Witness and Revelation in the Gospel of John* (Grand Rapids, 1970), p. 16, provides a useful summary of the debate about the witness terminology from Kattenbusch (1903) to Brox (1961).

[4] Cf. G. Fitzer, 'Der Begriff des *Martys* im Judentum und Urchristentum', Inaugural Dissertation, University of Breslau, 1929; T. W. Manson, 'Martyrs and martyrdom', *BJRL*, 39 (1957), 463–84; W. H. C. Frend,

In orienting investigation to this point, it has not been sufficiently recognized that the transition from 'witness' to 'martyr' represents only one development of meaning, and that several others, instead of contributing directly to what later became the standard usage, ran parallel courses which were briefer but which possess considerable independent interest for the history of early Christian thought. All of these developments begin with a metaphorical application of the legal term, but all do not converge at the point where μάρτυς first clearly and unmistakably signifies a witness who died for Christianity.[1]

It is our purpose to explore these developments as fully as possible in order to determine their significance for the New Testament concept of witness. The use of witnesses in the Old Testament will also be examined in detail.

To commence our study, however, some consideration must be given to the use of μάρτυς and its cognates in secular Greek, noting the legal situations in which they are employed. Attention will also be directed to the use of witnesses and evidence in non-legal situations, and to witnesses to convictions.

Martyrdom and Persecution in the Early Church (Oxford, 1965), pp. 1–103; J. Downing, 'Jesus and martyrdom', *JTS*, N.S. 14 (1963), 279–93, and T. E. Pollard, 'Martyrdom and resurrection in the New Testament', *BJRL*, 55 (1972), 240–51 – all of whom trace the roots of Jewish and Christian theologies of martyrdom back to the Maccabean revolt.

[1] R. P. Casey, 'Appended note on *martys*', *BC*, v, 31.

CHAPTER 2

THE WITNESS TERMINOLOGY OF SECULAR GREEK

THE USE OF WITNESSES IN HOMER

To understand the New Testament concept of witness it is necessary to study the vocabulary of witness in secular Greek, and also to look at the places where the idea may be found though the word itself is absent. This approach can be pursued with real profit, provided one constantly bears in mind James Barr's justifiable criticism of the linguistic fallacies frequently practised by philologists and theologians.[1]

First, attention may be directed to the famous trial scene depicted on the Shield of Achilles (*Iliad*, xviii.497–508). Here justice is a community affair, and one finds a real parallel to the Old Testament concept of justice in the gate. The elders in both cases are entitled to speak and take sides, and their function is to arbitrate disputes with a view to the welfare of the community.[2] Here judges and witnesses are not really differentiated; the ἵστωρ is both the one who helps a man to justice and the one who decides the case. His function as a daysman or arbitrator is not unlike the Old Testament *goʾēl* who takes the side of the litigant in a lawsuit. The Homeric passage sheds light on the place of the community in settling disputes in the ancient world, and the importance of legal procedure for the preservation of community life.

In Homer μάρτυρες are not mentioned in disputes involving arbitration. While the word μαρτυρίη appears in the *Odyssey*, it is not used in the technical sense of a witness in a lawsuit (*Odyssey*, xi.325). Occasionally, the word μάρτυρος is used of those familiar with some event or situation (*Iliad*, 1.338; ii.302), but they are not summoned either as formal or general witnesses.

---

[1] J. Barr, *The Semantics of Biblical Language* (Oxford, 1961).

[2] W. Leaf, ed., *The Iliad* (London, 1907), pp. 311–14, who compares the Homeric trial scene with the ancient judicial proceeding known to Roman law as the 'Legis Actio Sacramenti'.

THE USE OF WITNESSES IN DEMOSTHENES, ARISTOPHANES, ETC.[1]

According to Bonner–Smith, witnesses first appear in Hesiod,[2] and are certainly used in Athens before the time of Solon.[3] In the orators the litigant is generally represented as summoning his opponent with at least two witnesses (Isaeus, III.19).[4] In emergencies, however, a man might have to rely on those present to give testimony on his behalf (Aristophanes, *Clouds*, 494–6). The difficulty would arise when a vital matter depended on the testimony of a man who for some reason might not wish to testify; under such conditions, testimony could be demanded (Isaeus, IX.18). If the person had no knowledge of the matter, he could make a formal denial under oath (Aristophanes, *Ecclesiazusae*, 1026; Elephantine Papyri, XXXIV.1). On the other hand, if the person failed to appear to give testimony, legal action could be taken against him (Demosthenes, XLIX.19).

The only citizens competent to serve as witnesses in Greek courts were adult males. According to Demosthenes (XL.58), parties to a suit were not competent in their own cases. Certain types of information could be given in a speech without direct confirmation (Demosthenes, IV.23–4; XXVII.40). Sometimes a man could find no supporting witnesses, so he had to go to court simply with his speech (Isocrates, XXI; Antiphon, I). Such unconfirmed statements were sometimes believed (Demosthenes, XLIII.9–10, 30); in this respect Greek legal procedure differed from its Hebrew counterpart. Occasionally the advocate himself might be a witness (Isaeus, XII.4; Aeschines, II.170,184).

Another type of corroboration to which Athenian speakers appeal is the knowledge of the dicasts. Naturally the dicasts could be called upon as confirmatory witnesses only in matters

---

[1] For full details see R. J. Bonner and G. E. Smith, *The Administration of Justice from Homer to Aristotle* (2 vols., Chicago, 1938). On legal terms in Greek and Latin literature see C. D. Buck, *A Dictionary of Selected Synonyms in the Principal Indo-European Languages* (London, 1949), pp. 1419–61.

[2] Bonner–Smith, *op. cit.*, I, 49.

[3] *Ibid.* I, 173ff. For a useful collection of the Attic orators see R. C. Jebb, *Selections from the Attic Orators* (London, 1888).

[4] Unlike the OT, however, only one witness was required (Aristophanes, *Clouds* 1218; *Wasps* 1408, 1416), and occasionally witnesses were entirely absent (Isocrates XXI).

of public knowledge (Demosthenes, XXI.18). The force of such arguments was to remind the court of the public evidence which was favourable to the accused.

Hearsay evidence was strictly forbidden in Athenian courts (Demosthenes, LVIII.4);[1] the only exception to this occurred when the person who knew the facts was either dead or ineligible.[2] Otherwise, the witness must confine himself to matters of which he had personal knowledge (Demosthenes, XLVI.6).

On the other hand, the evidence of persons unable to attend court could be taken in writing before witnesses, and they in turn could later attest the statement of the original witness by means of an affidavit (Aeschines, II.19; Demosthenes, XLVI.7). The evidence was not taken by an official appointed by the court, for it was the task of the litigant who desired the evidence.

Certain people were incompetent in Greek courts. Women were not allowed as witnesses; the same was true of minors (except in homicide cases),[3] though on reaching majority they could testify on what they had known as minors.[4] The testimony of slaves was inadmissible except when given under torture,[5] and the evidence of interested parties was frowned upon (Demosthenes, XL.58). The failure of a party to appear in court or to give his testimony was sufficient evidence for a verdict (Lycurgus, 117; Demosthenes, XXXI.81; Lysias, VI.24; XII.7).[6]

In ancient Greece it was considered important to plead a cause effectively (Xenophon, *Memorabilia*, IV.8.1). In Athens a whole class of professional speech-writers developed to supply litigants with clever speeches. These paid special attention to the grounds on which the credibility of a witness could be attacked, such as: (1) by showing that his accounts of the matter in question were inconsistent (Demosthenes, XXIV.II.18ff.,46), (2) by proving conclusively that his evidence was false (Isocrates, XVIII.53ff.), (3) by demonstrating that the witness was guilty of offences which discredited his testimony (Demosthenes, LIV.31–7).

[1] Bonner–Smith, *The Administration of Justice* II, 130ff.
[2] *Ibid.*   [3] *Ibid.* II, 221ff.
[4] J. H. Lipsius, M. H. Meier and G. F. Schömann, *Das Attische Recht und Rechtsverfahren* (Leipzig, 1905–15), p. 874, note 32.
[5] Bonner–Smith, *The Administration of Justice*, II, 223ff.
[6] However, if the verdict went against a man by default, he could appeal. Cf. Lipsius, *op. cit.*, pp. 973ff.

THE USE OF WITNESSES IN ARISTOTLE

The Art of Rhetoric has much to say about witnesses and evidence.[1] Aristotle distinguishes between 'technical' and 'nontechnical' proofs (I.xv.I; cf. I.ii.2). The former are arrived at by careful skill, and it is with this category that forensic oratory is concerned. The latter include all those immediate means of proof which 'have not been furnished by ourselves but were already in existence' (I.ii.2).

Aristotle breaks down this group into five subdivisions: laws, witnesses, covenants, oaths and tortures.

Aristotle recognizes two kinds of witnesses – ancient and recent. 'By ancient I mean the poets and men of repute whose judgments are known to all', thereby including in this category both the interpreters of oracles for the future and proverbs. On the other hand, 'by recent witnesses I mean all well-known persons who have given a decision on any point, for their decisions are useful to those who are arguing about similar cases'. In addition, recent witnesses may include 'those who share the risk of the trial, if they should be held to be perjurers'.

After stating the arguments in regard to testimony, the author concludes: 'The evidence of witnesses may refer either to ourselves or to our antagonist, and either to fact or to character. Plainly, then, one can never be at a loss for serviceable testimony.' In other words, Aristotle has carefully distinguished between μαρτυρίαι περὶ τοῦ πράγματος and μαρτυρίαι περὶ τοῦ ἤθους. While Aristotle surely intended both to be legally admissible evidence, the point of his distinction is that those who are competent to give evidence about the occurrence of a fact are not therefore competent to give evidence about its quality. This is the task of the νομοί or the μάρτυρες παλαιοί.

The Art of Rhetoric reminds us of the frequently unprincipled way in which witnesses were used. The rhetorical art sought to influence the judge or jury not simply with scientific evidence, but 'with gesture...the arrangement of words used...and the inflexions of the voice'.[2] Often resorting to deception and pseudo-

---

[1] Aristotle, *The 'Art' of Rhetoric*, LCL (London, 1926), I.xv.13–18 (xv.1431b), pp. 155–9.

[2] Quintilian, LCL (London, 1921), I, 171; I.x.22. Cf. Cicero, *De Oratore* II.xxvii.116.

logic, it played upon the emotions, seeking compassion, sometimes ridiculing the opponent. Naturally testimonies also played
a part, for a testimony served to illustrate an argument proved
before by means of logic. Thus when some probability of guilt
could be reached, false witnesses could easily be found to illustrate and demonstrate the make-believe truth of a charge. Other
considerations worked in the same direction. Though witnesses
were questioned by the man who called them, they were not
cross-examined by the advocate for the opposite side, nor were
they tested for trustworthiness.

Under these circumstances it is clear that the evidential value
of testimony in Greek courts of law was relatively low. By
training witnesses to act as practising rhetoricians, the Greeks
lost confidence in their integrity and credibility. Then, too,
there was no special adherence to the formal principle of
establishing everything at the mouth of two or three witnesses.
In both of these respects Greek legal procedure differed markedly
from that of the Old and New Testaments, where witnesses were
considered valuable in establishing the facts and where at least
two were required to prove a case.

THE USE OF Μάρτυς IN LEGAL CONTEXTS

With this background it is now fitting that some consideration
should be given to the word itself. The Greek word that is
translated by 'witness' is μάρτυς and with it belong three other
words of the same derivation: to witness – μαρτυρεῖν; the act
or content of witnessing – μαρτυρία; the testimony or proof
(in an objective sense) – μαρτύριον.[1] All of these words are
found in classical literature, and all are used in the New
Testament, sometimes in a legal context, sometimes in a legal
metaphor.

The common use of μάρτυς in secular Greek sheds considerable light upon the New Testament's use of the same word.[2]

[1] S. de Dietrich, '"You are my witnesses"', *Int.* 8 (1954), 273; cf. R.
Asting, *Die Verkündigung des Wortes im Urchristentum* (Stuttgart, 1939),
pp. 526ff.
[2] Cf. the Greek lexicons, esp. those of Liddell–Scott–Jones, Moulton and
Milligan, Arndt and Gingrich.

Fortunately, there seems to be no semantic problem about rendering μάρτυς into English, for the word contains no special problems or obscurities. While its usage is varied, its meaning appears to be straightforward, regular and intelligible. Essentially one can only repeat here what has already been learned.[1] Therefore, it is sufficient to determine the basic meaning of the word and to note its application to various types of situations and circumstances. For the actual proof texts in the Greek literature attention may be directed to the general survey of the evidence in Kittel's *Theologisches Wörterbuch*, now available in English.[2]

Μάρτυς is originally a juridical term applied to a witness in a court of law.[3] In order to qualify and be called as a witness, a special kind of knowledge is presupposed on the part of the witness. On the basis of this first-hand knowledge he can testify concerning disputed circumstances and events. So men present at the time of an occurrence and able to give an eye- or ear-witness account of what happened are frequently called upon to state what they have seen or heard. In other words, μάρτυς is used of one who has direct knowledge or experience of certain persons, events or circumstances and is therefore in a position to speak out and does so.[4] He may appear as a witness in a lawsuit, in which case he bears witness for or against someone, or as a witness in a number of different circumstances connected with the business of law.

Witnesses are often required to attest documents,[5] but even here witness is a by-product of the lawcourt, since their function is to attest the document in a lawcourt should the need arise. The Greek inscriptions and especially the papyri supply nume-

---

[1] For a useful summary of recent discussion on the witness terminology see J. M. Boice, *Witness and Revelation in the Gospel of John*, pp. 165–7.

[2] H. Strathmann, 'Μάρτυς', *TWNT*, IV, 477–520 and *TDNT*, IV, 474–514.

[3] Cf. Lipsius, *Das Attische Recht und Rechtsverfahren*, pp. 871–88, *et passim*.

[4] F. Kattenbusch, 'Die martyrtitel', *ZNW*, 4 (1903), 111, gives a similar definition. Cf. also Lipsius, *op. cit.*, p. 885.

[5] E. Leisi, *Der Zeuge im Attischen Recht* (Frauenfeld, 1908), pp. 142–56, discusses three kinds of witnesses: (1) gods used as witnesses in oaths, (2) witnesses in legal transactions, (3) witnesses in important acts concerning lawsuits. He cites an interesting example from Demosthenes (XLVIII.11) involving all three types in the attestation of a contract.

rous examples of witnesses to contracts, agreements and the like.[1] In the case of contracts, first of all there are the terms of the contract, followed by a formal conclusion such as ἡ συγγραφὴ κυρία. The term μάρτυρες then leads to the signature of the document in question. This general procedure is found in contracts concerning the buying of slaves,[2] loan contracts[3] and lease contracts.[4] In some cases the illustration takes the form of a double contract involving six witnesses.[5]

Similarly, in the case of wills, the basic Greek procedure remains unchanged, and the number of witnesses (six) is that required for an ordinary contract.[6] Usually an accurate personal description of the witness with all his characteristic scars, birthmarks, and the type of hair, etc., accompanies the listing of the witnesses.[7]

Witnesses often appear also in public records. So the Delphic records concerning sacred slave liberation regularly close with the phrase μάρτυρες οἱ ἱερεῖς καὶ οἱ ἰδιῶται or a similar one (*Corpus Inscriptionum Graecarum*, 1.1699,1702–6).

In other words, a man may appear as a witness in a lawsuit or in a considerable number and variety of activities connected with the law. In these circumstances μαρτυρεῖν means 'to be a witness', 'to appear as a witness', originally in the sense of 'to testify to something in a court of law', and μαρτυρία has first of all an abstract meaning – 'the bearing of a witness' and then it also comes to designate the witness itself.

[1] Cf. V. A. Tcherikover and A. Fuks, *Corpus Papyrorum Judaicarum* (3 vols., Cambridge, Mass., 1957ff.), who cite μάρτυρες in the following papyri: 1.6.18 (pp. 118ff.); XVIII.12.29 (pp. 148ff.); XXII.14.34 (pp. 158ff.); XXIV.23 (pp. 164ff.); XXV.20 (pp. 167f.). All examples are from Vol. I.

[2] Cf. P. L. H. Vincent, 'La Palestine dans les papyrus ptolémaïques de Gerza', *RB*, 29 (1920), 182f.; W. L. Westermann, 'Slave transfer: deed of sale with affidavit of vendor', *Aeg*, 13 (1933), 229ff.

[3] Cf. Friedrich Preisige and Friedrich Bilabel, *Sammelbuch griechischer Urkunden aus Ägypten* (5 vols., Berlin, 1915–50), III.6709.6.

[4] *Ibid.* III.6759.18.

[5] *Ibid.* v.7532.22ff.

[6] Cf. J. P. Mahaffy, *Cunningham Memoirs, No. 8, The Flinders Petrie Papyri* (Dublin, 1891), pp. 55ff., 1.19.30.

[7] Strathmann, *TDNT*, IV, 476 and *TWNT*, IV, 479.

THE USE OF Μαρτύριον

In contrast to μαρτυρεῖν and μαρτυρία, μαρτύριον exhibits no special affinity for the lawcourts, or for legal matters generally; it simply means 'evidence', literally or metaphorically. It is natural that there should be this difference; the act of giving evidence (μαρτυρία) is normally legal, the existence of an object as evidence (μαρτύριον) need not be. Numerous examples reveal the fact that μαρτύριον is used quite generally to refer to any immediate means of proof (e.g. Herodotus, VIII.120; Plato, *Laws*, XII.943c). Nevertheless, μαρτύριον is a by-product of the lawcourt, since its function is to provide evidence in a lawcourt should the need arise.

THE USE OF Μάρτυς AND ITS COGNATES IN NON-LEGAL CONTEXTS

It is very significant that the other technical terms also undergo extension, and are widely used in non-legal contexts. Thus there develops a very general application of μάρτυς, μαρτυρεῖν, and μαρτυρία beyond the legal sphere. Testimony is not restricted to immediate convictions and opinions of whose truth the speaker is convinced. Instead of the original situation where a witness to particular events or experiences was in view, now there is also the declaration of firmly held opinions. In this latter case one is dealing with contents whose very nature excludes empirical verification. The trustworthiness of the witness now rests in his unique conviction.

THE USE OF DIVINE WITNESSES

The idea of witness can also be extended to deity.[1] Just as men call upon their fellows to serve as witnesses to agreements, solemn affirmations and declarations, so they call upon God by

[1] Leisi, *Der Zeuge im Attischen Recht*, p. 142, notes the frequent use of the verbs ἐπιμαρτύρεσθαι and μαρτύρεσθαι in this connection. Cf. Cicero, *Topica*, xx.77: 'The testimony of the gods is at times adduced...in order to win conviction.'

means of an affirmation or oath to bear witness to the truth of what they say or to the facts of an agreement. In such cases the tacit assumption is that if one dishonestly or deceitfully calls upon the deity (i.e. if he lies or later breaks the agreement), he will be subject to the deity's displeasure and liable to severe punishment.[1]

THE USE OF WITNESSES IN PLATO'S 'GORGIAS'

The rhetorical use of witnesses is directly challenged in Plato's *Gorgias* (XXVII–XXXI, 471E–475E). A testimony is not true just because many and carefully scrutinized witnesses stand behind it, for these may in fact be false witnesses. In Socrates's view concern for the facts must be the supreme consideration. Through rational discussion of the issue the truth comes to light, and convinces a person rationally. He who has been convinced is termed a 'witness', that is, an announcer of the facts of the case. It is this concept which is presented in the *Gorgias*, e.g., XXIX(474)[2] and XXXI(475E).[3]

Plato has clearly seen the distinction between two concepts of witness, and has advocated the factual concept as the only true and worthwhile one. In his concern for the facts Plato has moved in the direction of the biblical concept of witness, but he differs from it in his attitude to a minimal number of witnesses. Instead of the formal principle of a number of witnesses, Plato would place the testimony of one man whose truthfulness and integrity can stand the test of rational cross-examination.

But testimony in Plato can mean 'the attestation of an opinion which someone cherishes' or 'the truth of which one is convinced'. In such cases, it is not a question of testimony concerning facts or proceedings, but a question of opinions or convictions which one approves, expresses and believes. The witness takes a stand for the truths of which he is convinced. Thus the trial of Socrates shows that the practical act of being willing to stand for one's convictions is necessary when the testimony is given against the background of hostility and persecution.[4]

[1] Strathmann, *TDNT*, IV, 478 (*TWNT*, IV, 481).
[2] Plato, *Works*, LCL (10 vols., London, 1925), V, 351.   [3] *Ibid.* p. 359.
[4] Cf. Plato's *Apology*, where the idea of witness in a real court of law is evident by the use of legal words such as κατήγορος, κατηγορία, κατηγορεῖν,

THE USE OF WITNESSES IN EPICTETUS

The ideas which Plato developed without using the actual word μάρτυς were later developed by others, and are found, for example, in the writings of Epictetus (c. A.D. 110), where the word μάρτυς is used. Here the genuine philosopher is his own witness for his mode of life. He stands the test as a μάρτυς if he is willing to suffer for God in the face of his accusers when they would question the divine government of the world (*Discourses*, 1.29.46ff.).[1]

In fidelity to his convictions, the Stoic-Cynic philosopher bears witness not only with his lips, but also with his life, accepting all kinds of difficulty and suffering as the divine will. He patiently endures, for he believes that he has been called into this very situation by God. In this behaviour his μαρτυρία consists (*Discourses*, III.26.28).[2]

Under certain circumstances the philosopher's testimony may involve his death, but that idea is not fundamental to Epictetus's understanding of μάρτυς.[3] Nevertheless, Epictetus exhibits a tendency to treat μάρτυς as a dead metaphor by largely ignoring the forensic background of witness and virtually identifying it with the idea of suffering or conflict. Epictetus is concerned with the notion that true μαρτυρία entails not only the spoken word, but also the manful courage to stand up for one's convictions in hard times and through practical, concrete deeds (*Discourses*, III.24.110).

The idea of witness and the idea of suffering or conflict, then, come very close together in times of persecution, as has been noted in the writings of Plato and Epictetus. However, these two ideas rest upon two quite different frames of reference. The idea of witness is used either literally or metaphorically with

ἀπολογία, ἀπολογεῖσθαι, μάρτυς, ἔγκλημα. This usage illumines the NT concept of witness, for all these words also appear in the NT, generally with reference to real courts of law or in forensic metaphors. Note also the word τεκμήριον, which means 'proof' and which occurs in both the *Apology* (24d) and the New Testament (Acts 1: 3).

[1] Epictetus, *The Discourses*, LCL (2 vols., London, 1926–8), I, 199; cf. II, 221 (III.24.112).

[2] *Ibid.* II, 237. Cf. T. A. Langford, 'Giovanni Miegge on Jesus as a martyr', *Int*, 18 (1964), 183–90.

[3] N. Brox, *Zeuge und Märtyrer* (Munich, 1962), p. 178.

reference to a court of law, whereas the idea of conflict is used either literally or metaphorically with reference to a battlefield. While Plato recognizes the close relation of the forensic and military images to each other, he restricts the word μάρτυς to its proper forensic frame of reference. Unlike Epictetus, Plato and the New Testament as well generally employ the idea of witness as a live metaphor, and therefore it is to be understood mainly in the light of the lawcourt and the metaphorical application of legal terms.

THE USE OF WITNESSES IN HISTORIOGRAPHY

So far attention has largely been focused on the use of witnesses and evidence in legal contexts, but both may be concerned with non-legal matters, as in the case of historical evidence. In this connection it is worthwhile noting the way Herodotus uses evidence.[1] He clearly recognizes the different kinds of evidence on which his narrative rests (II.99.1), and thus discriminates between that part of Egyptian history which rests upon the testimony of the priests (II.142.1) and that part which rests upon independent confirmatory testimony (II.147.1). He values eye-witness testimony (III.115), and realizes the need of testing and examining all the evidence (IV.154; V.85f.; VI.14).

A similar concern for reliable evidence in a non-legal context is observable in Thucydides (c. 460–395 B.C.). Concerning the use of speeches in historiography Thucydides claims he has reproduced what seemed to him the most probable and appropriate language, preserving as faithfully as possible the general sense – i.e. he gives what he can accurately, but the speeches are in the main what he thought appropriate.[2]

Here again the idea of witness is prominent, though the word is not used. Stress is placed upon an 'exact knowledge of facts' which is to be gleaned by sifting the evidence of those who were actually eye-witnesses of the events themselves. Recognition is given to the problem occasioned by the disagreement of wit-

---

[1] Cf. W. W. How and J. Wells, *A Commentary on Herodotus* (2 vols., Oxford, 1912), I, 33–4, who cite the pertinent passages.

[2] Thucydides, I.22, trans. A. J. Toynbee, *Greek Historical Thought* (London, 1952), pp. 40–1.

nesses, and the need of cross-examination of the evidence by the historian is admitted. Moreover, the place of speeches in historical writing and their use in producing 'a permanent contribution to knowledge' is acknowledged and defined in a way which sheds considerable light upon the concept of witness reflected in the speeches of the Book of Acts.

Polybius is another ancient historian who uses the idea of witness in non-legal contexts. In addition to literary sources and official documents, Polybius strongly insists on the questioning of eye-witnesses. Indeed, this is one reason for his choice of 220 B.C. as the opening date for his main history (IV.2.2); evidence for events of an earlier date would be mere hearsay, and would serve as a safe foundation for neither judgments nor statements of fact (IV.2.3). He saw it as part of his task to interview those who had actually taken part in important events and who could therefore testify concerning them (XII.40.2–5). In other words, he places the strongest possible emphasis upon the importance of witnesses to facts for historiography.

SUMMARY

Witnesses appeared frequently in Greek lawcourts and in a variety of legal transactions. They were often used in non-legal contexts, for example, in historiography. Wherever they were employed to establish facts, they emphasized the importance that the Greeks (and the ancients generally) attached to evidence. It is true that Greek concern for facts was weakened by the misuse of rhetoric in the hands of unscrupulous witnesses, but Plato reasserted the importance of the facts to a worthwhile concept of witness. The same concern for the facts is evident in the writings of the Greek historians, as evidenced in the writings of Herodotus, Thucydides and Polybius. The Greeks also had a place for witnesses to convictions, and loyalty to convictions might involve witnessing against a background of persecution in perilous times. Both witnesses to facts and witnesses to convictions are of the greatest significance for the New Testament concept of witness.

CHAPTER 3

THE WITNESS TERMINOLOGY
OF THE SEPTUAGINT

The Old Testament of the early church was the Septuagint
(hereafter called the LXX). The New Testament quotes mainly
from this text, and in this way the terminology of the Old
Testament frequently enters the New Testament. As with many
other words, the witness terms found in the New Testament have
been greatly influenced by the terminology of the LXX, and
are to be understood, in large measure, from it. Fortunately, the
usage of μάρτυς and its cognates is intelligible in the great
majority of cases.[1]

THE LEGAL USE OF Μάρτυς, Μαρτυρεῖν, Μαρτυρία

Μάρτυς belongs to the legal sphere in the LXX. It signifies first
of all one who bears witness before a judgment is made,
especially the witness for the prosecution (Num. 5: 13; 35: 30;
Deut. 17: 6f.; 19: 15). At least two witnesses were required to
establish any charge, and this was accepted as a fundamental
principle of Jewish law (Num. 35: 30; Deut. 17: 6; 19: 15; cf. I
(III) Kgs 21: 13; Sanhedrin 9b). From the complaints and
assertions of the Psalms and Proverbs the crooked witness was a
notorious figure; accordingly, the μάρτυς ἄδικος, δόλιος and
ψευδής are particularly abhorrent (Ex. 23: 1; Psa. 26(27): 12;
34(35): 11; Prov. 6: 19; 12: 17; 19: 5, 9; 21: 38).[2] So serious
was the witness's responsibility that he must cast the first stone
in the event of a death sentence (Deut. 17: 7; cf. 13: 9; Acts 7:
58; Mishnah, Sanhedrin vi.4a); in some cases warning by
witnesses to refrain from a forbidden practice was required for a
court's subsequent imposition of the death sentence (Pesikta
x.8, commenting on Ex. 32:27).

Important contracts and solemn agreements required wit-

[1] For the philological details see Strathmann, *TDNT*, iv, 482–6 and
TWNT, iv, 484–9.
[2] Strathmann, *TDNT*, iv, 483 and *TWNT*, iv, 488.

nesses, and it is this 'witness of a contract' that is meant in Jer. 32(39): 10, 12, 25, 44 and Ruth 4: 9–11.[1] In other passages, it is a question of eye- or ear-witnesses to a proceeding (Lev. 5: 1; Isa. 8: 2).

An application is readily made to God in all these relations. He is called as a witness to an agreement between David and Jonathan in I Sam. (I Kgs) 20: 23, 42, and as a witness to the agreement of the Jews striving with Jeremiah concerning Egypt (Jer. 42(49): 5). When there is no witness to substantiate the innocence or prove the guilt of the suspected person, God is called to witness by means of a solemn asseveration or oath (Ex. 22: 10f.; cf. I (III) Kgs 8: 31–2). This theme also appears in I Sam. (I Kgs) 12: 5f., where Samuel calls upon God as a witness to his innocence, and it recurs in Job 16: 19, where Yahweh acts as a witness to Job's innocence. God also serves as a witness when trial is by ordeal (Num. 5: 16–22; cf. Sotah II and Numbers Rabbah IX.10, which cites Mal. 3: 5).

On the other hand, God appears as a witness in judgment in Mal. 3: 5 and Jer. 29(36): 23; and in his lawcourt the Song of Moses bears witness against Israel (Deut. 31: 19, 21)[2] and the Israelites appear as witnesses against themselves (Josh. 24: 22).

Μαρτυρεῖν appears in the legal sense of 'to bear witness in a court of law' in Num. 35: 30, Deut. 19: 18 and 31: 19, 21. In Lam. 2: 13 it simply means 'say' or 'declare'. Μαρτυρία has a forensic connotation in Ex. 20: 16, Deut. 5: 17(20) and Prov. 25: 18. In a few other places the meaning is unclear, as in Ex. 21: 36, I Sam. (I Kgs) 9: 24, I (III) Kgs 17: 20, and II Chron. 28: 10.

All these passages appear quite ordinary when they are compared with the common extra-biblical usage of secular Greek.

[1] The Code of Hammurabi also required witnesses to a contract (Section 7); see C. Edwards, *The Hammurabi Code: and the Sinaitic Legislation* (London, 1921), pp. 14–15.

[2] Cf. M. G. Kline, *The Structure of Biblical Authority* (Grand Rapids, 1972), *passim*, and D. J. McCarthy, *Old Testament Covenant* (Oxford, 1972), p. 38, n. 7.

THE USE OF Μαρτύριον

Μαρτύριον means a piece of objective evidence or an immediate means of proof. It can be a demonstration of the factuality of an event or the correctness of an assertion. So Ruth 4: 7 makes the removal of a man's shoe the evidence for the cessation of his previous claims. Similarly, the seven lambs which Abimelech receives from Abraham serve as evidence of the fact that Abraham has dug the wells of Beer-sheba (Gen. 21: 30). Jacob and Laban make a covenant to refrain from aggression on each other's territories and erect a cairn whose existence is to serve as an evidence of that covenant (Gen. 31: 44). In the same way the tribes of Reuben and Gad and the half tribe of Manasseh build an altar in the borders of Jordan not for burnt offerings and sacrifices, but as evidence of the reported arrangement (Josh. 22: 27). Even the Davidic dynasty provides evidence of God's grace and power; it is a μαρτύριον ἐν ἔθνεσιν (Isa. 55: 3-4).

Evidence for the factuality of an event can serve to accuse people. In Josh. 24: 27, for instance, the people of Israel, having made their vow to serve the Lord, are reminded by Joshua that the stone which he has set up by the sanctuary serves as evidence for the facts of the covenant with God; if Israel breaks this covenant, the stone assumes a threatening function. So also the book of the law, like the Song of Moses, serves as evidence for the prosecution, εἰς μαρτύριον ἐν ὑμῖν (Deut. 31: 19, 26). In Hos. 2: 14(LXX) God is to lay waste settlements of Israel εἰς μαρτύριον, that is, as evidence of the reality of their sins and as evidence of the reality of his judgment upon them. Μαρτύριον is also used, however, to refer to the revelation of God especially in the phrases σκηνὴ τοῦ μαρτυρίου (Num. 1: 50, 53; 10: 11; II Chron. 24: 6) and κιβωτὸς τοῦ μαρτυρίου (Ex. 26: 33, 34; 40: 21; Lev. 16: 2; Num. 7: 89). This revelation has been achieved through the instrumentality of Moses, and its contents are the commandments of God. 'The full appropriation of the word μαρτύριον and its plural μαρτύρια for the self-witness of God in the Mosaic legislation is a highly significant process for the development of Old Testament nomism.'[1]

The witness terminology of the LXX reveals a number of

---

[1] Strathmann, *TDNT*, IV, 486 and *TWNT*, IV, 489.

ways in which μαρτύριον has developed variations from the original sense of the Hebrew equivalents. These variations cannot simply be attributed to carelessness or ignorance on the part of the LXX translators, since at times they show an acute awareness of what they are doing. This is the case when they equate μαρτύριον with *mô'ēd* in the Pentateuch, for here the translation is the characteristic product of a Torah-centred theology. On the other hand, sometimes the translators misread the text and produced a meaning foreign to the original Hebrew; but such cases are almost accidental and could not in the nature of things result in semantic change.

CHAPTER 4

THE USE OF CONTROVERSY IN THE
OLD TESTAMENT

THE LEGAL ASSEMBLY IN ISRAELITE LIFE

We turn now to the witness in his setting in the Old Testament controversy. Fortunately, considerable work has been done on this subject in recent years, so it will be sufficient to indicate the main lines of development, and to refer the reader to the works of Gemser,[1] Köhler,[2] and McKenzie.[3]

In early Israel legal disputes were settled by justice in the gate (Deut. 25: 7–10; Josh. 20: 4; Job 5: 4; Psa. 127: 5). The legal proceedings were held in an open place, generally in the square by the town gate (Deut. 21: 19; Job 29: 7; Prov. 22: 22; Isa. 29: 21; Amos 5: 10, 12, 15; Zech. 8: 16). There the accuser summoned his witnesses and the accused with his witnesses, together with the elders of the place who would consider the case. There was no public prosecutor; as in Greek courts, the injured party must bring the action. When the people gathered at the gate, the accuser or his *go'ēl* (Ruth 3: 12; 4: 1–11; cf. Job 19: 25; Jer. 50: 34) began the legal dispute; he charged the accused with a certain matter, and sought to prove the truth of his charge. For this purpose he summoned his witnesses. Then the accused would be challenged to bring forward counter witnesses on the other side. Before the proceedings were finished, both litigants and their respective witnesses probably spoke several times. Then, as in Homer's judgment scene on the Shield of Achilles (*Iliad* XVIII. 497–508), the elders discussed the matter among themselves, paying most attention to those who had a reputation for making wise and just decisions (cf. Job 29: 7–10, 21f.). When common agreements had been reached, they rose to announce their decision (Isa. 3: 13; Jer. 26: 16–19); some-

---

[1] B. Gemser, 'The *rîb* or controversy-pattern in Hebrew mentality', *Wisdom in Israel and in the Ancient Near East*, eds. M. Noth and D. W. Thomas (Leiden, 1960), pp. 120–37.

[2] L. Köhler, *Hebrew Man* (London, 1956), pp. 149–75.

[3] D. A. McKenzie, 'Judicial procedure at the town gate', *VT*, 14 (1964), 100–4; cf. R. de Vaux, *Ancient Israel* (London, 1961), pp. 155–7.

times the king would act in this capacity (II Sam. 15: 1–6; I Kgs 20: 40). The royal role is particularly striking in two juridical parables where the king is addressed as a judge in order to lead him unwittingly to pass sentence upon himself (II Sam. 12: 1–14; 14: 1–20).[1]

The Book of Ruth gives an excellent picture of such an assembly (Ruth 4: 1–2).[2] A citizen of Bethlehem desires to settle a dispute concerning the law of inheritance. The controversy is handled by 'the elders of the city', who sit in the gates and function as judges (cf. Prov. 31: 23; Deut. 16: 18). Here is a vivid illustration of justice in the gate.

There are other examples of such a process of judgment to be found in both biblical and extra-biblical sources. An illustration of the former is Jeremiah's controversy with the prophets, priests and people of Jerusalem (Jer. 26). An instance of the latter is found in one of the Mari texts, 'which involves a judgment given at the "gate" by the assembly of the city leaders and the mayor' (ARM III.73: 11–15).[3]

The chief method of proof was the testimony of witnesses. These witnesses were not in any sense merely objective informants.[4] Their role was similar to that played in a modern lawsuit by the counsel for the defence and the counsel for the prosecution. Thus the Hebrew word '$\bar{e}\underline{d}$ is used both of witnesses for (Isa. 8: 2; Jer. 32: 10; Job 16: 19) and against the accused (Num. 5: 13; Josh. 24: 22; I Sam. 12: 5). It was a serious thing to make false accusation, and in property cases this could result in double compensation to the party falsely accused (Ex. 22: 9).

Judges and witnesses were not always differentiated. The same man, in fact, might serve as witness and judge in the same legal assembly (Ruth 4: 11; cf. Mic. 1: 2; Zeph. 3: 8; Mal. 3: 5; Psa. 50: 6–7; Rosh Hashanah 25b).

Unlike Greek courts, no one could be condemned by the declaration of a single witness (Num. 35: 30; Deut. 17: 6f.;

[1] Cf. U. Simon, 'The poor man's ewe-lamb – an example of a juridical parable', *Bib*, 48 (1967), 221.
[2] Köhler, *Hebrew Man*, p. 151. Cf. E. W. Heaton, *Everyday Life in Old Testament Times* (London and New York, 1956), p. 61.
[3] A. Marzal, 'Mari clauses in "casuistic" and "apodictic" styles', *CBQ*, 33 (1971), 343, cf. p. 496.
[4] J. Jeremias, *Jesus' Promise to the Nations* (London, 1958), p. 44.

19: 15; cf. Sotah 2b; Baba Bathra 31b).[1] It is true that the parents of a stubborn son could bring him before the elders without witnesses, but even here a statement was probably expected from both parents (Deut. 21: 18–21). Generally speaking, the law demanded the concurrent testimony of at least two persons (cf. Numbers Rabbah ix. 29; CD ix. 16 – x. 3).[2]

Thus for hundreds of years in the villages and towns of Palestine the legal assembly met in the open air and administered justice. Its proceedings were generally by word of mouth, though in later times written accusations also seem to have been known (Job 31: 35f.). Justice in the gate dealt with such matters as rights to a well, a right of way, a theft of someone's cattle, an assault which had a serious sequel or a claim to an inheritance. To judge in these circumstances did not mean to condemn (though *šāpaṭ* occasionally had that meaning, e.g., Psa. 109: 31; Ezek. 23: 45), but rather to give assistance to justice. So the psalmist's prayer, 'Judge me, O God' is not a cry of the guilty for punishment, but the cry of the persecuted for help in the gaining of justice (Psa. 7: 8; 26: 1; 35: 24; 43: 1); to judge and to help are parallel ideas in Hebrew.[3]

These observations on the Old Testament legal assembly are important for a number of reasons. In the first place, they shed light on the task of witnesses and advocates in both the Old Testament and the New. In the Old Testament legal assembly the same man was both witness and advocate. He did not attempt to win a verdict from the judge but to convince his opponent and elicit an acknowledgment of surrender from him. Several examples of this type of forensic situation may be cited here. The dispute between Judah and Tamar, for instance, is a case in point (Gen. 38: 24–6; cf. Sotah 10b). Judah states the accusation, Tamar produces the evidence in the form of the signet, bracelets and staff, and forces Judah to 'acknowledge' it. A comparable recognition of evidence occurs in the preceding

[1] Köhler, *Hebrew Man*, p. 159, notes that if the nature of the case excluded the possibility of witnesses, the accused person had to vindicate himself by oath before the priests at the sanctuary.

[2] Cf. H. van Vliet, *No Single Testimony*, STRT, IV (Utrecht, 1958).

[3] Köhler, *Hebrew Man*, pp. 156–7. Cf. L. Morris, *The Biblical Doctrine of Judgment* (London, 1960), *passim*.

chapter where Jacob admits as legally admissible evidence Joseph's blood-stained coat by 'discerning' it (Gen. 37: 32f.; the Hiph'il of *nākar* is used in both cases, as it is in Gen. 31: 32; Deut. 21: 17). Similarly, if a man is entrusted with an animal and it is torn by a wild beast, he is to bring the mangled animal to its owner 'as evidence' which will convince the owner of his innocence (Ex. 22: 13; cf. Amos 3: 12; Baba Kamma 112a).[1] So serious was the need for evidence that a man on divorcing his wife was required to furnish her with a formal certificate of divorce (Deut. 24: 1, 3; cf. Mt. 5: 31; 19: 7; Mk 10: 4). This theme of producing witnesses or evidence is used in the lawcourt scenes of Isa. 40–55 (e.g., Isa. 43: 9; 45: 21), and it is basic to a proper understanding of the Paraclete passages in the Fourth Gospel.

In the second place, the Old Testament legal assembly helps the reader to appreciate the forensic character of the apostolic testimony – a point especially stressed in the Book of Acts. The emphasis upon persuasion, argument, reasoning and debate reflects the lawcourt background of the Old Testament legal assembly.

Thirdly, the Old Testament legal assembly illumines the use of witnesses in the Fourth Gospel; in particular it clarifies the Johannine references to accusing witnesses such as Moses and Abraham (Jn 5: 45; 8: 40, 56). Fourthly, the Old Testament lawsuit helps to explain the argumentative quality of the first twelve chapters of John's Gospel, which are patterned after the Old Testament controversy.

Nor is this all that can be said. The legal assembly, according to the *lex talionis*, punished false witness with the punishment due to the offence which it sought to establish (Deut. 19: 16ff.; cf. Code of Hammurabi, Section 3); this principle is given very interesting application in the New Testament (Rev. 11: 13ff.). And then we should note that the legal assembly, sometimes called the ἐκκλησία (Sir. 26: 5; 38: 33), prohibited false witness (Ex. 20: 16; Deut. 5: 20; Prov. 14: 5, 25; 19: 5, 9, 28); this probably explains Paul's abhorrence of it in I Cor. 15: 15.

Everything which has been written so far about the legal assembly has presupposed the frequency of disputes. This theme

[1] For other examples cf. D. Daube, *Studies in Biblical Law* (Cambridge, 1947), pp. 6ff.

receives such prominence in the Old Testament that it deserves special treatment in its own right.

FREQUENCY OF QUARRELLING IN ISRAELITE LIFE

The frequency of disputes in the life of the ancient Hebrews is amply attested in the Old Testament. The Book of Genesis is full of such quarrelling (Gen. 13: 5ff.; 21: 25–32; 26: 18–22; 31: 25–55). Bickering marred Israel's life in the wilderness (e.g., Num. 16: 1–11; 20: 3ff.), and Moses, according to the Deuteronomic tradition, complains of the people's contentiousness (Deut. 1: 12).

Disputes could arise over the virginity of a young woman, a fact reflected in the laws concerning chastity (Deut. 22: 13–21). In such cases the parents of the young woman were to 'take and bring out the tokens of her virginity to the elders of the city in the gate' as evidence that the charges made against her by her husband were unfounded. Here is another picture of justice in the gate with the elders serving as judges who arbitrate the dispute.

There is a dispute between two halves of the Israelite community in Joshua 22, and there are disputes in the Book of Judges (8: 1–3; 12: 1–6), not to mention the later encounters between Samuel and Saul (I Sam. 15: 10–35), David and Nabal (I Sam. 25: 39), David and Nathan (II Sam. 12: 1–15), Elijah and Ahab (I Kgs 21: 17–19),[1] Nehemiah and his contemporaries (Neh. 5: 7; 13: 11; 17: 25). Quarrelling was so common that Israel's 'wise men' frequently found it necessary to warn their pupils against it; indeed more than twenty proverbs provide evidence of their unending attack upon the vice.[2]

---

[1] Cf. F. I. Anderson, 'The socio-juridical character of the Naboth incident', *JBL*, 85 (1966), 46–57.

[2] Gemser, 'The *rîb* or controversy-pattern in Hebrew mentality', pp. 120–2. Cf. J. Begrich, *Studien zu Deuterojesaja* (Munich, 1963), p. 27, n. 72, and J. Limburg, 'The root *rîb* and the prophetic lawsuit speeches', *JBL*, 88 (1969), 291–304. The problem of strife is also recognized in the New Testament, particularly in the Pauline Epistles (Rom. 1: 29; 13: 13; I Cor. 1: 11; 3: 3; II Cor. 12: 20; Gal. 5: 20; Phil. 1: 15; cf. I Tim. 6: 4; Tit. 3: 9).

TERMINOLOGY

Since legal texts of the Old Testament do not give a clear picture of the course of judicial proceedings, one must look elsewhere for knowledge of the legal terminology of ancient Israel. Fortunately, this evidence has been collected and ably presented by B. Gemser in the H. H. Rowley *Festschrift*, and when a few details are added, one cannot do better than call attention to the evidence which has been assembled there.[1]

THE CONTROVERSY IN THE BOOK OF JOB

Perhaps the longest controversy in the Bible is found in the Book of Job.[2] Here in chapters 3–31 there is a whole series of individual speeches made by four speakers, who form two parties. Job sets out a statement, or rather he makes a complaint (3: 3–26). A friend answers him, reproaching him and contradicting him. Job speaks again without showing himself convinced; a second and a third friend interchange speech with him. This dialogue form is repeated a second time with all the speakers, and Job clearly represents the opposition; it is repeated even a third time, except that the third friend says nothing more. Finally, Job sums up in his last speech, which gives passionate expression to his own conviction of innocence and includes a conditional self-cursing of the accused, who in this way seeks to establish his innocence before the legal assembly (31: 1–40).

Now it is precisely the formal aspect of Job which is of interest to us. Job's speeches on the one side and the speeches of his 'friends' on the other are controversy speeches; this is clear

[1] Gemser, *op. cit.*, pp. 122–5. Cf. also McKenzie, 'Judicial procedure at the town gate', Begrich, *op. cit.*, p. 39, and Limburg, *op. cit.*, pp. 293–9.

In rabbinic judicial procedure it was normal practice for the litigants to stand and the judges to sit (Shebu'oth 30a, 30b; Tosefta, Sanhedrin VI.2). Cf. R. B. Ward, 'Partiality in the assembly: James 2: 2–4', *HTR*, 62 (1969), 87–97 and G. F. Moore, *Judaism* (Cambridge, 1927), II, 182.

[2] Cf. Köhler, *Hebrew Man*, pp. 158–61 and G. von Rad, *Old Testament Theology* (London, 1962), I, 409, who sees Job in the prologue and epilogue as a '*martys*, a witness in the best sense of the term, for he took up a clearly positive attitude to a concern of God's.'

2-2

from their construction. Speech and counter-speech continue back and forth until one side has nothing more to say. When a speaker withdraws from the controversy, he signifies this by putting his hand over his mouth (Job 21: 5; 29: 9; 40: 4; cf. Judg. 18: 19; Mic. 7: 16).

The controversy pattern explains the lack of real progress in the thought. The intention is not, as in Platonic dialogue, to find truth in speech and counter-speech, but the presentation of a point of view already determined beforehand with such forcefulness as to persuade the listeners. Indeed, one might well say that the aim is to 'talk them round'. The same method is used throughout these chapters, in so far as the content does not suppress the forms which belong to the legal assembly. Job, in fact, is a rich source of information on the vocabulary of the Old Testament lawsuit.

In other words, the Book of Job from a formal point of view can be understood as the record of a lawsuit between Job and God. So Job can say: 'I desire to dispute with God' (Job 13: 3), or complain: 'Yet he has discovered a charge against me, and he has reckoned me as an adversary' (Job 33: 10, LXX). On one side Job appears as prosecutor and plaintiff. On the other side Job's 'friends' appear as witnesses to vindicate God's honour and as judges to condemn Job. God himself is the accused, whom Job wishes would appear in court that he might be argued with, though ultimately the judge of both Job and his friends.[1] The forensic pattern of these speeches, their use of juridical questions (e.g., Job 13: 7–9; cf. Isa. 41: 2, 4, 26), their lack of any real progress in thought and their attempt to persuade by 'talking the opponent round' – all these are reasons why the Book of Job is of particular value in understanding the biblical use of the controversy motif.

[1] Cf. E. R. Fairweather, 'The Christian humanism of Thomas Aquinas', *CJT*, 12 (1966), 194–210, who thinks Thomas 'presents the discussion between Job and his friends as a kind of academic *disputatio* and introduces the Almighty, at the beginning of the great utterances, as the *quaestionis determinator* – the master who decisively concludes the debate' (p. 201).

LAWCOURT LANGUAGE IN RELIGIOUS NAMES,
PHRASES AND PSALMS

Lawcourt language frequently appears in traditional religious phrases, for example, in some Hebrew personal names which are really condensed prayers.[1] Thus the name Jehoiarib (I Chron. 9: 10; 24: 7) and its contracted form Joiarib (Ezra 8: 16; Neh. 11: 5, 10; 12: 6, 19) not only refer to specific persons but also express the prayer: 'May Yahweh (as judge) contend the cause for the bearer of the name.' Another illustration of lawcourt language in traditional phrases is the use of the local names Massah ('Proof') and Meribah ('Contention'), which recalls Israel's fault finding in the wilderness (Ex. 17: 1–7; Num. 20: 1–13; cf. Num. 27: 12–14; Deut. 6: 16; 9: 22; Psa. 95: 8; 106: 32). Similarly note the shortened forms Jeribai (I Chron. 11: 46) and Ribai (II Sam. 23: 29; I Chron. 11: 31).

In the Psalms the psalmist cries out to God for help, using traditional lawcourt language. In one place he prays: 'Contend, O Lord, with those who contend with me' (Psa. 119: 154). In the beautiful psalm passage added to the Book of Micah it is evident that it is the divine Judge who is asked to 'plead the cause' of his persecuted worshipper (Mic. 7: 9; cf. Psa. 74: 22). Similarly in the prophets, blessing can be promised to faithful Israel by him who pledges: 'I will plead your cause' (Jer. 51: 36; 50: 34; cf. Isa. 49: 25; 51: 22).

There are about twenty-six Psalms in which lawcourt language and imagery occur. A good example is Psalm 50, which speaks of Yahweh as the divine Judge who summons his people to appear in court (50: 1–6; cf. Deut. 4: 26; 32: 1; Isa. 1: 2). Then follows his indictment against them: 'Hear, O my people, and I will speak, O Israel, I will testify against you' (50: 7ff.; cf. 50: 21). This psalm is particularly instructive because the judge has become the accuser in the same lawsuit.

Often the phraseology of the Psalms is thoroughly juridical, but in other cases the image of the lawcourt is interchanged with others. Psalm 35, for instance, is full of the language of the lawcourt (1ff.; 4ff.; 7ff.; 19–28) but its use of the controversy is interspersed with the images of a battle (2f.), hunting (7f.) and

---

[1] For other examples see Gemser, 'The rîb or controversy-pattern in Hebrew mentality', pp. 125–8.

wild animals (17, 25). Note also Psalms 17 and 109 for other illustrations of the juxtaposition of juridical and non-juridical metaphors. Similarly in Psalm 110 we 'have now moved from the vindication of a defendant in a lawsuit to that of a warrior on the battlefield...evidence of the way in which different themes and a variety of different metaphors cross and overlap and interlace'.[1] In other words, it is no exaggeration to say that lawcourt language is prominent in the Psalms.

LAWCOURT LANGUAGE IN OATHS

Lawcourt language also appears in the use of oaths. In ancient times when no human witness was present it was natural to invoke the deity by means of an oath (Ex. 22: 10f.; Isa. 65: 16; cf. Cicero, *Topica* xx. 77). Since there is a good deal on oaths in the Bible, it is useful to consider the material under several headings.[2]

The nature of oaths

An oath can be defined as 'a calling upon God to attest the truthfulness of one's assertions or promises'. Thus every oath implies two things: first, a declaration or promise, and second, an appeal to the all-knowing and all-powerful Judge who punishes falsehoods (cf. Wisd. 14: 29–31). Lying under oath was considered a serious offence, for it involved a violation of the Third Commandment (Ex. 20: 7; Deut. 5: 11; cf. Zech. 5: 3f.; I Tim. 1: 9f.). The following points may be noted in connection with the nature of oaths:

(1) The principle on which an oath is held to be binding is incidentally laid down in Heb. 6: 16 viz., as an ultimate appeal to divine

[1] C. F. D. Moule, *The Phenomenon of the New Testament* (London, 1967), p. 83. Cf. H. Schmidt, *Das Gebet der Angeklagten im Alten Testament* (Berlin, 1928), *passim*.

[2] On the biblical terms for oaths see A. A. Trites, 'The New Testament conception of witness', a D.Phil. dissertation deposited in the Bodleian Library, Oxford University (1968), chapter 4, and G. Ferries, *A Dictionary of the Bible* (Edinburgh, 1900), III, 575; cf. A. C. Zenos, *A New Standard Bible Dictionary*, ed. M. W. Jacobus *et al.* (New York, 1936), and H. C. Brichto, *The Problem of 'Curse' in the Hebrew Bible*, JBL Monograph Series, Vol. 13 (Philadelphia, 1963).

authority to ratify an assertion... (2) On the same principle that oath has always been held most binding which appealed to the highest authority both as regards individuals and communities. (a) Thus believers in...[God] appealed to him, both judicially and extra-judicially. (b) Appeals of this kind to authorities recognized respectively by adjuring parties were regarded as bonds of international security [e.g., II Chron. 36: 13], and their infraction as being not only grounds of international complaint, but also offenses against divine justice. (3) As a consequence of this principle, (a) appeals to God's name on the one hand, and to heathen deities on the other, are treated in Scripture as tests of allegiance...[Deut. 6: 13; Isa. 48: 1; Jer. 12: 16]. (b) So also the sovereign's name is sometimes used as a form of obligation (Gen. 42: 15; II Sam. 11: 11; 14: 19). (4) Other forms of oath, serious or frivolous, are mentioned, some of which are condemned by our Lord (Matt. 5: 33; 23: 16–22; comp. James 5: 12), yet he did not refuse the solemn adjuration of the high priest (Matt. 26: 63, 64).[1]

Occasions

Oaths were used in the Old Testament under the following circumstances:

(1) Agreement or stipulation for performance of certain acts (Gen. 14: 22; 24: 2, 8, 9 etc.). (2) Allegiance to a sovereign, or obedience from an inferior to a superior (Eccles. 8: 2; II Chron. 36: 13; I Kings 18: 10). (3) Promissory oath of a ruler (Josh. 6: 26; I Sam. 14: 24, 28, etc.)... (4) Vow made in the form of an oath (Lev. 5: 4 [cf. the use of εὐχή in Jon. 1: 16 and Acts 18: 18; 21: 23]). (5) Judicial oaths. Public or judicial oaths were required on the following occasions: (a) A man receiving a pledge from a neighbour was required, in case of injury happening to the pledge, to clear himself by an oath of the blame of damage (Ex. 22: 10, 11; I Kings 8: 31; II Chron. 6: 22). (b) A person suspected of having found, or otherwise come into possession of lost property, was to vindicate himself by an oath (Lev. 6: 3). It appears that witnesses were examined on oath; a false witness, or one guilty of suppression of the truth, was to be severely punished (Lev. 5: 1; Prov. 29:24; Deut. 19: 16–19). (c) A wife

---

[1] M. F. Unger, 'Oath', *Unger's Bible Dictionary* (Chicago, 1957), p. 800. On oaths in rabbinic literature see J. Rapponoport, 'Oath', *The Jewish Encyclopedia* (12 vols., New York, 1905), IX, 365–7 and cf. Yoma 74a. On the importance of oaths in Near Eastern vassal treaties see M. G. Kline, *By Oath Consigned* (Grand Rapids, 1968), p. 21. Kline also notes that oaths were required by the Essenes, according to Josephus (*Wars* II, 8, 7f.), and at Qumran (1 QS 1, 16ff.; v, 8ff.), for entrance into the covenant.

suspected of incontinence was required to clear herself by oath (Num. 5: 19–22).[1]

Professor Judge has advanced the interesting suggestion that an oath of personal loyalty to the Caesarian household may provide an explanation of the 'decrees of Caesar' mentioned in Acts 17: 7.[2]

Forms of oaths

Oaths appear in the Old Testament in many different forms. A common oath was: 'May the Lord do so to me and more also, if' I do or fail to do such and such (Ruth 1: 17; I Sam. 3: 17; 14: 44; II Sam. 3: 9, 35; I Kgs 2: 23; II Kgs 6: 31). Even more common was the phrase: 'As the Lord lives' (Judges 8: 19; Ruth 3: 13; I Sam. 14: 39, 45; 19: 6; 20: 21; 26: 10, 16; 28: 10; 29: 6; II Sam. 2: 27; I Kgs 2: 24; 18: 10; Jer. 12: 16; 38: 16; Hos. 4: 15). An unusual form appears in the Joseph story, where Joseph twice is said to make solemn affirmations 'by the life of Pharaoh' (Gen. 42: 15, 16). Other oath formulae were: 'As the Lord lives and as your soul lives' (I Sam. 20: 3; 25: 26; cf. II Sam. 11: 11); 'As the Lord lives and as my lord the king lives' (II Sam. 15: 21; cf. I Sam. 17: 55); 'The Lord is between you and me for ever' (I Sam. 20: 23); 'The God of Abraham judge between us' (Gen. 31: 53). M. H. Pope's comment here is helpful: 'As God is the guardian of the oath and fulfils or nullifies the curses in accordance with justice, one may make his asseveration an oath by calling God to witness (Gen. 31: 50; I Sam. 12: 5; 20: 23 (reading 'ēdh instead of 'adh); II Cor. 1: 23; Gal. 1: 20; Phil. 1: 8) or to watch (Gen. 31: 49) or to judge (Gen. 31: 53).'[3]

In New Testament times Jews were swearing 'by heaven', 'by the earth', 'by Jerusalem', 'by your head' and 'by the temple' (Mt. 5: 34; 23: 16; James 5: 12). Some oaths were regarded as binding, others were not (ὀφείλει, Mt. 23: 16, 18) –

[1] Unger, op. cit. Oaths were sometimes used in juridical parables (e.g., II Sam. 12: 5; 14: 11–19). J. M. Robinson, *The Problem of History in Mark* (London, 1957), p. 37, notes an unusual use of an oath in Mk 5: 7, but cf. Acts 19: 13 and Paris Magical Papyrus, line 13, cited in C. K. Barrett, *New Testament Documents* (London, 1957), p. 32.

[2] E. A. Judge, 'The decrees of Caesar at Thessalonica', *RTR*, 30 (1971), 1–7.

[3] M. H. Pope, 'Oaths', *IDB* (4 vols.; New York, 1962), III, 576.

a casuistical distinction condemned by Jesus. Both Herod the tetrarch and Simon Peter make sinful oaths but the formula used in each case is not given (Mk 6: 22–8; Mt. 14: 6–11; 26: 72).

Divine oaths

In many passages of scripture reference is made to God swearing or committing himself to a promise by an oath: e.g. the promises made to the patriarchs (Gen. 50: 24; cf. Sir. 44: 21; Lk. 1: 73–5) to David and his family (Psa. 89: 35–7; cf. Acts 2: 30) and to the priest-king of Psa. 110. Theodore Mueller throws light on this phenomenon:

On God's part an oath is his most holy and solemn asseveration of the absolute truth of his divine word (Num. 23: 19 [cf. Psa. 132: 11]) in order that his people may trust all the more in his promises (Isa. 45: 20–4). Since God cannot swear by anyone greater than himself (Heb. 6: 13), as men do (Heb. 6: 16), he swears by himself (Heb. 6: 13 [cf. Gen. 22: 16]), by his holiness (Psa. 89: 35), by his great name (Jer. 44: 26), by his life (Ezek. 33: 11 [cf. Jer. 22: 24; Ezek. 17: 16; Zeph. 2: 9; Rom. 14: 11]). The immutable God (Mal. 3: 6), however, swears not only to assure men of his fatherly love and mercy, but also to impress upon them as unfailingly sure his chastisements or punishments threatened to those who refuse to obey his divine word...(Psa. 11: 4–6; [cf. Num. 14: 21–3; Deut. 1: 34–5; I Sam. 3: 11–14; Jer. 22: 5; Ezek. 5: 11]). In particular, God has confirmed with a most solemn oath the sure hope of man's salvation through faith in Jesus... (Heb. 7: 20–8).[1]

Symbolic actions accompanying oaths

Oaths were frequently accompanied by certain symbolic actions. Here the following points should be borne in mind:

(1) Originally the oath of a covenant was taken by solemnly sacrificing *seven* animals, or it was attested by *seven* witnesses or pledges, consisting either of so many animals presented to the contracting party, or of memorials erected to testify to the act (Gen. 21: 28–31). (2) Lifting up the hand [was the gesture that generally accompanied an oath (Gen. 14: 22; Deut. 32: 40; Ezek. 44: 12)]. In

[1] J. T. Mueller, 'Oath', *Baker's Dictionary of Theology*, ed. E. F. Harrison (Grand Rapids, 1960), p. 382; cf. J. G. S. Thomson, 'Oaths', *New Bible Dictionary*, ed. J. G. Douglas (London, 1962), p. 902.

Dan. 12: 7 both hands are mentioned; in Psa. 144: 8; Isa. 62: 8 and Rev. 10: 5–6, the right hand. Thus to 'lift up (the hand)' meant to 'swear' ((יָד) נָשָׂא); cf. in NEB: Ex. 6: 8; Num. 14: 30; Neh. 9: 15; Ezek. 20: 5–6). Witnesses laid their hands on the head of the accused [in initiating execution by stoning (Lev. 24: 14; Deut. 17: 7; cf. Sus. 34)]. (3) Putting the hand under the thigh of the persons to whom the promise was made [for the genitals symbolized the mystery and power of generation] was an old form of oath (Gen. 24: 2, 9; 47: 29)... (4) Oaths were sometimes taken before the altar, or, as some understand the passage, if the persons were not in Jerusalem, in a position looking toward the temple (I Kgs 8: 31; II Chron. 6: 22). (5) Dividing a victim and passing between or distributing the pieces [was sometimes associated with the conclusion of a covenant] (Gen. 15: 10, 17; Jer. 34: 18).[1]

The use of Amen

'Amen' was the customary response made to an oath. In Deut. 27, for example, the six tribes on Mount Ebal respond to each of the curses by saying: 'Amen' (Deut. 27: 15–26). Similarly, the oath taken by Nehemiah's contemporaries is followed by the assembled people crying: 'Amen' (Neh. 5: 13; cf. Jer. 11: 5). Another interesting use appears in Num. 5, where the woman suspected of infidelity answers the priest's adjuration with the reply, 'Amen, Amen' (Num. 5: 19–22; cf. 1 QS 11.18). In all such cases, 'Amen' in oaths involves a 'solemn acknowledgement of the validity of a threat or a curse affecting oneself'.[2] Perhaps, then, the Old Testament use of 'Amen' in oaths is suggestive of the Fourth Gospel, as Dalman long ago suggested, 'The double ἀμήν, occurring 25 times in John...is not an oath yet more potent than a simple "verily", because it gives the hearer to understand that Jesus confirms His own statement in the same way as if it were an oath or a blessing.'[3]

[1] Unger, 'Oath', p. 801; cf. Pope, 'Oaths', p. 576.
[2] C. E. B. Cranfield, *The Gospel according to St. Mark* (Cambridge, 1959), pp. 139–40. Other examples are cited by A. J. B. Higgins, 'The words of Jesus according to St. John', *BJRL*, 49 (1967), 363–86, esp. pp. 371–2. On the 'juridical quality' of the oath in Num. 5 see J. M. Sasson, 'Numbers 5 and the "Waters of Judgement"', *BZ*, 16 (1972), 249–51.
[3] G. Dalman, *The Words of Jesus* (Edinburgh, 1902), pp. 227–9.

SUMMARY

To sum up, at several points the use of oaths is related to the idea of witness in the New Testament. This is particularly true of Paul's references to God as his witness, of the two immutable things mentioned in Heb. 6 and of the use of the reduplicated 'Amen' in the Fourth Gospel.

LAWCOURT LANGUAGE IN THE PREACHING OF
THE PROPHETS

Lawcourt language is put to good use by Israel's eighth-century prophets and their successors.[1] These prophets proclaim the unpalatable message that Yahweh has a controversy with his own people; this is why he summons and accuses, lays charges and pronounces sentence against Israel. Amos (2: 4–16), Hosea (2: 1ff.; chapters 4 and 5; 12: 2–14), Isaiah (1: 1–18; 3: 13–15; 5: 1–7), Micah (2: 6–11; 6: 1–2), Jeremiah (2: 9; 12: 1; 15: 10) and Ezekiel (chapter 17; 20: 33–44) all make use of controversy imagery and terminology.

Lawcourt language is also prominent in Isaiah 56–66. The controversy is still between Yahweh and his people, and the point at issue is the reason for Israel's plight and Yahweh's delay in delivering her from it (Isa. 59: 1–11). In Isa. 57: 3–13 some of the formal elements of a controversy appear in the summoning, interrogation, accusations, resumption of interrogation and threats. Compare the controversy in Isa. 58: 1–14, which is similar in character, and the picture of the divine vindicator in Isa. 63: 1–6, where the juridical image is mingled with those of the treader of the wine press, the warrior and the executioner.

The last canonical prophet is Malachi, who employs a question-and-answer method of stating his case.[2] Malachi's

---

[1] Gemser, 'The *rîb* or controversy-pattern in Hebrew mentality', pp. 128–33. Cf. H. B. Huffmon, 'The covenant lawsuit of the prophets', *JBL*, 78 (1959), 285–95, and Claus Westermann, *Basic Forms of Prophetic Speech* (London, 1967), who observes that in 'the legal procedure texts' (e.g., Hos. 2: 4–17) 'God speaks as the judge directly and without any introduction (by a messenger formula)' (p. 199).

[2] Cf. J. A. Fischer, 'Notes on the literary form and message of Malachi', *CBQ*, 34 (1972), 315–20.

controversies are real disputes with contemporaries, and his sermons represent the answers he gives as inspired by his God. Even so, it is noteworthy that Yahweh is pictured as the one who will 'approach them for judgment' and will be a 'swift witness' against the sinners among them (3: 5–13).

Thus from Amos to Malachi the theme of a controversy between God and his people is very much in evidence.

There is one more passage which Gemser has not mentioned but which is very interesting from a legal point of view. It occurs in Dan. 7: 9–14 where the Ancient of Days appears on a fiery throne surrounded by his court (I Kgs 22: 19); the record books are opened and judgment is given. Dan. 7 also describes 'one like a son of man' coming 'with the clouds of heaven' to receive 'dominion and glory and kingdom' (7: 13–14).

In other words it is fair to say that 'the sight of the administration of justice...was so familiar to the people that metaphors drawn from the lawcourt...have profoundly affected Hebrew idiom.'[1] These metaphors are of value in providing the necessary background for an understanding of the New Testament concept of witness.

[1] R. H. Kennett, *Ancient Hebrew Social Life and Custom* (London, 1933), p. 92.

CHAPTER 5

THE CONTROVERSY IN ISAIAH 40–55

In Isaiah 40–55 there are two controversies (one between Yahweh and the world and the other between Yahweh and Israel), and it is important not to confuse the one with the other. Still it is useful to list the legal ideas of Isaiah 40–55, without suggesting that they all belong to a single pattern. Then the results will be applied to understand the use of controversy in Isaiah 40–55. Finally, a few characteristics of the prophet's use of controversy will be brought forward for brief discussion.

THE CONTROVERSY PASSAGES

It may be helpful to list the main passages of Isaiah 40–55 which make use of the language of the lawsuit. They include:

(a) 41: 1–29. The trial of the nations is here dramatically presented. The literary character of the poem reflects its setting in the lawcourt. The formal characteristics of lawcourt speech are particularly evident in 41: 1–5, 21–4, 26.

(b) 43: 8–13. This poem depicts another trial scene like that of chapter 41, where all nations and Israel are summoned into the divine presence. Witnesses are very prominent in this passage.

(c) 43: 22–8. This passage has the markings of a controversy speech.

(d) 44: 7–8. Hebrew legal terms are used in this passage, and Israel is mentioned as Yahweh's witness.

(e) 45: 20–1. The imagery of the lawcourt is apparent here.

(f) 48: 14–16. The prophet returns to his favourite judgment scene, but the formal characteristics of a controversy are weak.

(g) 50: 1–2a. This appears to be a controversy speech; observe the barrage of pointed questions.

(h) 50: 7–9. Legal terminology is notable throughout this passage.

Lawcourt speech, in other words, occupies a place of considerable importance in the thought of Isaiah 40–55,[1] and its formal characteristics must now be examined.[2]

SOME FORMAL CHARACTERISTICS OF CONTROVERSY SPEECH

There may be passages in Isaiah 40–55 which are merely poetic in character, not implying any necessary reference to courtroom procedure or imagery (cf. Isa. 42: 18ff.). Many other passages, however, seem quite definitely to reflect the background and characteristics of the Hebrew lawcourt, and these may be listed under headings covering different aspects of legal procedure.

1. The Summons before the Court

Isa. 41: 1, 'Let them approach, then let them speak; let us draw near together for judgment!'

Isa. 41: 21, 'Set forth your case!' 'Bring forth your proofs!' 'Case' = *rîb* 'Proofs' = *'aṣûmôth*.

Isa. 41: 22, 'Let them bring them and tell us... Declare to us...!'

Isa. 43: 8, 'Bring forth the people!'

Isa. 43: 9, 'Let them bring out witnesses to prove their case!'

Isa. 48: 14, 'Assemble, all of you, and hear!'

Isa. 48: 16, 'Draw near to me, hear this!'

2. The Appeal to the Witnesses

Isa. 43: 10, 'You are my witnesses.'

Isa. 43: 12, 'You are my witnesses.'

Isa. 44: 8, 'You are my witnesses!'

---

[1] Cf. J. Fischer, *Das Buch Isaias* (2 vols., Bonn, 1939), II, 40–1 and J. Begrich, *Studien zu Deuterojesaja* (Munich, 1963), pp. 26–48. On the question of authorship cf. R. K. Harrison, *Introduction to the Old Testament* (London, 1970), pp. 764–95.

[2] See L. Köhler, *Deuterojesaja Stilkritisch Untersucht* (Giessen, 1923), sections 83–7; cf. H. E. von Waldow, 'The message of Deutero-Isaiah', *Int.*, 22 (1968), 259–87.

3. The Affirmation on Oath

Isa. 45: 23, 'By myself I have sworn, from my mouth has gone forth in righteousness a word that shall not return' (cf. Deut. 32: 40; Amos 6: 8).

Isa. 49: 18, 'As I live' – is Yahweh's declaration – 'you shall put them all on as an ornament, you shall bind them on as a bride does' (cf. Jer. 46: 18).

Isa. 54: 9, 'For as I have sworn that the waters of Noah should no more go over the earth, so have I sworn that I would not be wroth with you or rebuke you.'

4. The Accusation of the Adversary (which is cited in order to be refuted)

Isa. 40: 27, 'Why do you say, O Jacob, and speak, O Israel, "My way is hid from the Lord, and my right is disregarded by my God"?'

Isa. 49: 14, 'Zion says, "The Lord has forsaken me, my Lord has forgotten me."'

5. Questions in Juridical Speech

The use of the interrogative is very common in Isaiah 40–55 (e.g., 40: 6; 42: 19; 43: 19; 44: 19f.), but in 41: 2, 4, 26; 43: 9; 45: 21 and 50: 1–2a it is an example of juridical speech. The one party interrogates the other, questioning its explanations (41: 28). The purpose of the questions is to shift the burden of proof to one's opponent (cf. I Sam. 12: 3); this is why the counter-questions of the opponent are explained as illegitimate (Isa. 45: 21; cf. Gen. 31: 36, 37; Job 13: 7–9). The use of pointed questions by persons making charges against others was common in ancient Israel, and was not limited to formal law-suits (e.g., Gen. 44: 4; Ex. 2: 13; 17: 3; I Sam. 2: 23; 22: 13; 26: 15).[1]

[1] H. J. Boecker, *Redeformen des Rechtslebens im Alten Testament* (Neukirchen-Vluyn, 1964), p. 42.

6. The Challenge to the Opponent

The opponent is challenged to bring forward facts forgotten by the speaker which favour his case: 'Put me in remembrance, let us argue together; set forth your case, that you may be proved right' (43: 26). Similarly, whoever can raise a stronger claim is invited to submit and prove it: 'Does anyone claim to be my equal? Let him stand up and say so. Let him speak out and state his case to me' (44: 7; cf. Gen. 31: 32).

7. The Appeal to the Judge

The appeal to the righteousness of the judge is made in 49: 4, 'Surely my right (i.e. 'my judgment', *mišpāṭî*) is with the Lord, and my recompense with my God.'

8. The Pronouncement of the Verdict

Isa. 41: 11, 'Behold, all who are incensed against you shall be put to shame and confounded, those who strive against you shall be as nothing and shall perish.'

Isa. 41: 24, 'Behold, you are nothing and your work is nought; an abomination is he who chooses you.'

Isa. 41: 29, 'Behold, they are all delusions; their works are nothing; their molten images are empty wind.'

9. Some Technical Terms of Controversy Speech

Several technical terms of controversy speech appear in 50: 8–9. The *maṣdîk* is the one who declares that an accused person is not guilty. The *ba'al mišpāṭ* is any adversary, my opponent. 'This is the only example of the idiomatic use of *ba'al* ("owner") with *mišpāṭ* ("suit in law", "case"; cf. Job xiii. 18). It could presumably mean "my legal adviser", had there been any such in OT times. But quite obviously it means "my antagonist" or "accuser".'[1] The verb *hiršî'a* in 50: 9 means 'to declare someone guilty', that is, condemn him in a court of law.

In 51: 22 Yahweh is the one who 'pleads the cause of his people' (*yārîb 'ammô*), acting as helper in their lawsuit.

---

[1] C. R. North, *The Second Isaiah* (Oxford, 1964), p. 204.

10. Examples of Controversy Speeches

An appeal speech of the accused occurs in Isa. 43: 22–8 (cf. Gen. 31: 32, 36ff.; I Sam. 12: 1–5; 24: 9–15), and an appeal speech of the plaintiff appears in Isa. 41: 1–4 (cf. Gen. 16: 5; Isa. 1: 18–20; Lk. 15: 29). The speech of the plaintiff before the court can be seen in Isa. 44: 6–8 (cf. Isa. 1: 2–3; 3: 14–15; 5: 3–4; Psa. 50: 7ff., 16ff.), and the speech of the accused in Isa. 50: 1–2a (cf. Jer. 2: 5–13; Mic. 6: 3–5; Joel 3: 4–8). The speech of the judge is met in Isa. 41: 21–9 (cf. Psa. 82: 1–7). An example of a legal proceeding occurs in Isa. 43: 8–13.

THE CONTROVERSY

As the above material has shown, Isaiah 40–55 has made abundant use of lawcourt imagery and terminology. In no place is this more evident than Isa. 41: 1–29. This passage is full of technical terms of the ancient Hebrew lawcourt: the 'plaintiff, the witnesses, the bystanders, the accusation, the demand for a reply to the accusation and the verdict are all present'.[1]

The nations are summoned to court to participate in a controversy (41: 1). The dispute is between Yahweh and the pagan nations with their gods. After the nations are admonished to silence by the convener of the legal assembly (cf. Job 13: 13), Yahweh challenges them with the meaning of the events of contemporary history, particularly the stunning victories of Cyrus of Persia (41: 2–3). Yahweh declares that he is 'the first, and with the last', and therefore at work in the whole historical process (41: 4). The nations are frightened by Yahweh's appeal to history and seek security in the works of their hands (41: 5–7).

As the trial proceeds, the judge suddenly turns from the nations to address Israel: 'But you, Israel, my servant, Jacob whom I have chosen, the offspring of Abraham, my friend' (41: 8). Here reference is made to an 'I–thou' relationship between Yahweh (*'ᵃnî*) and Israel (*'attāh*). Note also that Israel is described as God's servant in terms which parallel her role as God's witness (cf. 41: 9 and 43: 10, 12); for this great task God

[1] J. Muilenburg, 'The Book of Isaiah, Chapters 40–66', *IB*, v, 448ff.

promises his help and strength (41: 10). A similar feature is apparent in the prologue and epilogue of Job, where Job functions as a witness in taking God's side (Job 1: 21; 2: 10; 42: 8) and is expressly described as 'my servant' (Job 1: 8; 2: 3; 42: 7, 8).

In verses 11–13 of Isa. 41 the nations are judged, and in verses 14–16 Israel is described as an instrument of divine judgment upon the nations. Then after a lyrical interlude on Yahweh's lordship over nature (verses 17–20) the trial is resumed (verses 21–4), though now it is the pagan gods themselves who are addressed (verse 23). As in 41: 1–2, Yahweh is both judge and accusing witness. The gods are asked to present their case (*rîb*, verse 21), but to the persistent challenge 'tell...tell...tell' they can make no reply. They have nothing to say about history and they cannot foretell, so the verdict is inevitable (verse 24).

But if the pagan gods are ignorant of the past and the future, it is quite different with Yahweh. He knows the past and the future, predicts what is to happen, and speaks through his messengers (41: 25–9). History has meaning, for it is under the sovereign control of Almighty God. It is to such truths as these that Israel is called to bear witness in Isa. 43: 8–13 in a passage which closely resembles Isa. 41.

In both Isa. 41 and Isa. 43 there is an appeal to history, to the 'former things'.[1] This is one of the most frequently repeated ideas in the first part of Isaiah 40–55 (41: 22; 42: 9, 18; 44: 7; 46: 9–11; 48: 3). 'Sometimes the stress lies on the event, sometimes on the prediction; but in reality the phrase includes both ideas – "past events as predicted".'[2] The challenge in both 41: 22 and 43: 9 is to produce past predictions which have subsequently been verified by the event. The silence of the pagan gods in Isa. 41 means that they lose their case. The trial of the nations concludes with the judge's pronouncement of the verdict (41: 29).

In 43: 8–13 another trial scene is introduced which is so important to this study that it is necessary to quote it in full:

[1] Cf. C. R. North, 'The "former things" and the "new things" in Deutero-Isaiah', *Studies in Old Testament Prophecy*, ed. H. H. Rowley (Edinburgh, 1950), pp. 111–26.

[2] J. Skinner, *The Book of the Prophet Isaiah, Chapters XL–LXVI* (Cambridge, 1898), p. 22; cf. the second edition (revised 1917, reprinted 1954), p. 25 and also pp. 33, 43, 46, 87ff., 240.

All the nations are gathered together,
   And the peoples are assembled.
Who among them can declare this,
   And show us the former things?
Let them bring out witnesses to prove their case,
   Or else let them listen and admit, 'That is the truth.'
You are my witnesses, says Yahweh,
   My servant whom I have chosen,
In order that you may know and believe me
   And understand that I am He.
Before me no god was formed,
   Nor shall there be any after me.
I, I am Yahweh, and besides me there is no Saviour.
   I declared, and I saved, and I proclaimed
And there was no foreign god in your midst.
   Therefore you are my witnesses, says Yahweh, I am God.
And also henceforth I am He,
   And there is none who can deliver from my hand.
I work, and who can hinder it?[1]

Here again the prophet has employed the literary form of a controversy to present his message. Once more Israel and the nations are summoned, as it were, into a lawcourt (verse 8), and once more the major parties in the controversy are Yahweh, the nations and Israel, with Yahweh as the speaker throughout (verses 9–13).

In this way the meaning of prediction; the significance of history; the election of Israel; the eternity, oneness and saving power of God; and the servant of the Lord all receive emphasis. Two major emphases of the poem, however, constitute a new element, new in the intensity with which they are asserted: the oneness of God and the mission of Israel as his witness.[2]

In 43: 8–13 Yahweh's people are summoned as witnesses in the controversy with the nations and their gods. At first sight, they appear quite unpromising witnesses, for they are described as both 'blind' and 'deaf' (43: 8). Still they have 'eyes' to see and 'ears' to hear. In the past they had witnessed God's mighty acts, although they had failed to perceive their spiritual significance (cf. 42: 20). Now the prophet pictures them acting as Yahweh's witnesses.

---

[1] This independent translation is the work of G. B. Caird.
[2] Muilenburg, 'The Book of Isaiah, chapters 40–66', p. 486.

Once again the nations are called before God, as in chapter 41, and confronted with the meaning of history. This time it is the foreign gods themselves who are addressed: 'Who among them can declare this?' (43: 9; cf. 41: 2; 42: 23; 48: 14). Who can explain 'the former things', the events that have taken place according to divine prediction? Thus Yahweh's opponents once more are invited to 'prove their case'.

Yahweh's challenge, then, is that the foreign gods *either* produce witnesses to testify to their past ability to foretell the future *or* be silent and listen to him when he presents his case and calls his witnesses, and, having listened, admit that Yahweh's claim is true. In other words, one litigant has to convince the other and win an admission of defeat. If one litigant makes no reply to the other, then it is assumed that he has conceded the case to his opponent. In this instance Yahweh has challenged the foreign gods, but they remain silent, for there is no reality behind them.

In view of the absence of witnesses on behalf of the nations and their gods, Yahweh turns to his own people and addresses Israel emphatically: 'You are my witnesses' (43: 8). Here the prophet is introducing one of his major themes:

He is describing Israel's mission in the world, and he follows the solemn commission with the oracle formula. The succeeding line supports this interpretation. The *witnesses* (plural) are identified with the *servant* (singular). Duhm and others read 'servants', but there is no evidence for this. Indeed, the plural *witnesses* and the singular *servant* are precisely what is needed, what the context demands, and what the prophet's thought concerning Israel throughout the poems requires. Israel does not exist for herself. She has a mission, and that mission is to be God's witness and elected servant. She exists to fulfil his purposes and to do his will...Through her witness and service Israel will come to know that Yahweh is God of all the nations. That God is God and the only God, this is Israel's witness, her mission as servant, and the meaning of her election.[1]

Israel's responsibility is reiterated as Yahweh once again reminds her: 'You are my witnesses' (43: 12).

Later in Isa. 43, however, the prophet turns from Israel's task to Israel as she really is. For this purpose he reverts to the form

[1] *Ibid.* p. 488. Cf. R. V. Moss, Jr, 'The witnessing church in the New Testament', *TaL*, 3 (1960), 263.

of a legal process. Thus 43: 22–4 can be called 'Yahweh's indictment' of his people for their failure to discharge their
religious obligations. But what if Israel pleads mitigating circumstances? The prophet anticipates the question, for he sees
Yahweh inviting Israel to come to court where the dispute may
be settled (43: 25–8). There Israel will have her chance to state
her case and to demonstrate why she merits Yahweh's special
consideration (43: 26)!

In 44: 7–9 the witness motif appears again:

> Does anyone claim to be my equal?
>> Let him stand up and say so.
> Let him speak out and state his case to me.
>> If he could foretell the future in advance
> He should be able to tell what is still to happen.
>> Fear not, nor be afraid;
> Have I not told you from of old and declared it?
>> And you are my witnesses!
> Is there a God besides me?
>> There is no Rock; I know not any.[1]

In 44: 7 the gods and their supporters are again challenged
to a controversy (cf. 41: 1–5, 21–9; 43: 8–13). The text of the
verse has suffered in transmission, for the words 'let him stand
up' have fallen out. However, it may be restored from the LXX
(στήτω), for Hebrew legal terminology supports it (since
'āmad is used as a typical technical term) and the context resembles 41: 21ff. and 43: 9. Moreover the verb 'ārak is used
here of setting forth a legal case (cf. Job 13: 18; 23: 4).[2] In other
words, this passage presents a summary of legal procedure: the
plaintiff rises in his place, raises his voice and states his case (i.e.,
argues it; cf. Job 35: 5).

These verses, then, constitute a lawsuit, as it were, in which
men are to decide who is really God – Yahweh or the gods of
the nations. The nations appear in the dual role of judges and
witnesses. As judges they must decide the case; as witnesses they
must appear to testify to the divinity of their gods. To the extent
that these witnesses are opponents of Yahweh, they will be
overcome (44: 11; cf. 45: 16), for they lack precisely that which
makes men witnesses, namely, the fact that they have seen and

[1] This independent translation is the work of G. B. Caird.
[2] North, *The Second Isaiah*, p. 136.

known something (44: 9). Consequently, when the pagan nations are challenged to prove the validity of the claims of their gods, they have no defence to present, and the case goes by default (44: 9–11).

In sharpest contrast to them, Israel is reminded: 'And you are my witnesses!' (44: 8; cf. 43: 10, 12). She is called as a vindicating witness to attest Yahweh's character, activity and purpose in the world. While the nations cannot produce witnesses to justify them, Israel is uniquely equipped to act in this capacity. Her task is to bear witness to all peoples and nations that Yahweh alone is God, and that beside him there is no Saviour (cf. Hos. 13:4). Perhaps nowhere in the Old Testament is lawcourt imagery used with more telling effect than here; certainly the reference to Israel as Yahweh's witness places the greatest stress upon her missionary task.

In chapter 45 the prophet reverts to the imagery of the law-court (45: 20–1) and puts to the nations the question which has been raised repeatedly concerning the meaning of Cyrus: 'Who told this long ago? Was it not I?' The juridical question leads to the great affirmation that Yahweh alone is God, a 'righteous God and a Saviour'. The way is thus prepared for God's invitation to the nations, in which they are graciously offered the gift of salvation (45: 22–3).

SUMMARY OF THE CONTROVERSY

What is one to make of these controversy passages? Several general remarks may be made. Isaiah 40-55 presents a great controversy or lawsuit in which Yahweh and his witnesses are placed on one side and the gods of the nations and their supporters on the other. Both the false gods and their would-be witnesses (the nations) are challenged to produce a case; they are invited to present cogent arguments such as fulfilments of predicted prophecies which can be duly attested. Their inability to do so is evidenced by their silence in the face of a challenge to speak from their legal opponents; therefore they forfeit the case. On the other hand, Yahweh's ability to predict the 'former things' can be established by the testimony of his witnesses, and this constitutes a convincing piece of evidence in favour of his claims. Israel can attest fulfilled prophecy, and she is to do so before the world (cf. 46: 2, where *'am* practically means 'the world', the singular *'am* standing parallel to *gôyîm*; cf. also 49: 8).

But there is also a second lawsuit in these chapters, namely, that between Yahweh and his people (variously called Jacob, Israel, Zion, etc.). Israel's complaint that her 'right' has been disregarded by her God is untrue: Yahweh is eternal, the indefatigable Creator of the whole earth, the never-failing source of strength available to his followers (40: 27–31). Israel thinks she has laboured in vain (49: 4), and complains that Yahweh has forgotten her (49: 14), but in view of his great love this is impossible (49: 15–16). Exiled Israel has been judged for her unfaithfulness (43: 21–8), but Yahweh can receive her back again. He does so that all men may recognize that he is the Lord of history (41: 17–20).

In other words, there are two groups of material which relate to the prophet's use of controversy, and they deal with two quite different kinds of controversy. Against the false gods Yahweh is the accuser; against Israel, the accused. The gods must defend themselves, but it cannot be done; they and their witnesses have nothing to say. Yahweh willingly defends himself, for he is quite capable of doing so.

THE IMPORTANCE OF ISAIAH 40–55 FOR THE NT CONCEPT OF WITNESS

Now it is possible to make a few comments on the significance of the controversy theme in Isa. 40–55. Here some characteristics of the prophet's concept of witness may be singled out for brief discussion:

(1) Isaiah 40–55 presents a sustained use of the controversy. Here the controversy between Yahweh and the false gods is really a lawsuit between God and the world. God is represented by Israel (43: 10, 12; 44: 8) and the world is represented by the pagan nations (41: 1; 43: 9; 45: 20). In Isaiah 40–55 the debate is over the claims of Yahweh as Creator, the only true God and the Lord of history (40: 25–31; 44: 6–8; 45: 8–11, 21). Isaiah 40–55 has a case to present, and for this reason it advances

arguments, asks juridical questions and presents witnesses after the fashion of the Old Testament legal assembly.

(2) The lawsuit between God and the world involves parties who serve both as witnesses *and* as advocates, and in this respect Isaiah 40–55 follows the general practice of the Old Testament legal assembly. It is the task of the witnesses not only to attest the facts but also to convince the opposite side of the truth of them (41: 21–4, 26; 43: 9; 51: 22; cf. Gen. 38: 24–6).[1]

(3) Special stress is laid upon predictive prophecy – a fact indicated by the frequent use of the phrase 'the former things' (41: 22; 42: 9; 43: 9, 18; 46: 9; 48: 3).[2] The nations are repeatedly challenged to give instances in which their gods have predicted the meaning of history. While they are unable to do so, Yahweh, on the other hand, can produce instances in which he has predicted something and it has later come to pass; the startling conquests of Cyrus are a case in point (41: 2–4). Yahweh's evidence is attested by Israel who is in a position to bear witness both to the prediction and to its subsequent fulfilment, and this is one of the main arguments for the case that Yahweh is God and the only Saviour (43: 1–13; 44: 7f.; 46: 8–11; 48: 3–5).

(4) The silence of the witnesses in these chapters is instructive. Again and again the pagan gods or their representatives are challenged to set forth their case and bring their proofs (41: 21–3; 43: 9; 44: 7), but they remain silent. Why? Because the pagan gods have never predicted anything, know nothing of the meaning or goal of history, and do not even exist (41: 24, 26–9). Their 'witnesses neither see nor know' (44: 9), and therefore they have nothing to say. Accordingly, by their silence the nations (the legal representatives of the false gods) acknowledge that Yahweh has won the lawsuit. The silence of the pagan nations in these chapters is similar to the silence of Job's third 'friend' in the third round of speeches in the Book of Job; in both cases the opponent has nothing to say and the

---

[1] Cf. D. R. Griffiths, 'Deutero-Isaiah and the Fourth Gospel', *ExpT*, 65 (1953–4), 358.

[2] Cf. D. R. Jones, 'Isaiah', *Peake's Commentary*, eds. M. Black and H. H. Rowley (London, 1962), p. 520, who observes that 'the idea of witness to the fulfilment of prophecy is marked' in the first part of the book as well, being explicit in 8: 2, 18 and implicit everywhere.

case goes by default to the other party. In Isa. 40–55 the silence of the nations is in marked contrast to Israel's role as Yahweh's witness (43: 10, 12; 44: 8).

(5) The 'Book of Consolation' makes abundant use of the ἐγώ εἰμι formula.[1] This is indicated by the fact that the phrase is used about sixteen times in these chapters to refer to Yahweh. Thus the LXX's ἐγώ εἰμι translates *'ᵃnî* or *'anoki* in such phrases as *'ᵃnî hû'* (41: 4; 43: 10; 46: 4; 52: 6), *'ᵃnî yhwh* (45: 8, 18, 19; 48: 16); *'ānokî, 'ānokî* (43: 25; 51: 12), *'ānokî 'ēl* (46: 9) and *'ᵃnî 'ēl* (45: 22). The formula is used by the prophet to declare solemnly the nature of Yahweh's claim as Saviour, Redeemer and Lord of history against the background of unbelief and rival claims.

(6) Isaiah 40–55 thinks of Israel both as God's witness and servant (43: 10, 12; cf. 41: 8f.; 44: 8). This combination appears later in the Fourth Gospel, where both Jesus and the disciples are described in this dual capacity.

[1] Cf. E. Stauffer, *Jesus and His Story* (London, 1960), pp. 142–59 and D. Daube, *The New Testament and Rabbinic Judaism* (London, 1956), pp. 325–9.

CHAPTER 6

THE IDEA OF WITNESS IN OTHER JEWISH WRITINGS

THE APOCRYPHA AND PSEUDEPIGRAPHA

The idea of witness is not absent in the Apocrypha and Pseudepigrapha, a fact attested by the use of a considerable number of words drawn from the vocabulary of witness. Since a study of these words contributes to an understanding of the New Testament concept of witness, it is imperative that such a study be undertaken.

There are several parallels between the Wisdom of Solomon and the Fourth Gospel, and these may be cited to begin with. Thus ἐλέγχειν is 'used in Wisdom as it is in John (Wisd. 1: 3; 4: 20; Jn 16: 8). The same applies to the notion of God bearing witness (Wisd. 1: 6; Jn 5: 32)... [Similarly,] Wisdom ordains man to "execute judgment"; so Christ has authority to "make judgment" "because he is son of man" (Wisd. 9: 3; Jn 5: 27) ... And there are other echoes.'[1] For example, the reference to 'signs and wonders' (Wisd. 8: 8; 10: 16; Jn 4: 48; cf. Acts 4: 30; 15: 12).[2]

God is described as a μάρτυς in Wisd. 1: 6 – a use which is later to be reflected in the writings of the Apostle Paul (Rom. 1: 9; II Cor. 1: 23; I Thess. 2: 5, 10; Phil. 1: 8). In Pirke Aboth IV.29 God is not only 'the judge' and 'the witness', but also 'the adversary' in the lawsuit (the ba'al dîn), suggesting that here the idea of witness is very much a live metaphor. As in the Old Testament, heaven and earth sometimes serve as witnesses (II Esdras 2: 14).

Men also act as witnesses (e.g., Pirke Aboth 1.9). Thus children born of unlawful unions serve as 'witnesses of evil against their parents when God examines them' (Wisd. 4: 6). Like the accusing witnesses in the Old Testament lawsuit, they

[1] E. M. Sidebottom, *The Christ of the Fourth Gospel* (London, 1961), p. 206. The second Wisdom reference has been corrected to read 4: 20 instead of 4: 27.

[2] Cf. J. P. M. Sweet, 'The theory of miracles in the Wisdom of Solomon', *Miracles – Cambridge Studies in their Philosophy and History*, ed. C. F. D. Moule (London, 1965), p. 122.

will rise in the day of judgment to give evidence which will secure a conviction – an idea which later reappears in both the Synoptics and John, though the word for 'witness' is not used (Mt. 12: 41f. = Lk. 11: 31f.; Jn 5: 45ff.; cf. Lk. 11: 19b). In another passage the witnesses are the prophets (Jubilees 1: 12): 'And I will send witnesses unto them, that I may witness against [or "to"] them, but they will not hear; and will slay the witnesses also, and they will persecute those who seek the law, and they will abrogate and change everything so as to work evil before My eyes.'[1] This passage can be compared with Rev. 11: 7, for there too the witnesses are killed after they have finished bearing witness.

The word for 'evidence' (μαρτύριον) is also used (e.g., Wisd. 10: 7), but it is not developed with special reference to the law-court; as in the Old Testament, when used in the plural with the definite article it can simply refer to 'the testimonies' or statutes of God (Sirach 45: 17). Similarly, μαρτυρία is occasionally found in the Apocrypha (e.g., Sirach 34(31): 23f.)[2] and 'testimony' is mentioned frequently in I Enoch (e.g., 67: 12; 89: 63, 76; 96: 4; 97: 4; 99: 3), but the giving of evidence is in no way restricted to formal depositions before real courts of law.

The verb μαρτυρεῖν appears once or twice in the Apocrypha. The most interesting example is found in I Macc. 2: 37, where the sabbatarian Jews cry: 'Let us all die in our innocence; heaven and earth testify for us that you are killing us unjustly.' This passage recalls the role of heaven and earth as witnesses in the Book of Deuteronomy (4: 26; 30: 19; 31: 28), and helps one to understand the use of μαρτυρεῖν in the Synoptic Gospels (Mt. 23: 31; cf. Lk. 11: 48). In addition, it deserves to be compared with Judith 7: 28, where a similar reference to heaven and earth as accusing witnesses is made by the use of μαρτύρεσθαι. See also Sirach 46: 19, where ἐπιμαρτύρεσθαι is used with reference to Samuel's calling men 'to witness before the Lord and his anointed' that he is blameless. This last passage, together with its Old Testament parallel (I Sam. 12: 3ff.), forms an excellent background for the understanding of such Pauline passages as I Thess. 2: 10.

---

[1] R. H. Charles (ed.), *The Apocrypha and Pseudepigrapha of the Old Testament* (2 vols., Oxford, 1913), II, 12.

[2] J. Downing, 'Jesus and martyrdom', *JTS*, N.S. 14 (1963), 279–93.

The story of Susanna is 'intended to illustrate the value and necessity of cross-examination of witnesses. It also seeks to vindicate the execution of false witnesses, although their victim may be delivered before his sentence was carried out.'[1] The two lustful elders are accusing witnesses in Susanna's trial; by their testimony they seek to establish her alleged adultery (verses 36–41; note the phrase ταῦτα μαρτυροῦμεν in verse 41, LXX). The 'elders of the people' are the 'judges' who decide the case and sentence Susanna to death. Before she can be executed, however, Daniel raises a protest on her behalf and summons the legal assembly to return to 'the place of judgment' (verses 45–9). There he is invited to act as an 'elder' by participating in the arbitration (verse 50). He does so by separating Susanna's accusers and 'examining' them individually (ἀνακρινῶ, verse 51). Daniel follows the procedure laid down in Deut. 19: 18 of making 'diligent inquisition' (R.V.). Under his searching cross-examination the testimony of the accusing witnesses breaks down, for they differ on a point of circumstantial evidence and therefore Daniel is able to convict them of bearing false witness (verses 54, 58, 61).[2] Acting in accordance with the Old Testament law of malicious witness, the judges put Susanna's accusers to death (verse 62), and Susanna is completely vindicated.

Susanna's story is important to this inquiry for several reasons: (1) It illustrates what has already been observed in the Old Testament, namely, the fact that one person can serve as judge and witness in the same legal assembly. In Susanna the two roles are virtually synonymous, for the judge helps the innocent person by acting as a witness in her defence.[3] Here the witness is not the eye-witness, but rather the advocate who takes the litigant's side and pleads her case. (2) Susanna's story offers an interesting application of the law of malicious witness mentioned in Deut. 19: 16–21. Since this law also appears in the New Testament (cf. Rev. 11: 13; 18: 20b), here is another link between the idea of witness in the Old Testament and the New. (3) Susanna employs καταμαρτυρεῖν (verses 21, 43, 49) and

[1] Charles, *Apocrypha and Pseudepigrapha*, I, 638. Cf. R. A. F. MacKenzie, 'The meaning of the Susanna story', *CJT*, 3 (1957), 211–18 and Sanhedrin 41a.
[2] But cf. Sanhedrin 69a.
[3] Cf. L. Morris, *The Biblical Doctrine of Judgment* (London, 1960), pp. 15–16.

ψευδομαρτυρεῖν (verse 62), offering parallels to the Synoptic uses of the same verbs in connection with the trial of Jesus (Mk 14: 50, 56, 57; Mt. 26: 62; 27: 13). (4) Daniel convicts the false witnesses 'out of their own mouth' (Sus. 61). Similar convictions on the basis of one's own evidence appear in the Old Testament and later in the Synoptic Gospels (II Sam. 1: 16; Job 9: 20; 15: 6; Lk. 19: 22; Mt. 12: 37). (5) The story highlights a dispute between the Pharisees during the time of Alexander Janneus (105–79 B.C.). As Charles and others have pointed out (*Apocrypha and Pseudepigrapha*, I, 651), the Sadducees advocated carrying out the sentence only if the falsely accused had actually been put to death, while the Pharisees held that the death penalty was in force from the moment when the unjust sentence was passed (Mishnah Makkoth 1.6; Sifre on Deut. 19: 19; Gemara, Makkoth 5B). According to the Pharisaic interpretation of Deut. 19: 19, the two lustful elders must be executed for malicious witness. (6) Susanna 51–9 may shed light on the interpretation of Jn 1: 48, 50. Professor Moule, commenting on the Susanna story, has directed attention to the importance which the rabbinical tradition attached to the scrupulous examination of evidence (cf. Mishnah Sanhedrin v.2 and Bab. Sanhedrin 41a). Thus he interprets 'under the fig tree' in Jn 1: 48, 50 as indicating 'the accurate knowledge of a person's whereabouts and movements' which is characteristic of a good witness.[1]

Many other legal words are used in the Apocrypha and Pseudepigrapha which will be encountered later in the New Testament. Two of the most interesting ones are *pārāklîṭ* and *kᵉṭîgôr*, both of which appear in Pirke IV. 13: 'He who does one precept gains for himself one *advocate*; and he who commits one transgression gains for himself one *accuser*.'[2] The Hebrew words represent παράκλητος and κατήγορος, words which we will return to later in considering the concept of witness developed in the Fourth Gospel, I John and the Book of Revelation (cf. Jn 5: 45; 14: 16, 26; 15: 26; 16: 7; I Jn 2: 1; Rev. 12: 10).

[1] C. F. D. Moule, 'A note on "under the fig tree" in John I. 48, 50', *JTS*, N.S. 5 (1954), 210–11. Cf. C. H. Dodd, *Historical Tradition in the Fourth Gospel* (Cambridge, 1963), p. 310, n.2.

[2] Charles, *Apocrypha and Pseudepigrapha*, II, 705. Cf. T. F. Glasson, *Moses in the Fourth Gospel* (London, 1963), p. 105.

Other legal words also appear, sometimes in forensic contexts where the idea of witness is prominent. A list of such words would include κρίμα, κρίσις, κριτής, κατακρίνειν, κατάκριμα, αἰτία, ἀντίδικος, ψευδομαρτυρεῖν and ὁμολογεῖν. As these words, generally speaking, are not integrated into any unified concept of witness in the Apocrypha and Pseudepigrapha, it is not necessary to look at them in great detail. Their importance lies in the fact that they show the presence of the linguistic raw materials on which the writers of the New Testament were to draw in the formulation of their ideas of witness.

THE DEAD SEA SCROLLS

The idea of witness is also present in the Dead Sea Scrolls, usually with reference to forensic situations. The Qumran community made use of witnesses in settling disputes. Thus *The Manual of Discipline* (1QS v. 24–vi.1) says:

When anyone has a charge against his neighbour, he is to prosecute it truthfully, humbly and humanely. He is not to speak to him angrily or querulously or arrogantly or in any wicked mood. He is not to bear hatred...Furthermore, no man is to bring a charge publicly against his neighbour except he prove it by witnesses.[1]

Similarly, *The Damascus Document* has some interesting things to say about the use of witnesses (CD ix.2–4):

If any of those that have entered the covenant bring charges against his neighbour without proving them by witnesses...he ranks as one who takes vengeance and bears a grudge.[2]

The same document also shows some interest in the question of the number of witnesses, and in the importance of testimony generally to the life of the covenant community (CD ix.16–x.3):

In the case of offences against the Torah, if a man sees such an offence committed but is alone at the time, and if the matter be one of a capital nature, he is to disclose it to the overseer by bringing a

[1] T. H. Gaster, *The Scriptures of the Dead Sea Sect* (London, 1957), p. 58; cf. G. Vermes, *The Dead Sea Scrolls in English* (London, 1963), p. 80.
[2] Gaster, *op. cit.*, pp. 83–4. Cf. M. Burrows, *The Dead Sea Scrolls* (London, 1956), p. 358.

charge in the presence of the alleged culprit. The overseer is then to make a record of it. If the man repeat the offence, this time also in the presence of one man only, and if the latter come in turn and inform the overseer – in that case, i.e., if the offender do it again and be again caught by one person – the case against him is to be regarded as complete.

However, if there be two witnesses, and they concur in their statements, the culprit is to be excluded from his customary degree of purity only if those witnesses are trustworthy and if they lay information before the overseer on the very day when they saw the man (committing the offence).

In cases involving property, two trustworthy witnesses are required. In those, however, that involve (no question of restitution but simply of) exclusion from the degree of purity, one alone is sufficient.

No man who has not yet completed his probationary period with the community and has not yet passed the statutory examination as a truly God-fearing person is to be permitted as a witness before its judges in a capital case.

No man who has flagrantly transgressed the commandment is to be deemed a trustworthy witness against his neighbour until he has succeeded in winning re-acceptance into the community.[1]

The Manual of Discipline is also worth considering. There it is explicitly laid down that a man

is not to have carnal knowledge of a woman until he is twenty years old and has reached the age of discretion. Furthermore, it is only then that he is eligible to give testimony in matters involving the laws of the Torah or to attend judicial hearings...No one who is feeble-minded is to take part in litigation or in rendering judgments in any matter affecting the community as a whole...If public notice is posted for a juridical or consultative assembly,...everyone is to observe a three-day period of sanctification.[2]

Two more passages call for brief attention. The first is found in the opening passage of *The Damascus Document* (CD 1.1), where God 'has a controversy with all flesh, and will execute judgment upon all who despise him'.[3] Here the controversy theme is a live metaphor and the phrase 'execute judgment' calls to

[1] Gaster, *op. cit.*, p. 85.
[2] *Ibid.* p. 286.
[3] Burrows, *The Dead Sea Scrolls*, p. 349.

mind similar judicial expressions in the Book of Wisdom and the Fourth Gospel (Wisd. 9: 3; Jn 5: 27). The second passage is in *The Manual of Discipline* (1QS VIII.6), where the sectarians are called 'witnesses to truth' because of their devotion to it. The point to note here is the parallel with the Fourth Gospel: 'Only in the Fourth Gospel, where it is used both of John the Baptist [5: 33] and of Christ [18: 37], does this phrase occur in the New Testament.'[1]

In summary, the idea of witness in the Dead Sea Scrolls appears mainly in real legal situations, usually in connection with community disputes. Because of this fact, the Scrolls furnish some interesting parallels to similar disputes in the Christian community where witnesses are involved (Mt. 18: 15ff.; cf. I Cor. 5: 1–8). The Scrolls also show the importance of witnesses in establishing facts, and indicate the restriction of witnesses to *bona fide* members of the covenant community. The number of witnesses is another matter to which attention is drawn. Finally, controversy language can be used metaphorically in the Scrolls, as when Yahweh is said to have a *rîb* with all flesh (CD 1.1).

THE WRITINGS OF JOSEPHUS AND PHILO

Josephus

Josephus has a number of informative things to say about witness.[2] In *The Antiquities* (IV.219) he remarks: 'Put not trust in a single witness, but let there be three or at least two, whose evidence shall be accredited by their past lives.'[3] He adds, however, two traditional rulings not found in Scripture with respect to those who give evidence: 'From women let not evidence be accepted, because of the levity and temerity of their sex; neither let slaves bear witness because of their soul, since whether from cupidity or fear it is likely that they will not

---

[1] R. E. Brown, 'The Qumran Scrolls and the Johannine Gospel and Epistles', *The Scrolls and the New Testament*, ed. K. Stendahl (New York, 1957; London, 1958), p. 197; cf. M. Black, *The Dead Sea Scrolls and Christian Doctrine* (London, 1966), p. 11.

[2] Josephus, *Works*, LCL (8 vols., London, 1926–34), which follows Niese's subdivision of the Greek text.

[3] *Ibid.* IV, 581; cf. Ḳiddushim 65b.

attest the truth.' (Cf. Yeb. 88b, 115a; Mishnah, *Rosh Hashana* 1.8.) The reference to women as unsuitable witnesses is significant for the New Testament, and may help to explain why Paul does not include the resurrection appearances to women in I Cor. 15: 3–8. Josephus concludes on the sombre note of the law of malicious witness: 'If anyone be believed to have borne false witness, let him on conviction suffer the penalty which would have been incurred by him against whom he hath borne witness.' In thus citing Deut. 19: 15ff., Josephus provides a link between the Old and New Testaments in their use of the law of malicious witness.

Josephus speaks of the Jews deciding their controversies with one another, using ἀντιλογία for 'dispute', as in Heb. 6: 16 (*Ant.* IV.235). We may also note his use of ἀντιλέγειν with the meaning 'to oppose in court' (*Ant.* XIV.325).

But the idea of witness is not confined to legal contexts in Josephus; it can also be used in legal metaphors. Thus Josephus reminds Justus that eye-witnesses are no longer available to furnish confirmation of his account of the Jewish War (*Life* 360): 'You had it written twenty years ago and could have obtained the evidence of eye-witnesses to your accuracy. But not until now, when those persons are no longer with us, and you think you cannot be refuted, have you ventured to publish it.'[1] Here is a use of μαρτυρία with reference to historical evidence, namely, that furnished by those who were present and who could therefore serve as witnesses concerning disputed facts. Living witnesses thus serve as a check upon the historian who would distort the truth and misuse the facts. In the eyes of Josephus it is intellectually dishonest to fail to make use of eye-witnesses in the critical task of sifting historical evidence (cf. *The Jewish War* 1.15). Josephus claims to be an eye-witness (αὐτόπτης) of most of the events which he reports (*Apion* 1.55), and he insists that the historian must first master 'the facts himself, either by following the events in person or by ascertaining them from those who know' (*Apion* 1.53; cf. Lk. 1: 1–4).[2] He tries to be faithful to these principles in both *The Antiquities* and *The Jewish War*.

There is another passage in *The Jewish War* (VI.134) in which

[1] *Ibid.* I, 133.
[2] *Ibid.* I, 185.

55

Josephus unites the two words signifying 'witness'.[1] Describing an episode in the capture of the temple, the historian places Titus on the scene, directing a night attack of which he is αὐτόπτης καὶ μάρτυς, 'spectator and witness'. Titus, in effect, assists in the conflict, appreciating for himself the gallantry of his men and rewarding them according to their deserts. As P.-H. Menoud has pointed out, this example provides clear evidence that μάρτυς involves more than simple eye-witness: 'The witness does not passively, objectively, function as a witness of the facts which unfold before his eyes; he understands them and he sees them in their ultimate consequences.'[2]

In addition to historical evidence, Josephus speaks of evidence to fact in a more general sense. He refers to the Greeks in one instance and to the Egyptians in another as 'witnesses' (μάρτυρες) of the antiquity of the Jewish people (*Apion* 1.4 and 1.93).[3] In each case there is no reference to a lawcourt, for the evidence is completely general in character.

Another point concerns Josephus's use of σημεῖον – a word which later proves to be important in both the Lukan and Johannine concepts of witness. G. MacRae cites examples of the use of σημεῖον in *The Antiquities* (II.274ff.; VI.91), and adds: 'The combination of σημεῖον with τέρας is familiar from the Septuagint and the New Testament; Josephus uses it of the promise of the false prophets in the procuratorship of Felix',[4] who invoke 'wonders and signs to be accomplished by the providence of God' (*Antiquities* xx.168).

One final passage calls for attention in Josephus. It is found in *The Antiquities* (IV.286): 'For by all means, from the mere knowledge that he has of his own conscience, ought everyone to act aright – let him be content with that for witness and do all that will bring him praise from others – but chiefly from his knowledge of God, whose eye no criminal escapes.'[5] This passage has a double interest for us. In the first place, the eye-witness of God is treated as a major motive for ethical action.

---

[1] *Ibid.* III, 415. For other examples of αὐτόπτης in Josephus see: *Ant.*, XVIII. 342; XIX. 125; *War*, III. 432.

[2] P. -H. Menoud, 'Jésus et ses témoins', *EeT*, 23 (1960), 11.

[3] Josephus, *Works*, I, 165 and I, 201.

[4] G. MacRae, 'Miracle in The Antiquities of Josephus', *Miracles – Cambridge Studies*, pp. 129–47, esp. p. 143.

[5] Josephus, *Works*, v, 613.

In the second, the term συνείδησις is employed – a word which is used sometimes by Paul in forensic contexts (Rom. 2: 15; 9: 1).

Philo

The idea of witness appears with considerable detail in the writings of Philo of Alexandria, and because he is virtually contemporary with the New Testament, his remarks are especially noteworthy.[1]

Witness in Legal Contexts. First of all, witnesses to contracts are mentioned in Philo. Thus he can say: 'Formal loans are guaranteed by contracts and written documents, and articles lent openly without such formality have the testimony of eye-witnesses' (*Spec. Leg.* IV.30).[2] This usage is perfectly normal; witnesses to contracts are very common both in secular Greek and in the Old Testament, so it is not at all surprising that they should find a place in Philo.

Next, the idea of witness must be scrutinized in legal contexts where there is a reference to courtroom procedure. This study leads naturally into a consideration of Philo's views of the single witness, the false witness, hearsay evidence, and the accuser in a court of law.

Philo sheds considerable light on the Jewish rejection of the single witness when he writes (*Spec. Leg.* IV.53f.):

He [Moses] added another excellent injunction which forbade them to accept the evidence of a single person [cf. Num. 35: 30; Deut. 17: 6, of death sentences; Deut. 19: 15, of all offences], first because the single person may see or hear imperfectly or misunderstand and be deceived, since false opinions are numberless and numberless too are the sources from which they spring to attack. Secondly, because it is most unjust to accept a single witness against more than one or even against one; against one, because the witness has not got the preponderance of number, and equality is incompatible with predominance. For why should the statement of a witness made in accusation of another be accepted in preference to the words of the accused spoken in his own defence? Where there is neither deficiency nor excess it is clearly better to suspend judgment.[3]

---

[1] Philo, *Works*, LCL (10 vols., London, 1929–42).
[2] *Ibid.* VIII, 25.   [3] *Ibid.* VIII, 41.

In other words, Philo has illuminated the Old Testament passages which deal with the rejection of testimony by only one witness. In doing so, he has also shed light upon the New Testament's firm adherence to the same principle.

Philo also offers some clear-cut reasons for the strict prohibition of false witness (*Dec.* 138–41):

Having denounced theft, he [Moses] next proceeds to forbid false witness [ψευδομαρτυρεῖν], knowing that false witnesses are guilty under many important heads, all of them of a grave kind. *In the first place, they corrupt truth*, the august, the treasure as sacred as anything that we possess in life, which like the sun pours light upon facts and events and allows none of them to be kept in the shade. *Secondly*, apart from the falsehood, *they veil the facts* as it were in night and profound darkness, take part with the offenders and against those who are wronged, by affirming that they have sure knowledge, and thorough apprehension of things which they have neither seen nor heard. And indeed they commit a third transgression even more heinous than the first two. For when there is a lack of proofs, either verbal or written, disputants have resort to witnesses whose words are taken by the jurymen as standards in determining the verdicts they are about to give, since they are obliged to fall back on these alone if there is no other means of testing the result. The result is that *those against whom the testimony is given suffer injustice when they might have won their case*, and the judges who listen to the testimony record unjust and lawless instead of just and lawful votes...It was for these reasons, I believe, that He [i.e., God] forbade false witness.[1]

If Philo's attitude is typical of Jewish thinking on this point, it is easier to understand Paul's tremendous abhorrence of being found a 'false witness of God' (I Cor. 15: 15; cf. II Cor. 11: 31). If being a 'false witness of men' entailed such bad consequences, how much more sinful it must be to bear false witness against God!

Philo has something to say on hearsay evidence (*Spec. Leg.* IV.59–61):

The first instruction that the law gives to the judge is that he should not accept idle hearing...If men listen to hearsay given as evidence their listening will be idle and unsound. Why so? Because the eyes are conversant with the actual events; they are in a sense in contact with the facts and grasp them in their completeness through the co-

---

[1] *Ibid.* VII, 75–7.

operation of the light which reveals and tests everything. But ears, as one of the ancients has aptly said, are less trustworthy than eyes, they are not conversant with facts, but are distracted by words which interpret the facts but are not necessarily always veracious. And therefore it seems that some Grecian legislators did well when they copied from the most sacred tables of Moses the enactment that hearing is not accepted as evidence, meaning that what a man has seen is to be judged trustworthy, but what he has heard is not entirely reliable.[1]

Philo here provides a link between the Greek and the Hebrew legal traditions. Whether the Greeks did or did not copy from the Torah the prohibition against hearsay evidence is not important here; the significant point for our study is that *both* Greek and Hebrew legal traditions were opposed to the use of hearsay evidence. It is this kind of hearsay evidence which the Apostle Paul comes up against in Rome when he meets the local leaders of the Jews (Acts 28: 22). Similarly, in both the Fourth Gospel and Acts great stress is placed upon the apostles as those who have *seen* as well as heard Jesus in the days of his earthly ministry and after his resurrection (Jn 15: 27; Acts 1: 21–2). Evidence provided by the ears is supplemented and completed by eye-witness evidence.

The next passage is interesting for the light which it sheds both on the false witness and on the role of the accuser in biblical literature (*Spec. Leg.* IV.41–4):

'Thou shalt not bear false witness.' This is the ninth of the ten heads but the fourth in number of those on the second table...Reprehensible as is the false accuser, his guilt is less than that of the bearer of false witness... *The judge looks with disfavour on the accuser* [κατήγωρ] *as a person who cares little for truth in his eagerness to win his case, and this is the reason why introductory addresses are required to secure the attention of the hearer to the speaker.* But the judge starts with no lurking feelings of hostility to the witness [ὁ μαρτυρῶν] and therefore he listens with a free judgment and open ears, while the other assumes the mask of good faith and truth, names indeed of the most valuable realities, but the most seductive of names when used as baits to capture something which is earnestly desired.[2]

---

[1] *Ibid.* VIII, 45–7. Cf. *Conf.*, 141, IV, 87.
[2] *Ibid.* VIII, 33–5. Philo also mentions the role of the Παράκλητος (*Vita Mos.*, II. 134).

Philo here has drawn attention to the initial prejudice which the κατήγωρ has to overcome in presenting his evidence as the counsel for the prosecution; perhaps this helps to explain why Tertullus in Acts 24: 1–9 makes such an elaborate introduction in contrast to the simpler one of Paul. In addition, this passage from Philo contributes to one's general understanding of the place of the κατήγωρ in the New Testament (cf. Acts 23: 30, 35; 25: 16, 18; Rev. 12: 10), and sets in a new perspective those passages in John's Gospel where the Jews function as the accusers of Christ (see John, chapters 5–11).

Witness in Legal Metaphors. Having viewed a number of passages where witness is treated in legal contexts, it is fitting to take a brief look at its use in legal metaphors. One such instance occurs in Philo's *Spec. Leg.* 1.55:

If any members of the nation betray the honour due to the One they should suffer the utmost penalties. And it is well that all who have a zeal for virtue should be permitted to exact the penalties offhand and without delay, *without bringing the offender before jury or council or any kind of magistrate at all*...They should think that the occasion has made them *councillors* (βουλευτάς), *jurymen* (δικαστάς), *high sheriffs* (στρατηγούς), *members of assembly* (ἐκκλησιαστάς), *accusers* (κατηγόρους), *witnesses* (μάρτυρας), *laws* (νόμους), *people* (δῆμον), everything in fact, so that without fear or hindrance they may champion religion (by inflicting punishment without mercy on the impious)...[1]

Obviously in this passage one is not dealing with a formal scene in a court of law, as the italicized words make perfectly clear. Yet legal terms are employed, and the lawsuit images are used as live metaphors. Here the accusing witnesses, in true biblical fashion (cf. Deut. 17: 7), are to carry out the sentence for which their evidence has prepared the way; this executive role of witnesses appears again in the New Testament in the stoning of Stephen (Acts 7: 58; cf. Jn 8: 7).

On the other hand, Philo occasionally speaks of a παράκλητος. In one such passage Joseph discloses himself to his brothers and tells them not to ask for another 'advocate' (*Jos.* 239). This use bears comparison with Jn 14: 16. Another illustration of the use of a legal metaphor in Philo is found in *Plant.* 173: 'If, just

---

[1] *Ibid.* VII, 131.

THE WRITINGS OF JOSEPHUS AND PHILO

as in a court of law, we are to make use, not only of the logical or
dialectical proofs but also of the modes of persuasion that are
called "inartistic", we shall call as witnesses many distinguished
physicians and philosophers, who ratify their evidence by
writings as well as by words.'[1] Here Aristotelian 'dialectical'
and 'non-dialectical' types of proof are used 'just as in a court
of law', and witnesses are placed among the latter group. Stress
is placed on two kinds of evidence, namely, that furnished by
witnesses (in this case, eminent physicians and philosophers)
and that provided by written documents. Thus this passage
serves to illumine some of the connecting links between the
Greek and the Jewish ways of handling evidence. Moreover, by
its emphasis on the quality of those who bear witness it anticipates the New Testament idea that the apostles are specially
qualified; they are witnesses of their crucified and risen Lord,
not only in the sense of attesting the facts, but also in being
competent to interpret them.

Witnesses to Fact: Personal. Having looked at witness both in
legal contexts and in legal metaphors, it is now appropriate to
consider witnesses to fact, personal and impersonal.

Philo quite naturally acknowledges the importance of eye-
witness evidence (e.g., *Jos.* 242). He observes that there were
no witnesses present to see either the action of Joseph's steward
(*Jos.* 208)[2] or the sacrifice offered by Abraham (*Abr.* 190).[3]
This meant that no eye-witnesses could come forward with the
evidence either to convict Joseph's steward of treachery, or to
attest the nobility of Abraham's action. That is, accusing
witnesses were lacking in the one case, and advocating witnesses
in the other, in so far as testimony was restricted to the evidence
of eye-witnesses. This principle of eye-witness testimony will
come repeatedly to the fore in the New Testament's use of the
idea of witness.

But eye-witness evidence is not the only kind of personal
evidence. A case in point appears in *Spec. Leg.* 1.333ff. Philo is
discussing the relative merits of the mind and the senses.
Turning to the senses (1.340), he accepts the view that 'each of
the other members of the body has its appropriate and very

[1] *Ibid.* III, 303.   [2] *Ibid.* VI, 241.
[3] *Ibid.* VI, 95.

indispensable use', but goes on to assert that 'the eyes may be said to have a common value and to create the conditions under which these members and all others operate successfully'.[1] Then as evidence for this view he cites 'the maimed' (who in this context can only mean 'the blind') 'who cannot make the proper use of their hands and feet' (1.341).[2] Here obviously the concern is not with eye-witness testimony, but with evidence provided by the blind which supports Philo's assertion.

Similarly in *Jos.* 125ff. Philo has been arguing that human life is a 'dream', full of change, 'confusion, disorder and uncertainty', and that men, by and large, are incapable of interpreting its true meaning. He cites as supporting witnesses of this contention not only individual men like Croesus and Dionysius of Corinth, but also men viewed collectively as cities, nations, countries, Greeks and barbarians, etc. (*Jos.* 134).[3] All these people provide evidence of the change and instability of life (*Jos.* 135).[4] In their corporate character these witnesses remind one of the conception of Israel as God's witness developed in Isaiah 40–55. However, there the prophet's use of the legal metaphor is much more fully worked out than in this illustration from Philo, and is enriched by the personal nature of the covenant between God and his people, Israel. While Philo sees the collective groups of people as evidence of a proposition he is seeking to establish, Isaiah 40–55 sees Israel as living witnesses who can actually speak of the concrete dealings of Yahweh with them in the events of their national history. Any parallel between the two, then, seems to be quite remote and superficial.

Another reference to evidence furnished by persons is found in *Det.* 99, where the poets and historians are called upon to supply documentary proof of the evils which attend sexual indulgence.[5] This passage does not suggest that the historians and poets are eye-witnesses of actual cases of sexual indulgence, but rather calls upon them as witnesses who are competent to judge the quality of historical events and actions. In this sense they are similar both to Aristotle's μάρτυρες παλαιοί and to the apostolic witnesses whose testimony will be examined in considering the Book of Acts.

---

[1] *Ibid.* VII, 299. [2] *Ibid.* [3] *Ibid.* VI, 205.
[4] *Ibid.* [5] *Ibid.* II, 269.

Witnesses to Fact: *Impersonal*. A few illustrations of impersonal evidence in Philo may now be treated. The idea that ether is an unquenchable fire, for instance, 'is attested by a single part of the heavenly expanse of fire, namely, the sun' (*Conf.* 157).[1] Here Philo's use of μάρτυς refers to impersonal evidence, and makes no special contribution to this inquiry.

In some instances, as might be expected, Philo shows his indebtedness to both Jews and Greeks. A good instance of this is his reference to the 'Heap' which Jacob calls as a witness in his controversy with Laban (Gen. 31: 46f.). The heap of stones is an objective piece of evidence in the Old Testament, and Philo dutifully cites it as such (*Post.* 59). However, Philo goes on to give a thoroughly Platonic explanation: 'This conveys the deep truth that the mind is for each man the witness (μάρτυς) of his secret purposes, and the conscience an impartial scrutineer unequalled in veracity.'[2] In doing so, he has quite forsaken the Jewish context.

Several passages attract attention because the evidence to which they refer is that of Scripture. Thus Philo's assertion (*Som.* II.297) that knowledge of what is truly good is reserved for God alone and whoever are his friends is supported by the witness of Scripture, μάρτυς δὲ καὶ χρησμός being used to introduce a quotation from Deut. 32: 39.[3] Similarly, after he has made an affirmation, Philo seeks confirmation of it by calling the 'law' as a witness (μάρτυς δ' ὁ νόμος), quoting Deut. 32: 15 (*Post.* 121).[4] See also *Leg. All.* III. 129, where Philo prefaces his quotation of Lev. 8: 29 with the words, μαρτυρεῖ δέ μου τῷ λόγῳ ὁ ἱερώτατος χρησμός, indicating that what he says is true because it is attested by Holy Writ.[5] There is nothing to suggest that Philo is departing from traditional Jewish reverence for the text of Scripture in these passages; in fact, all the evidence points to the conclusion that Philo is speaking as a typical Jew at this point. If this is the case, Philo provides an important parallel with the Fourth Gospel, where the witness of Scripture is advanced by Jesus as legitimate and powerful evidence in support of the claims he is making (Jn 5: 39). For both Philo and the writer of the Fourth Gospel the witness of Scripture was accepted as evidence of high value.

[1] *Ibid.* IV, 95. [2] *Ibid.* II, 361. [3] *Ibid.* V, 576–7.
[4] *Ibid.* II, 398–9. [5] *Ibid.* I, 386–9.

In the minds of their Jewish contemporaries this would be readily accepted, as the debates in the Fourth Gospel make quite clear; the authority and evidential value of Scripture was common ground between Jesus and his Jewish opponents.

Divine Witness. Several passages in Philo speak of God as a witness. He can be a witness of a private transaction. Thus *Spec.Leg.* IV.31 declares: 'This unseen transaction has assuredly the unseen God as its intermediary, to whom both naturally appeal as their witness.'[1] In this connection God is said to be 'the most veracious of witnesses who sees and hears all whether they intend or do not wish to do what they say' (*Spec. Leg.* IV.32).[2] This passage is similar to several Old Testament passages where God is called upon as a witness to an agreement (e.g., Gen. 31: 44; Judg. 11: 10).

Another use of the witness of God is in the case of oaths (cf. Josephus, *Jewish War*, VI.127). An oath, to use a definition which frequently appears in Philo, is 'an appeal to God as a witness on matters in dispute' (*Dec.* 86; cf. *Spec. Leg.* II.10).[3] Thus an 'oath represents the surest form of trustworthiness which carries with it the testimony of God' (*Plant.* 82).[4] The reason given for this opinion is that 'the man who swears calls God as a witness of the points in dispute' (*Plant.* 82).[5] The thought is that God is the best witness because he knows all things. It is the same notion which has already come to expression in Jeremiah, where at the close of his letter to the exiles in Babylon come the solemn words: 'I am the one who knows, and I am witness, says the Lord' (Jer. 29: 30). This idea, prominent in the Old Testament (cf. I Sam.12: 5–6; Jer. 29: 23; Mal. 2: 14), is taken up again in the New Testament by the Apostle Paul (Rom. 1: 9; II Cor. 1: 23; Phil. 1: 8; I Thess. 2: 5).

So Philo's use of God as a witness in the case of oaths serves as a real link between the Old Testament and the New Testament in their treatment of this theme. To Philo, as to the Old Testament and Paul, 'to call upon God as a witness to a lie is the height of profanity' (*Dec.* 86);[6] they all hold that God is

---

[1] *Ibid.* VIII, 25–7.   [2] *Ibid.* VIII, 27.
[3] *Ibid.* VII, 49; cf. *ibid.* VII, 311–13.
[4] *Ibid.* III, 255.   [5] *Ibid.*
[6] *Ibid.* VII, 49.

'at once an absolutely true witness and an incorruptible judge' (*Mig. Abr.*115).[1] This last quotation suggests a very close relationship between God's roles as witness and judge, and reminds one of such Old Testament passages as Mal. 3: 5, where God appears as a witness to execute judgment upon the ungodly. In Philo, as in the Old Testament, there appear to be some passages in which the two roles are virtually indistinguishable.

Finally, there are several passages in which the witness of God appears through the witness of Scripture. In *Cher.*40, for instance, God the lawgiver has testified (μεμαρτύρηκεν) to the virtue of certain persons who are represented as not having sexual intercourse with women.[2] Here it is the silence of Scripture which is adduced as testimony to the virtue of Abraham, Isaac, Jacob and Moses. That is to say, the witness of God is thought to be expressed through the witness of Scripture, as in Hebrews 11.

A more difficult illustration of the same point is found in *Leg. All.* II. 54f., where a thoroughly Platonic explanation is given of the 'tent of testimony'.[3] Here God bears witness to the godly man in the words of Scripture, calling him the 'tent'.

To sum up Philo's contribution in a sentence, one can say that he serves as a bridge between the Greek and the Hebrew worlds, and helps one to see the links between the Old and the New Testament ideas of witness.

---

[1] *Ibid.* IV, 199.   [2] *Ibid.* II, 33.   [3] *Ibid.* I, 259.

CHAPTER 7

THE WITNESS TERMINOLOGY OF THE NEW TESTAMENT

The New Testament, like the LXX and secular Greek, makes considerable use of words relating to the idea of witness. In fact μάρτυς and its fourteen cognates appear over two hundred times in the New Testament. The most frequent use is in the Johannine writings, where witness terms are found about eighty-three times. Witness terms are also used some thirty-nine times in Acts and about thirty-five times in the Pauline literature, counting twelve references in the Pastorals. It is appropriate to begin the specifically New Testament part of our study with a philological consideration of μάρτυς and its cognates.[1] Other words pertaining to the New Testament concept of witness will be dealt with at the relevant places in the succeeding chapters.

THE USE OF Μάρτυς

The noun μάρτυς appears thirty-five times in the New Testament. It is most prominent in the Book of Acts, where it is found thirteen times, but it also appears six times in the Pauline Epistles, five times in the Apocalypse, three times in the Pastorals, twice in Matthew, Luke and Hebrews and once in Mark and I Peter.

The Acts passages raise no special philological problems. The only exception is Acts 22: 20, where μάρτυς is used, as in Rev. 2: 13 and 17: 6, 'as a designation of those who have suffered death in consequence of confessing Christ... This, however, must not be misunderstood (as in ecclesiastical Greek) to denote that their witness consisted in their suffering death, –

---

[1] Strathmann, *TDNT*, IV, 489ff. and *TWNT*, IV, 492ff. O. Michel examines the various traditions about 'witness' to be found in the New Testament in B. Reicke and H. Baltensweiler (eds.), *Neues Testament und Geschichte: historisches Geschehen und Deutung*, Festschrift für Oscar Cullmann (Tübingen, 1972), pp. 15–31.

cf. Constit. Apos. v.9.923... – it refers rather to the witnessing of Jesus, which was the cause of their death.'[1]

The Pauline passages mainly refer to God as Paul's witness (five times – Rom. 1: 9; II Cor. 1: 23; Phil. 1: 8; I Thess. 2: 5, 10), and once cite the Old Testament law of evidence (II Cor. 13: 1; cf. Deut. 19: 15), which is also cited in Matthew and Hebrews (Mt. 18: 16; Heb. 10: 28; cf. Deut. 17: 6). The other reference in Matthew is to the witnesses in the trial of Jesus (Mt. 26: 65; Mk 14: 63), and the other reference in Hebrews concerns the cloud of witnesses (Heb. 12: 1). These passages will be discussed in Chapter 11, as will the references to the Pastorals and I Peter. The use of μάρτυς in the Apocalypse requires special study, but this has been attempted elsewhere.[2]

THE USE OF Μαρτυρία

The noun μαρτυρία occurs even more frequently than μάρτυς (thirty-seven times to thirty-five). Its main use is in the Johannine literature, but it is also found three times in Mark (14: 55, 56, 59), twice in the Pastorals (I Tim. 3: 7; Tit. 1: 13) and once each in Luke's Gospel and the Book of Acts (Lk. 22: 71; Acts 22: 18).

Μαρτυρία frequently appears in the Fourth Gospel (fourteen times) and the First Epistle of John (seven times). Often it is connected with a genitive. A subjective genitive is used of: the testimony of the Baptist (Jn 1: 19; 5: 36); of Jesus (3: 11, 32; 5: 31, etc.); of two men (8: 17); of the Gospel eye-witness (19: 35); of God and man (I Jn 5: 9). The noun also appears in the phrase 'to receive testimony' (Jn 3: 33; 5: 34; I Jn 5: 9).

In the Apocalypse the only phrase requiring special treatment is ἡ μαρτυρία 'Ιησοῦ. This phrase occurs six times in the book, and is of very great significance for the seer's concept of witness (Rev. 1: 2, 9; 12: 17; 19: 10 (twice); 20: 4). In view of the frequency and importance of the phrase, it seems wise

[1] H. Cremer, *Biblico-Theological Lexicon of New Testament Greek* (4th ed., Edinburgh, 1895), p. 413.

[2] A. A. Trites, '*Martys* and Martyrdom in the Apocalypse – a semantic study', *NovT*, 15 (1973), 72–8.

THE WITNESS TERMINOLOGY OF THE NT

to postpone consideration of the grammatical problem until the meaning of 'the testimony of Jesus' can be considered in all its aspects in Chapter 10.

The other New Testament uses of the noun require little comment at this point. The Markan uses of μαρτυρία all occur in connection with the trial of Jesus; Mk 14: 55 is interesting, for here μαρτυρία is sought κατὰ τοῦ Ἰησοῦ. Lk. 22: 71 represents only a slight alteration of the Markan text, Luke using the genitive singular of μαρτυρία where Mark and Matthew employ the genitive plural of μάρτυς (Mk 14: 63; Mt. 26: 65); all three Synoptists use χρεία with a noun in the genitive case. In Acts 22: 18 the risen Lord tells Paul in a vision that the people of Jerusalem will not accept his μαρτυρία. In I Tim. 3: 7 the substantive is used with ἔχειν in defining the qualifications of the office of bishop; here μαρτυρίαν καλὴν ἔχειν bears much the same meaning as the participle μαρτυρούμενος in Acts 6: 3 and 10: 22. In Tit. 1: 13 μαρτυρία is used with ἀληθής to endorse the quotation from Epimenides in the preceding verse.

THE USE OF Μαρτύριον

The substantive μαρτύριον is found about twenty times in the New Testament. It is used three times each in Matthew, Mark and Luke, twice in Acts, three or four times in the Pauline Epistles (depending on the reading of I Cor. 2: 1), twice in the Pastorals and once in Hebrews, James and Revelation.

In two passages the word is used in the phrase ἡ σκηνὴ τοῦ μαρτυρίου (Acts 7: 44; Rev. 15: 5). Here it obviously refers to the 'tent of witness' so frequently mentioned in the Old Testament.[1]

Acts 4: 33 is a striking passage, for we are told that the apostles kept on giving (the force of ἀπεδίδουν) their μαρτύριον with great power. The context makes it quite clear that the primary content of the apostolic testimony concerned the resurrection of the κύριος – a theme which is constantly reiterated in the Book of Acts (1: 22; 2: 24, 31, 32, etc.). The apostolic evidence is specially important because it is supplied by eye-witnesses.

[1] Cf. *TDNT*, iv, 482–6.

Since the passages in the epistles which use μαρτύριον will all be discussed in Chapter 11, the only references left to be considered are those found in the Synoptic Gospels. These passages raise an important question: How is one to treat the recurring phrase εἰς μαρτύριον αὐτοῖς? More specifically, what kind of a dative is αὐτοῖς in these passages? To answer these questions it is necessary to look at three kinds of dative.

(1) *The Dative of Indirect Object*, where the case serves simply to introduce the one for whom or in whose interest an act is performed; e.g., Mt. 18: 26: πάντα ἀποδώσω σοι; 13:3; I Cor. 5: 9.[1] Further examples are cited by A. T. Robertson.[2]

(2) *The Dative of Advantage (Dativus Commodi)*, where the dative is used in a more specific expression of personal interest; e.g., II Cor. 2: 1: ἔκρινα ἐμαυτῷ τοῦτο; Rev. 21: 2.[3] Blass, Debrunner and Funk cite as additional examples Lk. 4: 22; 18: 31; II Cor. 5: 13 (two examples); I Pet. 5: 9; James 3: 18.[4] Note also Jn 3: 26 and 16: 7.

(3) *The Dative of Disadvantage (Dativus Incommodi)*, where the dative is employed when a person's interest is adversely affected; e.g., Mt. 23: 31: μαρτυρεῖτε ἑαυτοῖς.[5] Nigel Turner notes two additional examples of the dative of disadvantage in Rev. 2: 5, 16, ἔρχομαί σοι,[6] and Swete thinks that 'Αὐτῷ may be regarded as the *dat. incommodi*' in Mk 6: 19.[7] Perhaps one of the most important examples for us is James 5: 3, where μαρτύριον is followed by ὑμῖν, a dative of disadvantage which is correctly translated 'against you'. Note also ἐμαυτῷ in I Cor. 4: 4, τῷ Παύλῳ in Acts 18: 12 and αὐτοῖς in Acts 26: 11, which are clearly datives of disadvantage.

With this grammatical background it is now possible to

---

[1] H. E. Dana and J. R. Mantey, *A Manual Grammar of the Greek New Testament* (London, 1928), p. 84.

[2] A. T. Robertson, *A Short Grammar of the Greek New Testament* (London, 1908), p. 112.

[3] Dana and Mantey, *op. cit.*, p. 85.

[4] Blass and Debrunner, pp. 101–3.

[5] A. T. Robertson, *A Grammar of the Greek New Testament* (3rd ed., New York, 1919), p. 538.

[6] J. H. Moulton, W. F. Howard and N. Turner, *A Grammar of New Testament Greek* (3 vols.; Edinburgh, 1906–63), III, 238; cf. C. F. D. Moule, *Idiom-Book of New Testament Greek* (2nd ed., Cambridge, 1968), p. 46.

[7] H. B. Swete, *The Gospel according to St. Mark* (London, 1898), p. 117.

consider each use of εἰς μαρτύριον αὐτοῖς in the Gospels. The first passage to study is Mk 1: 44 and its parallels, Mt. 8: 4 and Lk. 5: 14. In each case the αὐτοῖς plainly refers to 'the people' – a point recognized by the RSV's translation. Here the dative is dative of indirect object; the certificate obtained from the priest will serve as evidence to the people that the leper has been cured and is fit for readmission to society. The next passage is Mk 6: 11 and its parallels, Lk. 9: 5 and Mt. 10: 14. Notwithstanding Strathmann's view that αὐτοῖς in Mk 6: 11 simply means 'against them',[1] the dative is perhaps best interpreted as dative of indirect object, as this allows for the various nuances of thought which seem to be present in the phrase.[2] In Lk. 9: 5 the evidence is definitely 'against them' (RV, RSV) – a fact made clear by the use of: (1) ἐπί with the accusative and (2) the *dativus incommodi* in the parallel passage concerning the mission of the Seventy (ὑμῖν, Lk. 10: 11).[3] In the Matthean parallel the Markan phrase εἰς μαρτύριον αὐτοῖς is absent.

Mk 13: 9 and its parallels also invite our attention, particularly in view of the fact that both Mark and Matthew use the phrase εἰς μαρτύριον αὐτοῖς (Mk 13: 9; Mt. 10: 18). In Mark and Matthew the dative is the dative of indirect object, as is the case in a similar passage (Mt. 24: 14). In Mark αὐτοῖς refers to the recipients of the testimony (most probably the 'governors' and 'kings', but possibly also the 'councils' and 'synagogues' mentioned in the earlier part of the verse); in Matthew it refers to the governors and kings, and the Gentiles are specifically mentioned by the addition of the phrase καὶ τοῖς ἔθνεσιν (Mt. 10: 18; cf. 24: 14). Luke uses quite a different grammatical construction to emphasize the opportunity that such solemn moments would afford for bearing testimony (ἀποβήσεται ὑμῖν εἰς μαρτύριον, Lk. 21: 15). The content of the testimony cannot in any of the three Gospels be determined by philological arguments. Kilpatrick has suggested that in Mark at least it is eschatological rather than evangelistic, i.e.

---

[1] Strathmann, *TDNT*, IV, 503 and *TWNT*, IV, 509.

[2] Cf. C. E. B. Cranfield, *The Gospel according to Saint Mark*, CGT (Cambridge, 1959), p. 201.

[3] On the textual problem see B. M. Metzger, 'Seventy or seventy-two disciples?', *NTS*, 5 (1958–9), 299–306.

that it is a warning of the imminence of the end in which the rulers will be involved.[1]

There remains one further example to be discussed. Lk. 4: 22 is a puzzling passage, because αὐτῷ after μαρτυρεῖν may be taken either as a dative of advantage or disadvantage. Similar ambiguities appear in the Hebrew hē'ȋd when used with a suffix (which can mean either 'to bear witness for some one' as in Job 29: 11 and Lam. 2: 13 or 'to bear witness against some one' as in I Kgs 21: 10, 13) and in the Aramaic 'ashēd 'al. This ambiguity is readily explained when the Old Testament controversy is recalled. Jewish law had no counsel for the defence or prosecution, but rather relied on witnesses who brought evidence on behalf of the defendant or hostile witnesses who brought charges against him. Thus in Lk. 4: 22 it is by no means obvious whether the people bear witness in favour of Jesus or against him.

Jeremias has argued cogently for the dative of disadvantage here.[2] The fact that Jesus deliberately omits the Isaianic reference to divine vengeance upon the Gentiles would be sufficient to account for the hostility of his nationalistically-minded countrymen (Lk. 4: 19; cf. Isa. 61: 2). Interpreted in this way, Jeremias can paraphrase Lk. 4: 22 as follows: 'They protested with one voice and were furious, because he (only) spoke about (God's year of) mercy (and omitted the words about the Messianic vengeance).'[3] In other words, a good case can be made for taking αὐτῷ as a dative of disadvantage. This would be in keeping both with the antagonism expressed in the question at the end of verse 22, and with the murderous attempt to throw Jesus off the brow of the hill outside Nazareth (Lk. 4: 29). It would also be in complete harmony with the Old Testament conception of justice in the gate, where witnesses frequently function in a hostile manner against the accused.

[1] G. D. Kilpatrick, 'The gentile mission in Mark and Mark 13: 9–11', *Studies in the Gospels*, ed. D. E. Nineham (Oxford, 1955), pp. 145–58.

[2] J. Jeremias, *Jesus' Promise to the Nations* (London, 1958), pp. 44–6; cf. also *The Parables of Jesus* (6th ed., New York, 1963), p. 218.

[3] Jeremias, *Jesus' Promise to the Nations*, p. 45.

THE USE OF Μαρτυρεῖν AND Μαρτύρεσθαι

The verb μαρτυρεῖν is used approximately seventy-two times in the New Testament. It is particularly conspicuous in the Fourth Gospel (thirty-two times). There it most frequently occurs in the phrase μαρτυρεῖν περί (eighteen times), though three times it appears with the verb ἑωρακέναι (Jn 3: 11, 32; 19: 35) and once it is used to introduce a solemn 'Amen' saying of Jesus (13: 21).[1] Elsewhere μαρτυρεῖν is prominent in the Book of Acts (eleven times) and the Johannine Epistles (ten times), and appears eight times in Hebrews, six times in Paul, twice in the Pastorals (I Tim. 5: 10; 6: 13) and once each in Matthew and Luke (Mt. 23: 31; Lk. 4: 22).

The middle form μαρτύρεσθαι, on the other hand, is found only five times in the New Testament, three times in Paul (Gal. 5: 3; Eph. 4: 17; I Thess. 2: 12) and twice in Acts (20: 26; 26: 22). Acts 26: 22 and the Pauline references will be discussed in Chapters 9 and 11, so that leaves only Acts 20: 26 to deal with. The context is Paul's farewell speech to the Ephesian elders at Miletus, in which he solemnly affirms (μαρτύρομαι ὑμῖν) that he has fully discharged his obligations as an ambassador of Christ in their midst. While grammatically the verb μαρτύρεσθαι is followed by a dative of indirect object, the passage's chief interest lies in its similarity with the first part of Samuel's address to the people of Israel in I Sam. 12: 1–5. Twice Paul appeals to the knowledge of his hearers who can testify both to the faithful character of his ministry and the unstinting labour of his hands (Acts 20: 18, 34).

Returning to μαρτυρεῖν, we can discuss the major philological points under four headings: (1) μαρτυρεῖσθαι, (2) μαρτυρεῖν with the dative, (3) μαρτυρεῖν with μαρτυρίαν or ὁμολογίαν and (4) μαρτυρεῖν with prepositions.

(1) The passive form μαρτυρεῖσθαι occurs about twelve times in the New Testament. Sometimes it means 'be witnessed, have witness borne by someone', and so quite naturally it can be followed by ὑπό with a noun in the genitive case, as in Rom. 3: 21.[2] It can be used with ὅτι to introduce a quotation, as in Heb. 7: 8 (cf. 7: 17). A more common meaning of

---

[1] Cf. J. H. Bernard, *St. John*, ICC (2 vols., New York, 1929), II, 470.
[2] Arndt and Gingrich, p. 494.

THE USE OF Μαρτυρεῖν AND Μαρτύρεσθαι

μαρτυρεῖσθαι, however, is 'be well spoken of, approved'.[1] Here also ὑπό appears with a noun in the genitive to indicate the person or persons who give their approval. Cornelius and Ananias are said to be 'well spoken of' *by* the Jews (Acts 10: 22; 22: 12), and 'Demetrius has testimony *from* every one, and *from* the truth itself' (III Jn 12), ὑπό being used in each case. Others mentioned as well spoken of or approved are Timothy (Acts 16: 2), the Seven in Acts 6: 3 and widows seeking financial aid from church funds (I Tim. 5: 10, ἐν ἔργοις καλοῖς μαρτυρουμένη). Sometimes the person concerned is approved in the pages of the Old Testament (Heb. 11: 2, 39); this can be done by means of μαρτυρεῖσθαι followed by a nominative and infinitive construction (Heb. 11: 4a, 5).

(2) Μαρτυρεῖν is used with the dative some twenty times. Some of these passages have already been dealt with in discussing the use of the dative with μαρτύριον (Mt. 23: 31; Lk. 4: 22; Jn 3: 26). Concerning the remaining passages, certain observations may be made: (a) Three times in the Johannine writings μαρτυρεῖν takes ἀλήθεια in the dative (Jn 5: 33; 18: 37; III Jn 3), and once it takes ἀγαπή (III Jn 6). (b) Twice in the Book of Acts μαρτυρεῖν takes a dative when introducing a quotation from Scripture (Acts 10: 43; 13: 22). (c) The dative is probably the dative of indirect object in Jn 3: 28; Acts 15: 8;[2] 22: 5; Heb. 10: 15; Rev. 22: 16. (d) Three times Paul uses the phrase μαρτυρῶ γάρ plus a personal pronoun in the dative followed by ὅτι (Rom. 10: 2; Gal. 4: 15; Col. 4: 13). (e) In Acts 14: 4 the verb μαρτυρεῖν, followed by a dative, is used to introduce the fact that God gives consentient witness by 'signs and wonders', whereas much the same idea is conveyed in Heb. 2: 4 by the use of συνεπιμαρτυρεῖν followed by the nouns σημεῖα and τέρατα in the dative. (f) The dative in III Jn 12 is striking: Δημητρίῳ μεμαρτύρηται ὑπὸ πάντων κ.τ.λ.

(3) Μαρτυρεῖν is used with μαρτυρίαν or ὁμολογίαν only four times. In Jn 5: 33 the combination occurs on the lips of Jesus and concerns the Father's testimony to himself. In I Jn 5: 10 the phrase is interesting from a grammatical point of

[1] *Ibid.* Paul contrasts those well spoken of with their opposite number by the nouns εὐφημία and δυσφημία in II Cor. 6: 8. For other expressions of communal approval cf. Acts 5: 34; Gal. 2: 2; Phil. 2: 29.
[2] Cf. J. D. G. Dunn, *Baptism in the Holy Spirit* (London, 1970), pp. 81–2.

73

view as an illustration of a cognate accusative; the same is true of Rev. 1: 2. I Jn 5: 10 is also worthy of notice because God is the one who provides the testimony. I Tim. 6: 13 speaks of Jesus Christ, who bears the testimony which is described as ἡ καλὴ ὁμολογία; his 'confession' was offered before Pontius Pilate.

(4) Μαρτυρεῖν also appears with several prepositions. The use of μαρτυρεῖν with περί and ὑπό has already been noted. Μαρτυρεῖν appears with ἐπί plus the dative in Heb. 11: 4b and with διά plus the genitive in Heb. 11: 39. It takes εἰς with a noun in the accusative in Acts 23: 11, where μαρτυρεῖν appears in an accusative and infinitive construction. Μαρτυρεῖν is used only once with κατά plus a noun in the genitive. This occurs in a passage in which Paul is drawing the logical consequences which follow if one denies the possibility of resurrection. 'If there is no resurrection of the dead', Paul is saying, 'we are false witnesses who testify against God (κατά τοῦ θεοῦ; cf. Mk 14: 55; Acts 24: 1; 25: 2; Rom. 11: 2), and our testimony to the risen Christ is, *ex hypothesi*, false' (I Cor. 15: 15).[1] The use of μαρτυρεῖν κατά here reminds one of a similar use of '*ānāh bᵉ* in the Old Testament (Job 15: 6; Prov. 25: 18).

THE USE OF Διαμαρτύρεσθαι

The verb is found fifteen times in the New Testament, mainly in the Book of Acts (nine times), but also three times in the Pastoral Epistles (I Tim. 5: 21; II Tim. 2: 14; 4: 1) and once each in Luke, Paul and Hebrews (Lk. 16: 28; I Thess. 4: 6; Heb. 2: 6).

In Acts διαμαρτύρεσθαι refers to the solemn attestation of the apostolic message with a view to winning converts (e.g., 2: 40; 8: 25; 18: 5; 20: 24). The verb is used of Christian testimony before both Jews and Greeks (e.g., 10: 42; 20: 21; 23: 11; 28: 23), and of the Holy Spirit's testimony (20: 23; cf. 21: 4, 11). Several times this verb is combined with other verbs such as παρακαλεῖν (2: 40), λαλεῖν (8: 25), and πείθειν (28: 23). In the sole Lukan reference it virtually means 'warn'

[1] So W. D. Chamberlain, *An Exegetical Grammar of the Greek New Testament* (New York, 1941), p. 124.

(so RSV, NEB, JB), a usage which is paralleled in the LXX (Lk. 16: 28; cf. Ex. 19: 21; Deut. 8: 19; Neh. 9: 26; Jer. 6: 10). The verb has the same meaning in I Thess. 4: 6, where it is used with the defective verb προεῖπον. In the three passages in the Pastorals διαμαρτύρεσθαι is followed by the phrase ἐνώπιον τοῦ θεοῦ, and can be translated in each case as 'charge' (I Tim. 5: 21; II Tim. 2: 14; 4: 1). In Heb. 2: 6 the verb is used of the testimony of Scripture in introducing a quotation from Psa. 8: 4–6.

THE USE OF Ψευδομάρτυς, Ψευδομαρτυρία, AND Ψευδομαρτυρεῖν

The noun ψευδομάρτυς is found only twice in the New Testament and in both cases it is used in the plural. It appears in Matthew's account of the trial of Jesus (Mt. 26: 60) and in Paul's reasoned treatment of the resurrection. If the possibility of a general resurrection be denied on *a priori* grounds, Christ is not raised, the preaching of Paul and his fellow apostles (ἐγὼ εἴτε ἐκεῖνοι, I Cor. 15: 10) is meaningless, and they are detected as ψευδομάρτυρες: 'not such as falsely claim to be witnesses; but those who bear witness to what is false, Matt. 26: 60.'[1] The reason why they can be described as 'false witnesses of God' is clear: it is because they have testified that God has done something which in fact he has not done, i.e., raise up Christ.[2] In other words, the phrase 'rests upon the significance which the apostles, as preachers of the Gospel, claim for their prerogative as witnesses of Jesus'.[3]

The noun ψευδομαρτυρία is absent from the New Testament except in Matthew's Gospel, where it appears twice. In Mt. 15: 19 false depositions (ψευδομαρτυρίαι) are mentioned despite their absence from the Markan parallel (Mk 7: 21), possibly because Matthew wishes to suggest that the later depositions at the trial of Jesus sprang out of the evil hearts of the ψευδο-

[1] C. Hodge, *An Exposition of the First Epistle to the Corinthians* (Grand Rapids, 1953), p. 320.

[2] Strathmann, *TDNT*, iv, 514.

[3] H. Cremer, *Biblico-Theological Lexicon of the New Testament* (4th ed., Edinburgh, 1895), p. 413.

75

μάρτυρες (Mt. 26: 60). This suggestion is strengthened by the fact that the other use of ψευδομαρτυρία in Matthew occurs in the trial of Jesus (Mt. 26: 59). Here the Sanhedrin keeps on seeking ψευδομαρτυρία against Jesus.

The verb ψευδομαρτυρεῖν, which appears in Josephus (*Ant.* IV. 219; III. 92), is found five times in the New Testament. In Mk 10: 19 and its parallels (Mt. 19: 18; Lk. 18: 20) several of the Ten Commandments are quoted. This fact accounts for the use of the verb, which is used in the LXX at Ex. 20: 16 and Deut. 5: 20 (17) to represent the Hebrew *'ānāh*. The other two references are Markan, and come in the trial of Jesus (Mk 14: 56, 57). They both contain the phrase ἐψευδομαρτύρουν κατ' αὐτοῦ, which is notable for its use of the imperfect tense of the verb and of ψευδομαρτυρεῖν with κατά.

THE USE OF Καταμαρτυρεῖν

This verb, already encountered in the LXX (e.g., I(III) Kgs 21(20): 10, 13; Job 15: 6; Prov. 25: 18), Josephus (*Ant.* IV. 219; cf.VIII.358, 359) and Philo (*Leg. All.* III.199), appears only three times in the New Testament, in each case in connection with the trial of Jesus. Matthew records the high priest's words in precisely the same language as Mark: τί οὗτοί σου καταμαρτυροῦσιν (Mt. 26: 62; Mk 14: 60). In Matthew the verb reappears in the following chapter in Pilate's challenge to Jesus: 'Do you not hear how many things they witness against you?' (Mt. 27: 13). In all three passages καταμαρτυρεῖν governs a personal pronoun in the genitive.

THE USE OF OTHER Μαρτ- WORDS

A few additional words related to μάρτυς and its cognates must be listed for the sake of completeness, though they do not substantially affect the development of the witness theme in the New Testament. With the sole exception of the adjective ἀμάρτυρος (meaning 'without witness'; found only in the New Testament at Acts 14: 17; cf. Thucydides II.41.4; Josephus, *Ant.* XIV.111), the miscellaneous words are verbs formed by adding prefixes to the verb μαρτυρεῖν. Thus συνεπιμαρτυρεῖν means 'to bear witness at the same time' (Heb. 2: 4). This illustration is striking because in addition to the testimony of Christ and those who heard him reference is made to the consentient divine testimony in signs and wonders. Other examples of verbs built up from the basic verb are ἐπιμαρτυρεῖν (I Pet. 5: 12) and the middle deponent verb προμαρτύρεσθαι (I Pet. 1: 11).

SUMMARY

It is now fitting to summarize our results. Generally speaking, we can say that as far as μάρτυς and its cognates are concerned, points of grammar and philology do not greatly advance one's understanding of witness in the New Testament. The obvious exceptions to this statement are the treatment of εἰς μαρτύριον αὐτοῖς in the Synoptics and ἡ μαρτυρία 'Ιησοῦ in the Apocalypse. The former phrase requires careful grammatical study of each passage to see whether the dative is dative of indirect object, dative of disadvantage, or dative of advantage. The latter phrase must be treated both grammatically and theologically, together with the semantic development of the noun μάρτυς and the verb μαρτυρεῖν (see Chapter 10).

CHAPTER 8

THE CONCEPT OF WITNESS IN THE FOURTH GOSPEL

The Fourth Gospel, like Isaiah 40–55, is of particular importance for it presents a sustained use of juridical metaphor. Here we must ask what is the issue being debated, who are the participants in the debate and what is the outcome.

The issue under debate is plainly the Messiahship and divine Sonship of Jesus. It is mainly to convince his readers of this proposition that the Evangelist has written his Gospel: 'But these are written that you may believe that Jesus is the Christ, the Son of God, and that believing you may have life in his name' (Jn 20: 31). Now it is possible, as Professor Moule has noted,

to interpret this as applying to those who have already come to believe, in the sense that the aim is to deepen or make constant that belief... But on the whole there is a strong case for the view that the Fourth Gospel is more intelligible as a skilful apology... than as primarily intended for the full believer.[1]

Similarly, Professor van Unnik has remarked that 'John did not write for Christians in the first place, except perhaps in chs. 13–17 which show a somewhat different character... His book was... a mission-book which sought to win.'[2] As Renan said a hundred years ago, the Fourth Gospel evinces 'the desire to prove a thesis, and to convince adversaries'. It has a definite case to present: 'briefly, the purpose of John's Gospel is to prove to his readers who Jesus is, and that faith in him means salvation'.[3]

[1] C. F. D. Moule, 'The intention of the evangelists', *New Testament Essays*, ed. A. J. B. Higgins (Manchester, 1959), p. 168, *contra* R. V. G. Tasker, R. E. Brown and A. J. B. Higgins, for which see Higgins, *The Tradition about Jesus* (Edinburgh, 1969), pp. 23–4, 45.

[2] W. C. van Unnik, 'The purpose of St. John's Gospel', *The Gospels Reconsidered*, ed. F. L. Cross (Oxford, 1960), p. 195.

[3] E. Renan, *The Life of Jesus* (1863; Everyman Edition, 1927), p. 15 and O. J. Fjelstad, 'The purpose of John's Gospel', *TF*, 1 (1929), 161–2. Cf. J. Muilenburg, 'Literary form in the Fourth Gospel', *JBL*, 51 (1932), 43.

THE JURIDICAL CHARACTER OF THE FOURTH GOSPEL

That John is concerned to prove a case is clear from a number of considerations which may be listed here for the sake of convenience, and explored in greater detail later.

To begin with, the sayings of Jesus in the Fourth Gospel are often described as 'discourse', but are rather more commonly juridical debate. The discussions of Jesus with 'the Jews' sound like a lawsuit: indeed, the first twelve chapters have as their main theme the conflict of Jesus with the 'Ιουδαῖοι, who represent the unbelieving world in its hostility to God. 'This whole section', Professor Johnston has pointed out, 'has the form of a great contest or assize.'[1] The 'argumentativeness' which Burkitt found 'so positively repellent' is an integral element in the Fourth Gospel, and provides just the context of contention and debate in which one would expect to see witnesses called and evidence presented to substantiate the claims of Christ.[2]

These general considerations are strengthened by observing that the Fourth Gospel presents a controversy very similar to the one found in Isaiah 40–55. There the controversy between Yahweh and the false gods turns out to be a lawsuit between God and the world. God is represented by Israel and the world by the pagan nations. Similarly, in the Fourth Gospel God incarnate has a lawsuit with the world. His witnesses include John the Baptist, the scriptures, the words and works of Christ, and later the witness of the apostles and the Holy Spirit. They are opposed by the world, represented by the unbelieving Jews. In Isaiah 40–55 the debate is over the claims of Yahweh as the Creator, the only true God and the Lord of history (Isa. 40: 25–31; 44: 6–8; 45: 8–11, 21); in John it is over the Messiahship and divine Sonship of Jesus (Jn 20: 31; cf. 3: 15–16). John, like his Old Testament counterpart, has a case to present, and for this reason he advances his arguments, chal-

---

[1] G. Johnston, *The Spirit-Paraclete in the Gospel of John* (Cambridge, 1970), p. 155. On the juridical aspect in John see T. Preiss, *Life in Christ* (London, 1954), pp. 9–39, and M. C. Tenney, 'The meaning of "witness" in John', *BS*, 132 (1975), 229–41.

[2] F. C. Burkitt, *The Gospel History and its Transmission* (Edinburgh, 1911), pp. 227–8. Cf. C. Masson, 'Le témoignage de Jean', *RHPR*, 38 (1950), 120–7.

lenges his opponents and presents his witnesses after the fashion of the Old Testament legal assembly.

'Witness' is one of John's favourite words. C. K. Barrett has made this point very clear:

'Witness' (μαρτυρεῖν, μαρτυρία) holds an important place in the thought of the gospel. The Baptist (1.7f., 15, 32, 34; 3.26; 5.33), the Samaritan woman (4.39), the works of Jesus (5.36; 10.25), the Old Testament (5.39), the multitude (12.17), the Holy Spirit and the apostles (15.26f.), God the Father himself (5.32, 37; 8.18), all bear witness to Jesus. Jesus himself...bears witness to the truth (18.37; cf. 3.11), in conjunction with the Father (8.13–18) whose consentient testimony validates his own. Witnesses in turn testify to the truth of the gospel record (19.35; 21.24). In 18.23 the accusers of Jesus are invited to bear witness regarding the evil he is alleged to have done, that is, to establish by their testimony the fact alleged. This is normal Greek usage, it corresponds sufficiently to the use of the root '*wd* in the Old Testament (which also supplies the notion of God's testifying to, or against, his people), and is the common meaning of the words in John.[1]

The idea of witness in John's Gospel is both very prominent and thoroughly juridical,[2] and is to be understood in terms of Old Testament legal language.

Other juridical words are notably frequent in the Fourth Gospel in the context of hostility and debate; e.g., judge, cause, judgment, accuse, convince. The use of such Greek words as κρίσις (eleven times), κρίνειν (nineteen times), κρίμα (9: 39), κατηγορία (18: 29), κατηγορεῖν (5: 45, twice). ἀποκρίνεσθαι (5: 17, 19), ἀπόκρισις (1: 22; 19: 9); βῆμα (19: 13), 3ήτησις (3: 25), ἐλέγχειν (3: 20; 8: 46; 16: 8), ὁμολογεῖν (1: 20, twice; 9: 22; 12: 42), ἀρνεῖσθαι (1: 20; 13: 38; 18: 25, 27), αἰτία

---

[1] C. K. Barrett, *The Gospel according to St. John* (London, 1962). Cf. J. H. Bernard, *St. John*, ICC (2 vols., Edinburgh, 1929), I, xc–xciii, who finds seven major witnesses in John's Gospel. Marcus Barth, *Die Augenzeuge*, (Zurich, 1946), p. 272, thinks that John's neglect of μάρτυς and μαρτύριον in preference for the verb and μαρτυρία indicates a concentration on the actual witness-giving as opposed to the subject matter offered as evidence. So also Boice, *Witness and Revelation in the Gospel of John*, p. 25.

[2] R. Bultmann, *The Gospel of John* (Oxford, 1971) has drawn attention to the forensic use of μαρτυρία and μαρτυρεῖν on pp. 50, 145, 172, 293, 553. Cf. I. de la Potterie, 'La notion de témoignage dans Saint Jean', *Sacra Pagina*, II, eds. J. Coppens *et al.* (Paris, 1959), 194–6.

(18: 38; 19: 4, 6), εὑρίσκειν (18: 38; 19: 4, 6) and σχίσμα (7: 43; 9: 16; 10: 19) suggests the idea that the work of Christ is set against a background of opposition in which it would be natural to try to prove Christ's case when it was being questioned and challenged.

The work of the Holy Spirit appears to be interpreted in a juridical way in the Fourth Gospel. Not only is the Spirit described by the juridical word Παράκλητος (14: 16, 26; 15: 26; 16: 7; cf. I Jn 2: 1), but his activity is thoroughly in keeping with such a designation.[1]

The respect paid to the Old Testament law of evidence indicates that John has a case he is anxious to prove. Thus even Jesus' own declaration is not accepted as valid without confirmation (5: 31). Similarly, Jesus is presented as quoting the rule from the Old Testament that 'the witness of two men is true' (8: 17). This rule comes from Deut. 19: 15, and can be discovered in several places in John's Gospel – chapter 1 has the double witness of the Baptist and the disciples; chapter 2 establishes the reality of the miracle by two independent witnesses; chapter 5 records the witness of the Baptist, the works of Christ and the scriptures; chapter 20 has *two* angels at the empty tomb where Mark has only one. John is definitely concerned to present legally admissible evidence.

Belief is a central concept in the Fourth Gospel; indeed, 'no other evangelist speaks so often of belief and unbelief.'[2] Thus the verb πιστεύειν appears some ninety-eight times in the Gospel, usually with reference to Christ as the object of faith (e.g., 3: 16; 4: 39; 6: 29; 12: 44; 17: 20). This is not surprising in view of the testimonial and evidential character of this Gospel (20: 31), and supports the notion that the Evangelist is trying to convince people that Jesus is the Christ, the Son of God. He writes, to borrow a phrase from 19: 35, 'that you also may believe'.

[1] R. E. Brown, 'The Paraclete in the Fourth Gospel', *NTS*, 13 (1967), 116–17. On the different interpretations of 'Paraclete' cf. Johnston, *The Spirit–Paraclete*, pp. 80–118 and R. E. Brown, *The Gospel according to John* (2 vols., Garden City, N.Y., 1966–70), II, 1136–43.
[2] R. D. Potter, 'Topography and archaeology in the Fourth Gospel', *TU*, 73 (1959), 330. Cf. F. V. Filson, 'The gospel of life', *Current Issues in New Testament Interpretation*, ed. W. Klassen and G. F. Snyder (London, 1962), p. 112.

Another consideration has been succinctly stated by J. C. Hindley:

When Jesus makes affirmations about His heavenly origin and divine commission [e.g., 5: 43; 7: 28f.; 8: 14, 28] He is not only revealing the relationship between Himself and God: *He is presenting evidence for a verdict*, or rather a challenge to decision. His words have and are intended to have an existential impact on those who hear them... Closer examination shows that this is not merely an assertion. Certain arguments are used to justify it...: the often quoted 'which of you convicts me of sin?' (8: 46) is an argument of this type.[1] Similarly, the allusion to Psalm 82.6 ('I said you are gods') is intended as a proof amenable to human reason that the claim to be Son of God is not blasphemous (10.34). So, though less clearly, is the argument that Jesus 'does not seek his own glory' (8.50): that is to say, His religious dependence on God ought to be recognised as a proof of His integrity.[2]

Another feature, hinted at in the preceding points but deserving consideration in its own right, is the use of juridical questions in John. The interrogative frequently appears in the Fourth Gospel (e.g., 1: 48; 4: 27, 33; 9: 36; 11: 34; 14: 5; 18: 29; 20: 15), but in many places, particularly in John 1–12, it is an example of lawcourt speech. The parties in the controversy interrogate one another, questioning each other's explanations. The obvious aim of these pointed questions is to shift the *onus probandi* to one's opponent (cf. Mk 11: 27–33 pars.). This characteristic was observed both in Isaiah 40–55 (Isa. 41: 2, 4, 26; 43: 9; 45: 21) and Job (13: 7–9), and is also present in John's Gospel (e.g., Jn 5: 44, 47; 7: 15, 19, 20, 23, 52; 8: 48, 57; 9: 34; 10: 31). Taken with other evidence, this is another indication of the importance of the controversy theme in the Fourth Gospel.

The question of Messiahship, as van Unnik has pointed out, holds an important place in the Fourth Gospel.[3] The Baptist denies that he is the Christ (1: 20; 3: 28). The common people (7: 25–31, 40–3; 12: 34), the Jewish authorities (1: 19, 24–5) and the Samaritans (4: 25, 29) discuss Messiahship, and the first disciples confess: 'We have found the Messiah' (1: 41).

[1] On Jn 10: 34 see A. Hanson, 'John's citation of Psalm lxxxii reconsidered', *NTS*, 13 (1967), 363–7.

[2] J. C. Hindley, 'Witness in the Fourth Gospel', *SJT*, 18 (1965), 321–3.

[3] W. C. van Unnik, 'The purpose of St. John's Gospel', pp. 167ff.

Later a blind man is excommunicated for the same confession, for 'the Jews had already agreed that if any one should confess him to be the Christ, he was to be put out of the synagogue' (9: 22). Further, except in two cases, in the combination 'Jesus Christ' (1: 17; 17: 3), the word is always a title, and ὁ χριστός retains its full etymological force. John is so concerned to present Jesus as Messiah that he uses the title more frequently than Matthew (twenty-one times to seventeen), and more often than Mark (seven) and Luke (twelve) put together; this was the main thing he was concerned to prove.

The silence of the witnesses at the trial of Jesus is remarkable in the Fourth Gospel. This feature is reminiscent of the Book of Job, where a speaker withdraws from the controversy by putting his hand over his mouth (Job 21: 5; 29: 9; 40: 4). Silence is appropriate when one has nothing more to say (as is the case with Job's third 'friend', who does not participate in the third cycle of speeches), or when the case against one is unanswerable (cf. Neh. 5: 6–8; Mt. 22: 12). Now in John's Gospel, in contrast to Mark (14: 55–60) and Matthew (26: 59–62), there are no accusations by false witnesses in the trial of Jesus. This cannot be taken as accidental, for John presents Jesus as explicitly inviting the high priest to question the opposing witnesses (18: 21). Similarly, Jesus boldly challenges the officer who hits him on this occasion with the words: 'If I have spoken wrongly, bear witness to the wrong; but if I have spoken rightly, why do you strike me?' (18: 23, also 8: 46; cf. a similar challenge to one's legal opponents in Acts 24: 20). The fact that no reference is made to anyone taking up the challenge is intended by John to suggest that Jesus won the lawsuit; even Pilate thrice declares that Jesus is innocent (18: 38; 19: 4, 6).[1] Jesus bore witness at his own trial to the truth (18: 37), and his evidence, John implies, is ungainsayable.[2]

---

[1] Cf. J. A. Bailey, *The Traditions Common to the Gospels of Luke and John* (Leiden, 1963), p. 64.

[2] O. Betz, *Der Paraklet* (Leiden, 1963), pp. 36–116, has gathered an impressive amount of evidence showing parallels between Qumran and Johannine thought including ethical dualism, predestination concepts, the light of life, spirit of truth *and* witnessing to the truth (Jn 5: 33; 18: 37; 1 QS 8: 6). For an evaluation of Betz's contribution see A. R. C. Leaney, *The Rule of Qumran and its Meaning* (London, 1966), p. 53, and Johnston, *The Spirit-Paraclete, passim.*

Therefore, according to Old Testament legal procedure and in harmony with rabbinical practice (Kiddushin 65b) Jesus really won his case; it was a travesty of justice that he was crucified when no κατηγορία could be laid against him and when no αἰτία had been found in him (18: 29, 38; cf. I Sam. 12: 1–5). Pilate is really convicted of the sin of perverting justice.

This interpretation receives confirmation from Isaiah 40–55. Repeatedly there the pagan gods or their representatives are challenged to state their case and advance their proofs (Isa. 41: 21–3; 43: 9; 44: 7), but they remain silent. Why? Because they cannot predict or influence the course of events and because they have no real existence (41: 24, 26–9). Their 'witnesses neither see nor know' (44: 9), and therefore have nothing to declare. Accordingly, by their silence the nations, who function as the legal representatives of the false gods, acknowledge that Yahweh has won the lawsuit. The silence of the nations is in marked contrast to Israel's role as Yahweh's witness (43: 10, 12; 44: 8), and, it may be added, to Yahweh's own refusal elsewhere in the Old Testament to keep silent in court when acting as a witness or judge (Ps. 50: 3–7; Mal. 3: 5). This, then, is the probable background against which the silence of the witnesses in the Fourth Gospel is to be understood. Here is another indication both of the juridical character of the Fourth Gospel and of its creative use of Isaiah 40–55.

Participants in the lawsuit can serve both as witnesses *and* as advocates, just as they do in the Old Testament lawsuit or controversy. A like situation obtains in Isaiah 40–55, where it is the task of the witnesses not only to attest the facts but also to convince the opposite side of the truth of them (Isa. 41: 21–4, 26; 43: 9). In the Fourth Gospel both of these functions are stressed. John the Baptist is both a witness to Christ (1: 8, 15) and also an advocate who tries to convince unbelievers 'that all might believe through him' (1: 7). The same is true of Christ: as a good witness he speaks of what he knows and bears witness of what he has seen (3: 11, 32; cf. 1: 18; 8: 26), and as the ἄλλος Παράκλητος (cf. 14: 16) he presents his case (5: 30–47; 10: 32–8). After Christ's departure to the Father, the lawsuit over his claims continues; the apostles are both eye-witnesses of his public ministry (15: 27), and also advocates who try to convince people of his redemptive significance (17: 20; 19: 35).

But they are not alone in this work, for the Holy Spirit also serves in the dual role of witness and advocate (15: 26; 16: 8–15).

The details of Jn 19: 34–5 appear to have an evidential significance. The account of the soldier piercing the side of Jesus and the immediate outrush of blood and water is important, for 'John intended to provide evidence that Jesus was a real man, and that he really died...This is emphasized by the stress laid on the eye-witness in v. 35' – a fact indicated by the use of both μαρτυρεῖν and μαρτυρία.[1] John's concern for eye-witness testimony here is interesting for several reasons: (a) 'The fact that he is at pains to protect the truthfulness of a single witness is a definite sign that he is working upon a historical basis.'[2] This reminds us of the Book of Acts, where Luke's emphasis on the apostolic witness serves a similar purpose. (b) The phrase 'he knows that he speaks the truth' is similar to Paul's use of the phrase 'God is my witness' when asserting some fact of his inner life for which his word is the only guarantee (Rom. 1: 9; II Cor. 1: 23; Phil. 1: 8; I Thess. 2: 5).

Pilate in the Fourth Gospel virtually assumes the role of a witness or advocate. This is indicated by: (a) his repeated, emphatic declaration that Jesus is innocent of the charge laid against him (18: 38; 19: 4, 6); (b) his stout refusal to change the superscription to 'He said, I am the King of the Jews' (19: 19–22); (c) his attempt to release Jesus instead of Barabbas, the revolutionary ληστής (18: 39–40); (d) his plan to scourge Jesus, and then, if possible, release him (19: 1, 4; cf. Lk. 23: 22); (e) his desire to turn the execution over to the Jews, thereby escaping judicial responsibility for a gross miscarriage of justice (19: 6); (f) his persistence in seeking to release Jesus (ἐζήτει, 19: 12) despite the determined cries of the Jews, for His crucifixion (ἐκραύγασαν, 18: 40; 19: 6, 15; ἐκραύγαζον, 19: 12); (g) his final appeal for the Jews to recognize and spare their king: 'Here is your King!' (19: 14f.) As Ellis Jansen has remarked:

[1] Barrett, *The Gospel according to St. John*, p. 462, Cf. H. P. V. Nunn, *The Authorship of the Fourth Gospel* (Oxford, 1952), pp. 13–14.
[2] A. Barr. 'The factor of testimony in the gospels', *ExpT*, 49 (1937–8), 406–7. Cf. E. Pond, 'The evidence of testimony', *BS*, 102 (1945), 179–93.

To Pilate Jesus truly was the King of the Jews in a religious sense, and so he refuses to make the change [on the superscription]. Thus even Pilate is aware that the people have committed the dastardly deed of rejecting their heavenly King, and adds his support to the main contention of the early Christian preachers to the Jews. He makes the same confession in his own way that Nathaniel had made much earlier: 'Thou art the Son of God; thou art the King of Israel.'...Thus even Jesus' judge adds his witness to Jesus' divinity.[1]

The resurrection accounts of chapters 20 and 21 have an evidential ring about them. Against all would-be objectors John is concerned to maintain the identity of Christ's risen body with the one which was crucified and laid in the tomb. This may possibly explain why John alone speaks of: (a) Christ's 'hands *and* side' (20: 20, 25, 27; but cf. Lk. 24: 40: 'hands and feet'); (b) the athletic condition of the witnesses – perhaps an eye-witness touch (Jn 20: 3, 4); (c) the state of the grave cloths (20: 6–8); and (d) Christ's invitation to doubting Thomas (20: 27; cf. Lk. 24: 40: 'Handle me'). This argument appears the more cogent in view of Christ's explicit challenge to the Jews: 'Destroy this temple, and in three days I will raise it up' (Jn 2: 19ff.). The resurrection is of juridical significance in that it constitutes Christ's last and greatest sign.[2]

'The Johannine idea of the mission of Christ as God's agent is seen within the context of a lawsuit', as Peder Borgen has shown by pointing out the striking similarities which exist between the halakhic principles of agency and ideas in the Fourth Gospel:

(a) the unity between the agent and his sender [Jn 12: 44; 13: 20; 14: 9; 15: 23] – (b) although the agent is subordinate [13: 16], (c) the obedience of the agent to the will of the sender [6: 38; 8: 29], (d) the task of the agent in the lawsuit [6: 44; 12: 31–2]; (e) his return and reporting back to the sender [13: 3; 17: 4], and (f) his appointing of other agents as an extension of his own mission in time and space [17: 16; 20: 21].[3]

---

[1] E. Jansen, 'The first century controversy over Jesus as a revolutionary figure', *JBL*, 60 (1941), 271. On Jn 13: 21 see E. C. Hoskyns, *The Fourth Gospel*, ed. F. N. Davey (London, 1947), p. 442.

[2] Cf. W. F. McClellan, 'Saint John's evidence of the resurrection', *CBQ*, 1 (1939), 253–5 and D. Guthrie, 'The importance of signs in the Fourth Gospel', *VE*, (1967), 78.

[3] P. Borgen, 'God's agent in the Fourth Gospel', *Religions in Antiquity*, ed. J. Neusner (Leiden, 1968), pp. 137–48.

It is point (d) that calls for further comment here:

According to the halakah the sender transferred his own rights and the property concerned to the agent. On this basis the agent might acquire the title in court and secure the claim for himself. The will of the sender, the Father, in John 6: 39 makes just this transfer clear:... The transfer is even more pointedly stated in 17: 6: 'thine they were, and thou gavest them to me'....

The next step is the actual acquiring of the title in court and the agent's securing of the claim himself. John 12: 31–2 pictures such a court scene...There is close resemblance between the two phrases 'I will draw all men to myself' (John [12: 32]) and 'secure the claim for yourself' (halakah [Baba Kamma 70a: 'Go forth and take legal action so that you may acquire title to it and secure the claim for yourself']).[1]

In other words, Christ, as the one sent from the Father, functions as his agent in the cosmic lawsuit with the world; ἐντολή describes the 'charge' or 'commandment' the agent has received from his superior (10: 18; 12: 49f.: cf. Barn. 6: 1).

The 'signs' of Christ can have evidential value.[2] A good example of this is furnished by Nicodemus, who admits that Jesus is 'a teacher come from God, for no man can do these signs that you do, unless God is with him' (3: 2). Similarly, the evidential value of signs is recognized in 6: 2, where the multitude follows Christ 'because they saw the signs which he did on those who were diseased' (cf. 12: 17–18). John believed that signs were important in presenting his case (20: 30–1); this is the reason that the blind man can declare: 'Unless this man came from God, he would not be able to do a thing' (9: 33). The Evangelist definitely attached some apologetic significance to signs; to the unbelieving they posed a difficult question: 'How can a man who is a sinner do such signs?' (9: 16). For the Jewish leaders who persisted in unbelief, the signs raised an embarrassing issue: 'What are we to do? For this man performs many signs. If we let him go on thus, every

---

[1] *Ibid.*

[2] For a useful study of 'sign' and 'work' see W. Nicol, *The Semeia in the Fourth Gospel* (Leiden, 1972), esp. pp. 113–19. Cf. P. Riga, 'Signs of glory – the use of "semeion" in John's Gospel', *Int*, 17 (1963), 402–24. On the historical and philosophical problems raised by appealing to miracles as evidence see G. F. Woods, 'The evidential value of the biblical miracles', *Miracles – Cambridge Studies*, pp. 21–32.

one will believe in him, and the Romans will come and destroy our holy place and our nation' (11: 47–8).

John, like Isaiah 40–55, makes abundant use of predictive prophecy. Repeatedly the reader is told that Jesus predicted something which later came to pass. He predicts his own crucifixion (8: 28; 12: 32f.; 18: 31f.) and resurrection (2: 19–22; 16: 16, 19; cf. 20: 18, 25), the defection of Judas (6: 70f.; 13: 18f., 21; 17: 12; cf. 18: 2f., 5), the denials of Peter (13: 38; cf. 18: 17, 25, 27), his return to the Father (14: 28; 16: 10, 17, 28; the sevenfold use of μικρόν in 16: 16–19 suggests the imminence of the *Wiederkehr*), the coming of the Spirit (14: 16f., 26; cf. 20: 22) and the persecutions which his disciples will experience (15: 18–25; 16: 1–4). Now it is possible, using the methods of *Religionsgeschichte*, to interpret this phenomenon in terms of a gnostic myth of the θεῖος ἀνήρ. Hans Conzelmann, following Rudolf Bultmann, has done just that in his *Outline of the Theology of the New Testament*.[1] However, in the light of the cumulative evidence of links between Isaiah 40–55 and the Fourth Gospel it is far more reasonable to suppose that John has patterned his debates after the controversy found in Isaiah 40–55. Interpreted in this way, the predictions of Jesus are presented as evidence for his claims as Messiah and Son of God; the argument from fulfilled prophecy is adduced 'so that when it takes place you may believe' (14: 29; cf. 13: 19; Isa. 43: 9f.). Here one may observe a similarity with Isaiah 40–55, where Yahweh's evidence is attested by Israel, who bears witness both to the prediction and to its subsequent fulfilment. Both John and Isaiah 40–55 want people to know and understand and believe the case they are presenting (Jn 20: 31; Isa. 43: 10; cf. 45: 22–5) and for this reason they bring forward the evidence of fulfilled prophecy.

The Fourth Gospel frequently employs the ἐγώ εἰμι formula both with a predicate nominative (e.g., 8: 12; 10: 7, 9, 11; 11: 25; 14: 6) and also absolutely (e.g., 6: 20; 8: 24, 28, 58; 13: 19).[2] Taken by itself, this formula could be interpreted

[1] H. Conzelmann, *An Outline of the Theology of the New Testament* (London, 1969), pp. 344–5. Cf. R. Bultmann, *Theology of the New Testament* (2 vols.; London and New York, 1955), II, 61ff. Nicol, *Semeia in the Fourth Gospel*, pp. 48–94, has subjected the θεῖος ἀνήρ theory to searching criticism.
[2] Cf. D. Daube, *The New Testament and Rabbinic Judaism* (London, 1956), pp. 325–9.

purely as a teaching device to lay emphasis upon the claims of Jesus. Unquestionably the formula does this, but in view of the repeated use of the same phrase in the controversy in Isaiah 40–55, the phrase *may* have a juridical significance.

In Isaiah 40–55 ἐγώ εἰμι is used in the solemn declaration of Yahweh's claim as Saviour, Redeemer and Lord of history against a background of unbelief and in the face of rival claims. Similarly, in the Fourth Gospel Jesus uses this formula to make the strongest asseveration of the case which he is submitting to the world's verdict. The possibility that ἐγώ εἰμι may have a juridical significance gains strength from its congruity with other, more clearly defined indications of the juridical character of the Fourth Gospel which have been outlined in the preceding points.

Isaiah's 'Book of Consolation' speaks of Israel both as God's witness and as his servant (Isa. 43: 10, 12; cf. 41: 8f.; 44: 8); the same combination appears in John's Gospel. Jesus plainly assumes the role of a servant in John 13: 1–17 (in fact he deliberately gives them a ὑπόδειγμα, 13: 15), and great stress is laid on his task as a witness (Jn 3: 32–4; 8: 13–4, 18; 18: 37). Similarly, the disciples of Jesus are called to be both servants (13: 14–17; 15: 20) and witnesses (15: 27; cf. 1: 6–8, 15, 19ff.; 19: 35; 21: 24). The controversy-pattern of Isaiah 40–55 once again appears to illuminate the use of controversy in the Fourth Gospel.

Another point may be mentioned, though it too should not be pressed. It comes from a study of the use of lawcourt language in oaths, and concerns the use of ἀμήν in John's Gospel. 'In the Fourth Gospel it is always in the double form, occurs only in sayings attributed to Jesus and, like the synoptic single form, always precedes the words "I say to you" (λέγω ὑμῖν, twenty times; λέγω σοι, five times).'[1] Dalman long ago suggested an explanation for the use of 'Amen' in the Gospels:

An oath had been pronounced by Jesus, Matt. 5: 37, as displeasing to God; He had therefore to seek for some other mode of emphasis, and found it in the solemn 'Amen'. This is not an oath, yet more potent than a simply 'verily', because it gives the hearer to under-

[1] A. J. B. Higgins, 'The words of Jesus according to St. John', *BJRL*, 49 (1967), 371–2.

stand that Jesus confirms His own statement in the same way as if it were an oath or a blessing.[1]

Higgins is in basic agreement with this statement, noting that 'the double "amen" in John is an asseveration', but denying, on the basis of Old Testament usage, that the double form is more emphatic than the single form used in the Synoptics.[2] For our purposes the point to be observed is that such a solemn affirmation would be particularly meaningful in the context of a lawsuit over the claims of Christ, even if one accepts Jeremias's suggestion that the double ἀμήν in the Fourth Gospel reflects liturgical practice.[3]

THE LAWSUIT OF THE MINISTRY

Viewed from a juridical perspective, the Fourth Gospel has a case to present. As van Unnik has pointed out, the Fourth Evangelist avoids excessive reliance upon proof texts because he is aware of the type of reproach later represented in the words of Trypho: 'All the words of the prophecy which, Sir, you adduce, are ambiguous and contain nothing decisive in proof of your argument' (Justin Martyr, *Dialogue with Trypho* 51: 1).[4] Unlike Justin Martyr, John does not seek to support his case by a large string of Old Testament quotations, for he realizes that unbelievers can give completely different explanations of the same texts. Instead he introduces a number of independent witnesses who testify on behalf of Jesus of Nazareth, whose claims have been called into question by the Jews. Thus John presents witnesses and offers evidence to substantiate the Messiahship and divine Sonship of Jesus (20: 31). This concern for testimony plainly appears in the very first chapter, where the

[1] G. Dalman, *The Words of Jesus* (Edinburgh, 1902), pp. 226-9.

[2] Higgins, *op. cit.*, p. 372.

[3] J. Jeremias, *The Prayers of Jesus* (London, 1967), pp. 112-15.

[4] Van Unnik, 'The purpose of St. John's Gospel'. On the dangers of overplaying the role of the Christian apologist see A. J. B. Higgins, 'Jewish messianic belief in Justin Martyr's *Dialogue with Trypho*', *NT*, 9 (1967), 298-305. On John's use of the OT see C. K. Barrett, 'The Old Testament in the Fourth Gospel', *JTS*, 48 (1947), 155-69, and E. D. Freed, *Old Testament Quotations in the Gospel of John* (Leiden, 1965).

two prose passages on the Baptist are wedged into the poetic-like structure of the Prologue (1: 6–8, 15).

The Testimony of John the Baptist (1: 6–8, 15, 19–34)

John is the first and one of the most important witnesses to Jesus, and his testimony is a three-fold one, as the Prologue makes clear: (1) He is not the Light. (2) He is sent to bear witness to the Light. (3) The purpose of his witness-bearing is that all may believe in Christ (1: 6–8). This pattern is followed in subsequent sections dealing with the Baptist.[1] John is mentioned at the beginning of the Fourth Gospel, for he is the first to point his fellow men to Jesus, and in that sense all believers have been brought to Christ through him (1:7b). While there had been other men sent from God, John's task was unique. He bore witness to the incarnate Word, to His superiority to himself and to His prior existence.[2]

In 1: 19ff. the Evangelist returns to the Baptist's testimony (ἡ μαρτυρία τοῦ Ἰωάννου, 1: 19). When the Jews send a deputation of priests and Levites from Jerusalem for the express purpose of interrogating him (ἵνα ἐρωτήσωσιν αὐτόν), John testifies that: (1) He is not the Messiah, not Elijah, not the Prophet, but only a voice (1: 20–23); (2) He bears witness to Jesus as Lamb of God, Son of God, and Baptizer with the Holy Spirit (1: 29–34); (3) His testimony results in the first believers coming to Christ (1: 35–7).

If the question is asked why the Evangelist included this material in his case for the Messiahship and divine Sonship of Jesus, the key is perhaps given in 1: 20. Here the emphatic use of ὁμολογεῖν and ἀρνεῖσθαι makes it clear that John is claiming the Baptist as the first Christian witness or 'confessor'[3] in contrast to the Synoptic notion that he is not in the kingdom of God (Mt. 11: 11; Lk. 7: 28). While the Synoptists note the Baptist's appearance, life style, fiery preaching and baptism,

[1] Cf. C. H. Dodd, *Historical Tradition in the Fourth Gospel* (Cambridge, 1963), pp. 248–9.
[2] The notion that the Baptist refers both to space and time is supported by E. C. Hoskyns, *The Fourth Gospel*, ed. F. N. Davey (London, 1947), p. 151.
[3] Dodd, *op. cit.*, p. 299. The contrast between 'confession' and 'denial' appears clearly in the Shepherd of Hermas (*Sim.* IX. 28. 7).

and record his subsequent incarceration and beheading by Herod Antipas (Mk 1: 14; 6: 14–29; Mt. 4: 12; 11: 2–15; 14: 1–12; Lk. 3: 19–20), the author of the Fourth Gospel concentrates on the witness which he bears to Christ. This witness is seen as resting upon divine revelation (1: 31–4). When John's work is done and people begin to leave his side to follow Jesus, he shows no resentment, but only pleasure at the accomplishment of his task (1: 35–42). John is the Messiah's forerunner (1: 23; cf. Mk 1: 3); he is misunderstood if he is taken to have any greatness of his own (1: 19–27; cf. 3: 25–30). His one job is to make the Messiah known to Israel (1: 31).

In summary, the Baptist's whole function, in the eyes of the Fourth Evangelist, is simply that of a witness. For this task he is commissioned by God, who prepares, equips and sends him. The central purpose of his testimony is to point men to Christ, which is another way of expressing the purpose of John's Gospel as a whole (1: 7; 20: 31). John's testimony is a help to the Jews, and later Jesus is to cite it for this reason (5: 31–4). The probable life situation is one in which it was desired that the Baptist's followers should be recognized as adoptive members of the Christian community.[1]

The Testimony of the First Disciples (1: 35–51)

The Fourth Evangelist, however, believed that evidence must be presented by two or three witnesses to be legally acceptable (5: 31; 8: 17), and therefore the Baptist's testimony had to be corroborated by the testimony of others. John's testimony seems to set off a chain-reaction: he leads Andrew to Christ, Andrew probably brings Philip, and Philip introduces Nathanael.

By this time interest has shifted to a different theme:

The main purpose of the passage, from verse 40 onwards, is to deploy a series of 'testimonies' supplementary to that of John, and these are

[1] The evidence for this view appears in the following facts: (1) Luke knows of people at Ephesus who: (a) had some connection with John the Baptist (Acts 18: 25; 19: 3), (b) were Christians (for μαθηταί, used absolutely, never means anything else in the NT), but defective Christians (Acts 18: 25f., 19: 1–7). (2) Behind the whole of Luke–Acts there is evidence of a tradition which has contact with the Johannine tradition (cf. G. B. Caird, *The Gospel according to Saint Luke*, pp. 20–1).

so arranged that the several persons summoned as witnesses assign to Jesus, one after another, various titles of dignity: Andrew names him Messiah, Philip describes him as the Fulfiller of law and prophets, Nathanael acclaims him as Son of God and King of Israel. The passage works up to a climax in which Jesus takes up the theme and in mysterious terms speaks of the angels ascending and descending on the Son of Man, thus completing the series of Messianic titles by the addition of the one which in all the gospels alike is used by him alone.[1]

The stories of Andrew, Philip and Nathanael are narrated for the sake of the confirmatory testimony which they afford to the Messiahship of Jesus, in accordance with the Old Testament law of evidence (Deut. 19: 15). The Evangelist has summoned witnesses who corroborate the testimony of the Baptist by appealing to the scriptural expectation of a coming Messiah and by declaring that Jesus is the fulfilment of all the Messianic prophecies. Accordingly, these well-known or typical persons are intended to pose for the reader the question which the Fourth Evangelist has Jesus ask Nathanael, 'Do you believe?' (1: 50).

The Testimony of the First Sign (2: 1–11)

Human testimony, however, is not the only kind of evidence for the Messiahship of Jesus; there is also the evidence of the mighty words of Jesus, and to the first of these the Evangelist draws attention in the story of Jesus turning water into wine. Here John has passed from the 'witness' of the Baptist and the early disciples to the 'witness' of the works of Jesus.

In chronological order the Cana miracle was the first σημεῖον. This word is used more often by John than the other Gospel writers, and appears a full seventeen times in his Gospel. It is used of the mighty works of Jesus, which John never calls 'miracles' (δυνάμεις) or 'wonders' (τέρατα), except in 4: 48, where τέρατα is used in a disparaging way. John's selection of the σημεῖα of Jesus has been made, as he later tells his readers, 'that you may believe' (20: 30f.). While the Evangelist is aware of the fact that the spiritually blind see

---

[1] Dodd, *Historical Tradition in the Fourth Gospel*, p. 302; cf. H. F. D. Sparks, *The Formation of the New Testament* (London, 1952), pp. 116–17.

only miracles, he also knows that the spiritually sensitive see 'signs', that is, pointers to the true significance of Jesus.[1] This is very clear in the Cana incident, for the σημεῖον manifested Jesus' 'glory', which is a term expressive of his filial unity with the Father (2: 11; cf. 1: 14). The miracle thus served to strengthen the faith of Christ's immediate followers in him as Messiah and Son of God.

The Testimony of the Resurrection (2: 12–25)

In the Evangelist's view, however, Jesus must also prove himself Messiah in Jerusalem, 'the city of the great king' (cf. Psa. 48: 2), for he is 'King of the Jews' (Jn 18: 33, 39; 19: 2, 19, 21) and Judaea is his πατρίς (4: 44; contrast with Mk 6: 4 pars., where Jesus' home is Nazareth).[2] Consequently, after Cana the scene moves from Galilee to Jerusalem, where Christ cleanses the temple. His drastic action is challenged by the hostile Jewish leaders who demand a sign to vindicate his authority (2: 18; cf. Mt. 12: 39; Lk. 11: 29). In reply Jesus issues a counter-challenge which amounts to a prophecy of his own death and resurrection: 'Destroy this temple, and in three days I will raise it up' (2: 19).

In effect, then, Christ staked the truth of his mission on his resurrection, and when he rose from the dead, his claims were vindicated. This decisive proof led his disciples into a full-fledged faith in his Messiahship and divine Sonship based upon the corroborative evidence of scripture and the word of Jesus (2: 22). Since John is concerned to present evidence to convince people of the claims of Jesus (20: 31), it is easy to see why he should include this evidential challenge of Jesus to the Jews.

During this Passover many were brought to faith in Jesus because of the signs which they had seen him perform (2: 23). Their faith, however, was shallow and unstable; they were

[1] Hindley, 'Witness in the Fourth Gospel', pp. 328–9. On possible parallels to John's use of signs in Philo and the LXX see R. Formesyn, 'Le sèmeion johannique et le sèmeion hellénistique', *ETL*, 38 (1962), 869ff.

[2] But cf. R. H. Lightfoot, *St John's Gospel* (Oxford, 1956), pp. 34–6, who thinks that Jesus' real '*patris* is in heaven'.

convinced only 'while they were beholding' (θεωροῦντες, 2: 23), and such faith is later castigated as no more than second best (14: 11). Therefore, though 'many *trusted* in his name,... Jesus did not *trust* himself to them' (the verb πιστεύειν is used in both cases in 2: 23f.). He required no one 'to testify of man', for he knew the facts of human nature. A striking piece of evidence of Christ's knowledge is provided in his encounter with Nicodemus.

Christ's Testimony before the Representative Teacher (3: 1–21)

Christ's interview with Nicodemus allows him to present self-revelatory testimony before a man who is at once a representative Pharisee, teacher and ruler of the Jews. Jesus soon pierces the self-confidence of Nicodemus's opening words (οἴδαμεν, 3: 2) by emphatically showing him the necessity of the new birth (3: 3, 5). In this way Nicodemus is reduced to puzzled questioning (3: 4, 9). Jesus rebukes Nicodemus for his ignorance (3: 10), and continues with a solemn attestation: 'Truly, truly (note the juridical force of the reduplicated ἀμήν) I say to you, we speak of what we know, and bear witness to what we have seen; but you do not receive our testimony' (3: 11). Here Christ speaks not only for himself, but for all who have entered into a personal experience of his salvation. Christ's witnesses have actual knowledge of the new birth which he is attesting, and he therefore associates their testimony with his own. Their testimony, however, is limited to earthly things, while Christ's testimony includes heavenly things (note the change from the plural in 3: 11 to the singular in 3: 12); as the eye-witness of heavenly things, Christ can speak with a unique knowledge of τὰ ἐπουράνια (cf. 5: 20; 6: 46; 8: 38).

Thus Christ and his witnesses warn Nicodemus and the half-believing Jews represented by him that 'the truths about to be revealed must be received on the ground of testimony which can only be verified, as it were, from within; they cannot be established by external evidence, and are therefore unacceptable to the natural man (3: 11b).'[1] Nicodemus and other Jews had been impressed by the evidence of Jesus' signs (3: 2),

---

[1] *Ibid.* p. 117. Cf. H. Conzelmann, *An Outline of the Theology of the New Testament* (London, 1969), pp. 344–5.

but had ignored a far more important kind of evidence, namely, that which God makes clear in the hearts of men. This kind of testimony is inwardly perceived, and makes possible an acceptance of the claims of Jesus. Such divine illumination is granted only to those whom the Father attracts to the Son (6: 37, 44–6, 65; 12: 32; 17: 6; cf. Acts 16: 14). This is the fundamental kind of testimony, and it opens the way to all others.[1]

In 3: 12 the scepticism of Nicodemus and others like him is rebuked; the point is that earthly things, like physical birth, the wind and especially the observed activity of Jesus, ought to speak to the percipient of heavenly things. Just as 'the uplifted serpent drew the hearts of Israel to God for their salvation [Num. 21: 4–9], so the uplifted Jesus drew men to himself and so gathered to God those who were his children (cf. 12: 32; 11: 52)'.[2] Paradoxically, it later becomes apparent that the very uplifting which spells Christ's suffering and death is the means whereby he wins his case, is vindicated and draws all men to himself (12: 31f.). The exaltation of the Son of Man makes possible the salvation of those who believe (3: 15).

The testimony of Christ presents men with a challenge which they cannot escape; they must decide for or against his claims, and in the process of making a decision they themselves are undergoing a process of judgment: 'He who believes in him is not condemned [κρίνεται]; he who does not believe is condemned [κέκριται] already, because he has not believed in the name of the only Son of God' (3: 18; cf. Acts 13: 46). Christ's coming initiates a divine process of judgment: 'And this is the κρίσις, that the light has come into the world, and men loved darkness rather than light, because their deeds were evil' (3: 19; cf. 15: 22).

In other words, the Evangelist has introduced a theme which is of importance to his courtroom imagery. Jesus is on trial and evidence is being brought to support his case; men must make up their minds. But the assessment of the evidence, or their

---

[1] J. Bonsirven, *Theology of the New Testament* (London, 1963), pp. 135–8. Cf. Vanhoye, 'Notre foi, oeuvre divine d'après le quatrième évangile', *NRT*, 86 (1964), 337–54.

[2] Barrett, *St. John*, p. 178. On the double meaning of ὑψοῦν here and elsewhere in John see D. W. Weads, 'The Johannine double meaning', *RQ*, 13 (1970), 106–20.

willingness to confront it, depends upon moral qualifications. And so, while engaging in the act of judgment, they find themselves on trial – either acquitted or condemned. By the use of this courtroom imagery the Evangelist implicitly rebukes the unbelief of the Jews at Jerusalem who failed to understand Christ's cleansing of the temple as a Messianic act and the spiritual blindness of Nicodemus which made him stumble at the necessity of the new birth. At the same time, his use of courtroom imagery makes the evangelistic appeal of his Gospel the more compelling.

The Final Testimony of John the Baptist (3: 22–30)

The Evangelist has presented Christ's testimony in Jerusalem to the Jews; now he turns to consider his teaching in Judaea generally (3: 22). The outward similarity of Christ's work to that of John the Baptist leads him to mention the Baptist's final witness to the Messiah. On this occasion the setting is provided by a 'dispute' (ζήτησις, 3: 25) between some of John's disciples and 'a Jew' (the more probable textual reading)[1] about purification. Since John is unable to provide the true purification, he cannot be the Messiah: indeed, he emphatically disavows any claim to the role (3: 28; cf. 1: 20). His function is simply to introduce Israel to its Messiah – a function comparable to that of a best man at a wedding (3: 25–30). When his task is accomplished, he recedes into the background and 'rejoices greatly at the bridegroom's voice'. 'This joy of mine', the Baptist says, 'is now full.' Then he adds the words of a humble witness: 'He must increase, but I must decrease.' In this way the Evangelist informs his readers that John took pleasure in the fact that Jesus' ministry was superseding his own and accepted the situation as being of divine appointment (note the use of δεῖ in 3: 30).

The verses which follow (3: 31–6) are different in style from John's testimony, and probably contain the reflections of the Evangelist on the relation of John the Baptist to Jesus. Though John is divinely commissioned to be a forerunner of the Messiah, like other earthly witnesses he is earthly in origin and

---

[1] On the textual problem here see Barrett, *St. John*, p. 184, and Dodd, *Historical Tradition*, p. 280.

must of necessity use the language of earth (3: 31b). He is unable to speak of heavenly things with the same firsthand knowledge that can belong to him alone who has come directly from heaven and is far superior to all others (3: 31a, 31c). Such a heaven-sent witness speaks God's own words (3: 32, 34), is empowered by the Spirit (3: 34; cf. 1: 33f.), and everything that is to be made known about God has been given to him (3: 35). To accept his testimony is to confirm or attest (σφραγίζειν is used) that 'God is true'; to reject it is to make God a liar (3: 33; cf. I Jn 1: 10; 5: 10). In other words, the Evangelist has endorsed the Baptist's testimony and strengthened it by his corroborative testimony on behalf of the Son of God. Thus the whole section (3: 22–36) is in keeping with the Evangelist's stated purpose and warrants inclusion in his case for the claims of Christ.

The Testimony of the Samaritans (4: 1–42)

So far the Evangelist has dealt with Christ's public work in Judaea and in the Holy City (2: 13–3: 36). Now he turns to the testimony of the Samaritans which supports his case for the claims of Christ. Like the blind man of Jn 9, the Samaritan woman passes through a number of stages in spiritual perception. At first she sees Jesus simply as a 'Jew', a member of a hostile group that held her people in contempt as religious apostates (4: 8; cf. II Kgs 17: 24–34). Then she moves on to consider the possibility that he may be 'greater than our father Jacob' (4: 12). After further conversation she is led to exclaim: 'Sir, I perceive that you are a prophet' (4: 19). Finally she invites others to test her tentative discovery: 'Come see a man who told me all that I ever did. Can this be the Christ?' (4: 29). The use of μήτι and not οὐκ suggests her hesitation, but the corroborative testimony of the Samaritans after Jesus' two-day stay expresses their considered opinion: 'Now we believe, not because of your saying [D has μαρτυρίαν here instead of λαλιάν], for we have heard for ourselves (αὐτοί), and we know that this [οὗτος highlights the vigour of their conviction] is truly the Saviour of the world' (4: 42).

For both the woman and the men of Samaria it was the direct contact with Jesus himself which produced conviction and confession regarding him. While some responded in faith because of the woman's testimony (τῆς γυναικὸς μαρτυρούσης, 4: 39), 'many more believed because of his (i.e. Christ's) own word' (4: 41). Clearly, the response of the Samaritans and their testimony to the Messiah is in keeping with the Evangelist's desire to help his readers to faith in Christ. It also prepares them for the testimony of the next sign.

The Testimony of the Second Sign (4: 46–54)

John is well aware that Jesus has done far more mighty works than he has related in his Gospel (3: 2; 6: 2; 20: 30; 21: 25), but he considers his selection adequate in view of his stated purpose. This consideration accounts for the inclusion of the healing of the nobleman's son. The Evangelist organizes the whole story around the nobleman's faith: first, it is said that 'the man believed the word that Jesus had spoken to him' (4: 50), and later it is noted that the petitioner and his whole house 'believed' (without further qualification).

For John it was important that these mighty acts of Christ had actually been done, and that it was impossible to deny them:

While arguing from evidence is not ultimately satisfactory, it is not completely dismissed [15: 24, for example, shows that men can be blamed for being roused into opposition by evidence which should have led them at least to become inquirers]...The miracles therefore have a subordinate place in Christian apologetic. Used in this way, however, for their evidence-value, they are not the basis for true faith, and do not bear the 'glory of God'. To see the glory of God one must see them as 'signs'.[1]

To summarize the first four chapters, one can say that they commence the controversy over the claims of Christ. The evidence for Christ is conveyed both in the self-revelatory testimony of Christ and in the testimony of his disciples, as well as in the testimony of the signs performed. All the material is presented in order to achieve the purpose which the author has stated at the end of chapter 20. However, John knows and

---

[1] Hindley, 'Witness in the Fourth Gospel', p. 331. Cf. G. L. Phillips, 'Faith and vision', *Studies in the Fourth Gospel*, ed. F. L. Cross (London, 1957), pp. 84–5.

frankly admits that this evidence by itself is insufficient to lead men to make a whole-hearted commitment to Christ; for that to take place there must be the indispensable witness of God within the heart of man.

A change is noticeable in chapters 5–12. Now the debate over the claims of Christ is intensified, and opposition becomes more outspoken. Step by step faith and unbelief are called out as the controversy develops around the miracles recorded in chapters 5, 9 and 11. Chapter 6 deals with the faith-crisis in Galilee; together with chapter 5, it serves as an introduction to the 'Great Controversy' of chapters 7–12.

The Testimony of the Third Sign (5: 1–47)

The evidence which the Evangelist has presented in the first two signs is strengthened and corroborated by the third sign, namely, the healing of the impotent man (5: 1–9). At the same time the healing leads to the resulting conflict with the Jews, who aim their criticism directly at Christ (5: 10–47). First, they attack his supposed breach of the sabbath (5: 16); then they hit out against his claim to a unique relationship with God (5: 18). To them Christ's claim in 5: 17 appears blasphemous: how can he whom they regard merely as a man (5: 12; cf. 6: 42; 9: 16) make himself equal with God? For this reason they seek to kill him (5: 18).

The debate is now fully under way. In the ensuing verses Jesus answers in words which attest with juridical solemnity the Son's relation to the Father and provide a justification of his works and claims as Messiah (5: 19ff.).

Up to this point Christ has been bearing witness of himself, so the question naturally arises: Can Christ's testimony be accepted in view of the Old Testament principle of evidence stated in Deut. 19: 15? It is to answer this objection that Christ appeals to the testimony of John the Baptist and the Father. The former is cited only as an *argumentum ad hominem* to those who attached great importance to the testimony of the Baptist (5: 33–5); the latter is of permanent value and significance. The Father's witness is the only witness that Jesus considers important for his own vindication, and it is this witness which is alluded to in 5: 32.

Christ recalls John's testimony for the part it might continue to play in the salvation of the Jews (5: 34–5). In one sense, John's witness would influence only those who lived near enough to feel the direct impact of his message; in another sense, though his testimony is completed (μεμαρτύρηκεν, 5: 33; cf. κέκραγεν, 1: 15), his words continue to bear witness (cf. μαρτυρεῖ, 1: 15). For this reason some exegetes have viewed the Father's testimony as embracing John's. This interpretation helps to explain: (1) the Gospel's emphasis on the divine character of the Baptist's mission (1: 6, 33; 3: 28), (2) the comprehensive purpose of his ministry: 'that all might believe through him' (1: 7), and (3) the permanent significance of his witness in holy history (1: 15, 23, 29–34).

The works of Christ constitute a higher testimony than John's and provide an important attestation of his person and work (5: 36). These certainly include the miracles of Christ such as that of 5: 1–9, but as the context makes clear, they are perhaps best expressed in terms of Christ's activity as life-giver and judge (5: 20–30). 'In the results of these two activities belief is able to discern the lordship of Jesus and therefore the activities, with their results, bear witness of and to him.'[1] Ironically, it is precisely this testimony which the unbelieving Jews refuse to accept.

The Old Testament also serves as a witness and provides corroborative evidence pointing to Christ (5: 39); John obviously thinks so, for he frequently uses ἵνα ἡ γραφὴ πληρωθῇ or a similar phrase (13: 18; 17: 12; 19: 24, 36; cf. 19: 28). But in John's Gospel the Jews remain unbelieving. They form a striking contrast with the Beroean Jews, who not only searched the scriptures, but 'received the word with all readiness of mind', with the result that 'many of them therefore believed' (Acts 17: 11–12). By their stubborn refusal to come to Christ the Johannine 'Jews' shut themselves off from eternal life, and display ignorance of the true meaning of their own scriptures – a motif which is given special attention in Matthew's Gospel (Mt. 12: 3, 5; 19: 4; 21: 16, 42; 22: 31).

Why then does this multiple testimony to Christ fail to gain acceptance (cf. 5: 11, 32)? Because men cannot believe unless they have received what the Fourth Gospel terms 'the witness

---

[1] Lightfoot, St. John's Gospel, p. 146.

of the Father'. The witness of the Father in John is not the miraculous voice mentioned in 12: 28, for this seems to be excluded by 5: 37b. It is not simply the works of Jesus, for 5: 36–7 draws a distinction between 'the works which the Father has granted me to accomplish', which 'bear witness that the Father has sent me', and the fact that 'the Father who sent me has borne witness to me'. The witness of the Father is rather the internal divine witness which leads to faith.[1] Without this witness, all other witness and evidence is inadequate, for it falls short of convincing people of the claims of Christ.

In chapter 5 Christ solemnly concludes his indictment of the Jews by citing Moses as a prosecuting witness. The Jews are at fault when they appeal to Moses to oppose Christ (5: 45; cf. 9: 28), 'for he wrote of me' (5: 46; cf. 1: 45). His witness is not to be confined to a few Messianic references like Deut. 18: 15, for the whole Mosaic Law, with its demand for total love and obedience, also bears witness to Jesus. Jesus is the one true law-keeper, because he does the works of God (5: 36), and therefore the Mosaic Law bears witness to him. Because the Jews do not see that, Moses will become their accuser and not their advocate and defender (5: 45ff.). Like the men of Nineveh and the Queen of the South (Mt. 12: 41f.; Lk. 11: 31f.), Moses will rise up and give evidence against the unbelieving Jews, using the very writings which they profess to honour.[2]

Here, then, is an echo of Isaiah 40–55 where we observed a great controversy between God and the world. In this cosmic lawsuit Christ is the representative of God, and the Jews are the representatives of the world. In their pleading the Jews base their arguments on the law, and Jesus appeals to the testimony borne to him by John the Baptist, his own works and the scriptures. Belief is invited and unbelief made inexcusable by the three witnesses presented by Jesus. To those who receive these witnesses and accept their evidence, there is granted a divine self-authentication of the mission of Christ, namely,

[1] Hindley, 'Witness in the Fourth Gospel', p. 326. Cf. R. Bultmann, *Theology of the New Testament* (2 vols., London and New York, 1955), II, 68.
[2] Cf. L. Roth, *Judaism* (New York, 1961), pp. 61–2, who notes that if the Jews refuse to heed the Law, then 'the Torah is there to testify against them' (cf. Deut. 31: 19, 26).

the witness of God himself. This divine self-authentication is not to be conceived as independent of the other three witnesses; rather, it is found in the perception that: (1) John was from God; (2) Jesus is doing the works of God; (3) the voice of God in scripture is a testimony to Jesus.

The Testimony of the Fourth and Fifth Signs (6: 1–71)

The next sign takes place in Galilee when Jesus miraculously multiplies five barley loaves and two fish (6: 1–14). The Galileans, already intrigued by the signs wrought on the sick (6: 2), now accept Jesus as the promised Prophet (cf. Deut. 18: 15, 18f.) and prepare to take him by force to be their political ruler (6: 14f.). Thus the multitude substantiates the fact of the miracle, but is blind to its meaning as a sign pointing to Jesus as the 'bread of life' and therefore the promised Messiah (6: 26). It murmurs at Christ's claim to be the true manna (6: 31–41), accuses him of being Joseph's son (6: 42) and carries on disputes over his claims (ἐμάχοντο πρὸς ἀλλήλους, 6: 52). He for his part solemnly presents his case *sub specie iudicii* (6: 26, 32).[1]

The other sign recorded in John 6 is Christ's walking on the water (6: 16–21; cf. Mk 6: 45; Mt. 14: 22–33). The climax comes in verse 20 with Christ's emphatic declaration, Ἐγώ εἰμι. As we noted in studying Isaiah 40–55, this phrase was often used to refer to God himself. Now John picks it up and applies it to the presence of God in Jesus.

Chapter 6, in other words, presents evidence to substantiate the claims of Christ, and thus accords perfectly with the Evangelist's purpose in writing the Gospel. When taken with chapter 5, it constitutes an introduction to 'The Great Controversy' of chapters 7–12. In both cases the testimony of Christ's works and words divides his hearers into two classes and prepares the way for 'The Great Controversy' in which faith and unbelief are fully revealed.

'The Great Controversy' falls into two parts, the first

---

[1] Cf. P. Borgen, 'Observations on the midrashic character of John 6', *ZNW*, 54 (1963), 232–40 and his *Bread from Heaven* (Leiden, 1965), pp. 80–6, and I. de la Potterie, 'Jesus king and judge according to John 19: 13', *Sc*, 13 (1961), 97–111.

(chapters 7–10) containing the outline of the successive stages of the controversy itself and the second dealing with the decisive judgment (chapters 11–12). The revelation of faith and unbelief at Jerusalem centres on events and discourses connected with two national festivals, namely, the Feast of Tabernacles and the Feast of Dedication. Similarly, the decisive judgment consists of two parts: (1) the narrative of the final sign with its immediate consequences (ch. 11) and (2) three typical scenes (which mark the close of the work of Christ's public ministry) and two summary judgments upon the results of Christ's work (ch. 12).[1]

The Conflict in Chapters Seven and Eight

In John 7 the controversy between Jesus and the Jews becomes more intense and ominous, and the atmosphere of the lawcourt more apparent. The issue to be decided is the Messiahship of Jesus, and on this subject opinion is divided (7: 12). The opposition against the Son of Man, anticipated in chapters 5 and 6, is now hardening, and the Jewish leaders are preparing to seize him and put him to death (7: 1). He on his part has incurred the world's hostility 'because I testify of it that its works are evil' (7: 7). The lawsuit over his claims thus moves inexorably to its climax in the Passion when the Son of Man is glorified and the effects of the Spirit's work are made available to believers.

The appearance of Christ teaching in the temple sets the stage for three separate debates on his claims by three groups of people, namely, 'the Jews' (7: 14–24), 'some of the inhabitants of Jerusalem' (7: 25–31), and the representatives of 'the chief priests and the Pharisees' (7: 32–6). When the Jews question the authority of Christ's teaching, he replies by claiming that it has a double attestation: (1) The person who desires to do God's will cannot help but recognize the source of Christ's teaching. (2) The complete devotion of Christ to the Father who sent him is a sign of his truthfulness. The principle laid down is then applied to the condemnation of the Jews. They profess unbounded devotion to the Torah, and yet are prepared to murder him who came to fulfil it (7: 19). Christ

---

[1] Westcott, *The Gospel according to St. John*, II, 260.

therefore acts as an accuser, rebukes them for the superficial character of their judgment and challenges them to render a true verdict (7: 24).

In the second scene Christ answers popular objections to his Messiahship (7: 25–7), and declares his authority is derived from God, whom the Jews do not know (7: 28–9). His testimony is given publicly and with solemn emphasis (παρρησίᾳ λαλεῖ, 7: 26; ἔκραξεν, 7: 28), and, as on previous occasions, provokes a division concerning him (7: 30f.).

The third scene in the controversy is described in 7: 32–6. The ἀρχιερεῖς and Φαρισαῖοι, whose united opposition is frequently mentioned (7: 32, 45; 11: 47, 57; 18: 3), now send officers to seize him (7: 32), and in their presence Christ announces his speedy exit from the Jews (7: 33–5). Once again, the Jews completely fail to grasp the meaning of his words (7: 36), and Christ's claim to satisfy man's spiritual thirst precipitates yet another division of opinion over him (7: 37–44).

The chapter closes by recounting the Sanhedrin's meeting with the temple police (7: 45–52). On this occasion Nicodemus reminds the chief priests and Pharisees that a proper judicial hearing is demanded by Jewish law (cf. Deut. 1: 16), but his remarks are summarily rejected, allegedly on scriptural grounds (7: 50–2).

In passing, one may note that the textually suspect[1] *Pericope Adulterae* (Jn 7: 53–8: 11) both uses legal words (e.g., κατηγορεῖν and κατακρίνειν) and presupposes a juridical situation in which the woman is the accused, the scribes and Pharisees are her accusers, and Jesus is placed in the role of judge. The reference to stoning (λιθάζειν) is instructive, reminding us of the Old Testament practice which decreed that the accusing witnesses in the case of a death sentence must play a leading

---

[1] Martin Rist, 'Pseudepigraphy and the early Christians', *Studies in New Testament and Early Christian Literature*, ed. D. E. Aune (Leiden, 1972), pp. 75–91, dismisses the pericope as an 'interpolation', one of the recognized 'techniques of pseudepigraphy' (p. 76). Bultmann's commentary on John ignores the passage entirely.

For a striking defence of the passage on literary grounds see A. F. Johnson, 'A stylistic trait of the Fourth Gospel in the *Pericope Adulterae*?', *BETS*, 9 (1966), 91–6. Cf. H. Riesenfeld, *The Gospel Tradition* (Oxford, 1970), pp. 95–110.

part in casting the first stones against the condemned (Deut. 13: 9f.; 17: 6f.; cf. Acts 7: 58f.).[1]

In chapter 8 'The Great Controversy' continues following Christ's declaration that he is the light of the world (8: 12). The pronouncement at once leads the Pharisees to question the authority by which Jesus speaks and acts; is he not a witness in his own defence, giving invalid testimony to himself? In the debate recorded in chapter 5 Jesus made it clear that the real witness to himself was the Father. Now he claims that his own knowledge of his divine origin and destination gives him the right, if need be, to bear witness to himself; and asserts that it is precisely because the Jews refuse to recognize where he came from and where he was going that their judgment of him is inadequate and superficial (8: 14–18).

Judgment, in any case, is really God's prerogative, and his alone. Even Jesus does not exercise that judgment during his earthly life (8: 15), though his presence in the world leads men to pass judgment on themselves (3: 19ff.). If Christ were to pass judgment, however, he claims that his judgment would be true because of the unity between himself and the Father who sent him (8: 16). If the Jews demand *two* witnesses in order to satisfy the Jewish law of evidence, those two witnesses are Jesus and his Father (8: 18). 'Here the Old Testament and halakhic rule of two witnesses has been applied to the idea of Jesus as the Son of the (heavenly) Father: the Father and the Son both witness.'[2] In reality, however, the testimony of these two is one.

The Jews are unwilling to accept an invisible witness who cannot appear and give evidence before them (cf. the demand for a sign in Lk. 11: 29–32 = Mt. 12: 38–42). Jesus, in reply, admits that God cannot be a visible witness in the same way as human witnesses, but insists that he can still be known and understood. In their blindness concerning the nature of Jesus the Jews reveal their blindness concerning the nature of God (8: 19). They are puzzled about Christ's 'going away' to the

[1] For details see A. A. Trites, 'The woman taken in adultery', *BS*, 131 (1974), 137–46.
[2] P. Borgen, 'God's agent in the Fourth Gospel', *Religions in Antiquity*, ed. J. Neusner (Leiden, 1968), p. 147. Cf. C. H. Dodd, *The Interpretation of the Fourth Gospel* (Cambridge, 1954), p. 77.

Father (8: 21–2), and make a negative response to the challenge implied in the ἐγώ εἰμι declaration of 8: 24. Consequently, they stand under God's judgment. They are guilty of appealing to Abraham in order to oppose Christ (8: 39ff.), whereas Abraham actually serves as a witness for Christ (8: 56). Abraham, like Moses (5: 45ff.), will serve as an accusing witness against the very ones who claim his support. Refusal to believe in Christ severs them from Abraham, who 'rejoiced' in the hope of the coming Messiah (8: 56). The Jews, unable to lay any charges against Christ (8: 46), are themselves charged with lacking the moral qualifications which would enable them to make a proper assessment of the evidence for his claims (8: 43ff.). Despite their unbelief, the Son of Man will be vindicated by death and resurrection: 'When you have lifted up the Son of Man, then you will know that I am he' (ἐγώ εἰμι, 8: 28).

Summing up chapters 7 and 8, it is accurate to say that these chapters are

more continuously occupied with controversy than any others in John; and at their close light and darkness, good and evil, Jesus the Son of God (8: 38) and the Jews the children of the devil (8: 44), are left diametrically opposed...In accordance with the teaching of 3: 18, 19, chapter 9 will now show what the result is, both for the disciple of the light, who does welcome him (1: 12), and for the children of darkness.[1]

The Testimony of the Sixth Sign (9: 1–41)

In John 9 the lawsuit of Christ's public ministry continues. Jesus heals a blind man on the sabbath, and sets off another dispute. Despite undeniable evidence of a miracle, the Pharisees level charges and others raise questions (9: 16). The debate continues back and forth, and reminds one of the speech and counter-speech characteristic of the Old Testament legal assembly, so amply illustrated in the Book of Job.

The miracle here, as elsewhere in John's Gospel, is a 'sign' pointing to the nature and character of Jesus. Because men differ in their spiritual perception, they differ also in the way they read this sign and this precipitates a division among them. To some the miracle only serves to solidify their opposition

---

[1] Lightfoot, St. John's Gospel, p. 199.

to Christ; to others, it is an encouragement to believe (9: 16, 24). In John 9 the clearest instance of the miracle acting as a stimulus to faith is the blind man himself. At first he speaks of 'the man called Jesus' (9: 11), then he acknowledges that Christ is a 'prophet' (9: 17), 'a man from God' (9: 33), and finally, the 'Lord' (9: 38). The sign and its effects are well summarized by Christ's words: 'For judgment (εἰς κρίμα) I came into this world, that those who do not see may see, and that those who see may become blind' (9: 39; cf. 3: 19).

The lawsuit of the ministry implies that Jesus confronts men with a choice. When evidence is offered for the claims of Christ, men must decide for or against him, and by their choice they judge themselves. The chapter also suggests that those who bear witness for Christ may encounter persecution (9: 22, 34)– an idea which is developed at some length in the second half of the Fourth Gospel (15: 18–16: 4).

The Conflict in Chapter Ten

In chapter 10 the lawsuit of the ministry continues to move towards its climax. Christ presents himself as the good shepherd, again using an ἐγώ εἰμι saying which identifies him with God (10: 7, 11, 14). Once more his words produce a division of opinion among the Jews. Earlier Christ had been opposed on the grounds of being a sabbath breaker and therefore a sinner (9: 16, 24); now the opposition takes the stronger form of a charge of demon possession (10: 19). Others, however, are inclined to take Christ's side in view of the healing of the blind man (10: 20).

After the fashion of the Old Testament lawsuit Christ's opponents now summon him to state his case (10: 24). David Catchpole thinks the setting of Jn 10: 24–39 is quasi-juridical, but adds the significant comment: 'And when those who speak of blasphemy are themselves lawyers, even if the setting is non-juridical, we cannot allow too wide a gap between usage inside and outside the court-room.'[1]

Christ answers his critics by insisting that he has told them the true facts of the case already; his works have provided

[1] D. Catchpole, '"You have heard his blasphemy"', *TB*, 16 (1965), 10–18.

sufficient evidence to accept his claim as God's Son, whose works have been done in the Father's name. The Jews who oppose Christ have not been prepared to receive the evidence and act accordingly; for they do not possess the prerequisite moral qualifications to evaluate the evidence. While they can bear witness to facts, they are in no position to bear witness to their meaning or quality – a distinction which has already been observed in Aristotle's *Rhetoric* (i.xv.). Therefore, in the nature of the case, they cannot appreciate the unity between Christ and the Father, and consequently disbelieve (10: 29–31). Furious at Christ's remarks, the Jews plan to stone him (10: 31; cf. 8: 59).

When Christ challenges their action, they assert that they are fulfilling the Torah's command to stone the blasphemer (10: 32–3; cf. Lev. 24: 16). Christ counters by an *a fortiori* argument from scripture, and appeals again to his works as evidence for his claims (10: 34–8). Like the Old Testament prophet, he is concerned that the Jewish people 'may know and understand' and 'believe' (Jn 10: 38; cf. Isa. 43: 10). However, when they refuse to believe and try to arrest him again (10: 39; cf. 7: 30), he is forced to flee to the area where John the Baptist performed his first baptisms. Here his ministry is more successful. Many believe when they see the correspondence between the Baptist's testimony and the actual life and ministry of Jesus (10: 40–2)

The Testimony of the Seventh Sign (11: 1–57)

In Jn 11 Jesus raises Lazarus from the dead and performs one of the greatest signs recorded in the Fourth Gospel. In addition to providing the setting for the 'I am' saying and prefiguring Christ's own resurrection, this sign is introduced by the author as a strong piece of evidence for the claim of Jesus. Mary and Martha, together with the disciples of Jesus, are witnesses to the fact of the miracle (11: 7, 15–16). So also are the Jewish neighbours who accompany Mary to the tomb, though some of these reveal their hostility to Christ by reporting this miracle to the Pharisees (11: 46). The fact that the chief priests and the Pharisees believe the story of Lazarus's resurrection is indicated by their remark that 'this man performs many signs' (11: 47), and by their deliberate plans to put Christ to death (11: 53).

Thus while the miracle helps to crystallize the faith of Mary, Martha, the disciples and 'many of the Jews' (11: 45; cf. 11: 15), it also serves to prepare the way for the crucifixion. It leads Caiaphas to prophesy that 'one man should die for the people, and that the whole nation should not perish' (11: 50; cf. 10: 16). Here is a clear example of John's use of 'unconscious testimony to Jesus'.[1] The purpose of Christ's death, the Evangelist adds, is to gather into one the people of God who are 'scattered abroad' (11: 52). The miracle, together with its 'I am' saying, both serves as evidence for Christ's case as Messiah and also points to the means whereby he is going to win his case and convince his scattered people of his claims (11: 52; cf. 12: 32). The chapter closes with a reference to the chief priests and the Pharisees, who had given orders that anyone who knew where Jesus was should 'give information' leading to his arrest (μηνύσῃ, 11: 57; cf. Jos., Ant. IV.220). The case against Christ is being prepared, and his opponents are anxious to obtain any data which will secure his conviction.

The Climax of the Lawsuit of the Ministry (12: 1–50)

The lawsuit of the public ministry reaches its climax in chapter 12. The chapter opens with an account of a supper given in Bethany at which both Jesus and Lazarus are present. The crowds are attracted to the scene 'not only on account of Jesus, but also to see Lazarus, whom he raised from the dead' (12: 9). The chief priests, angered on learning that many of the Jews are believing on Jesus because of Lazarus, plan to put Lazarus to death as well as Jesus (12: 10f.).

The next day Passover pilgrims welcome Jesus with palm branches and hosannnas as he rides into Jerusalem on an ass's colt (12: 13–15). The Palm Sunday incident is important for John as it is one of several instances in his Gospel where a fulfilled prophecy or prediction is taken as evidence for the Messiahship and divine Sonship of Jesus (cf. 12: 37–40; 13: 18f.; 14: 28f.; 16: 1–4). This emphasis upon prediction and fulfilment was one of the major arguments in Isaiah 40–55 for establishing the case that Yahweh was God and the Lord of

---

[1] E. L. Titus, *The Message of the Fourth Gospel* (New York, 1957), pp. 34–5. Cf. Johnston, *The Spirit-Paraclete*, p. 89.

history. Similarly, in John's Gospel Jesus predicts something 'so that when it does take place, you may believe' (14: 29; cf. 13: 19). For this reason the Evangelist comments on this incident: 'His disciples did not understand this at first; but when Jesus was glorified, then they remembered that this had been written of him and had been done to him' (12: 16; cf. Psa. 118: 25–6; Zech. 9:9). For John, as for the writer of Isaiah 40–55, the fulfilment of prophecy and prediction is taken as evidence for the establishment of his legal case.

The third incident in chapter 12 is the arrival of the Greeks (12: 20f.). When they request an interview with Jesus, he sees the coming of his 'hour' when the benefits of his work will become available to all men (12: 23f.; cf. 7: 30, 39; 8: 20; 13: 1; 17: 1). The means whereby this is achieved is his death; the lawsuit of the public ministry is won by the uplifting of the Son of Man to suffer and die (12: 32–4). Paradoxically, this uplifting is also his exaltation to glory; it is the 'hour' when the Son of Man is 'glorified' (12: 23, 28).

The tragedy of the unbelieving Jews is their failure to receive the light of the world, Jesus (12: 35f.; cf. 8: 12; 12: 46). Despite his many signs wrought before them, they persist in wilful unbelief (12: 37). Yet John sees even the stubborn fact of Jewish *Ungläubigkeit* as an evidence for the claims of Jesus. This very thing had been foretold by the prophet Isaiah; as a witness in the Council of Yahweh Isaiah 'saw his (i.e., Christ's) glory and spoke about him' (12: 41; cf. Isa. 6: 1).[1] Isaiah's prophecy was now being fulfilled, and this was an evidence that Christ was the promised Messiah (12: 38–40; cf. Isa. 6: 9f.; 53: 1).

Despite widespread unbelief, John does not want to give the impression that Christ's claims were totally unacceptable to the Jews. For this reason he records the Pharisees' expostulation, 'Look, the world has gone after him' (12: 19), and later notes that 'many even of the authorities believed on him' (12: 42). On the other hand, John wants to make it perfectly clear that there was a reason which prevented the authorities from 'confessing' Christ – they loved the praise of men and they feared lest they should be 'put out of the synagogue' (12: 42f.). Two points should be observed here: (1) The use of ἀποσυνάγωγος in this passage, as in 9: 22 and 16: 2, recalls the costliness of

---

[1] Cf. H. W. Robinson, 'The Council of Yahweh', *JTS*, 45 (1944), 154.

Christian commitment in John's time, and suggests the anti-pathy of the Jewish leaders to Christ and his cause (cf. Mt. 5: 11f.; Lk. 6: 22). It is significant that some believers like Nico-demus remained secret disciples for 'fear of the Jews' (19: 38; cf. 7: 13; 9: 22; 20: 19). (2) The same verb ὁμολογεῖν appears here which is used in the Johannine Epistles to refer to the solemn confession of Jesus Christ as the incarnate Son of God (I Jn 2: 23; 4: 2f., 15; II Jn 7). John's implication is that faith which falls short of full confession is defective (cf. Rom. 10: 9f.). Perhaps this is why Christ warns those who reject (ἀθετεῖν is used) his testimony that his words will serve as accusing wit-nesses to convict men on the last day (12: 48; cf. Mt. 12: 41f.; Lk. 11: 31f.).

Summary of the Lawsuit of the Ministry

In chapters one to twelve John uses forensic language to describe a cosmic lawsuit between God and the world,[1] and in this respect he resembles Isaiah 40–55. In this lawsuit Christ is the representative of God and the Jews are the representatives of the world. In their pleading the Jews base their arguments on the law, while Jesus appeals to the witness borne to him by John the Baptist, his own works and the scriptures, and refers also to precedents in Old Testament history and fulfilled pre-dictions.[2] The lawsuit reaches its climax in the proceedings before Pontius Pilate in which Christ is sentenced to death. Paradoxically, however, Christ's death is the means whereby he is glorified and draws all men to himself (12: 28, 32). By his apparent defeat on Calvary Christ wins his case and 'overcomes the world' (cf. 16: 33, where the perfect tense of νικᾶν is used).[3] Instead of the cross being his judgment, it is really the judgment

---

[1] Cf. T. Preiss, *Life in Christ*, p. 17, n. 1.

[2] N. A. Dahl, 'The Johannine church and history', *Current Issues in New Testament Interpretation* (London, 1962), p. 139. Cf. R. Lievestad *Christ the Conqueror* (London, 1954), pp. 259–60.

[3] Arndt and Gingrich, p. 154, note that νικᾶν is used with the meaning of 'conquer in a legal action' in Aristophanes, the papyri, the inscriptions and Josephus. In the NT it is found in the legal sense of 'winning a case' in Rom. 3: 4. In I John νικᾶν is used to refer to the participation of Christians in Christ's victory over Satan and the world (I Jn 2: 13f.; 5: 4a, 4b, 5).

of the world;[1] by it every mouth is stopped and the whole world is found guilty before God (12: 31; cf. Rom. 3: 19). The διάβολος is active in opposing Christ (8: 44; 13: 2); as ὁ Σατανᾶς he makes use of Judas, ὁ υἱὸς τῆς ἀπωλείας, in engineering the betrayal and arrest (13: 27; 17: 11; cf. 18: 2–12 and 6: 70, where Judas himself is termed a διάβολος). However, the cross entails the legal defeat of Satan. The ἄρχων τοῦ κόσμου, mentioned in 12: 31, 14: 30 and 16: 11, is 'cast out' of the heavenly lawcourt, so that he can no longer accuse those who follow Christ; he has been vanquished by the uplifting of the Son of Man (12: 31f., where note the double meaning of ὑψοῦν; cf. Job 1: 6–12; 2: 1–6; Zech. 3: 1f.; Rev. 12: 9–12). The charges of the world and of the Jews against Jesus have been proven untrue – a point suggested apocalyptically by the ejection of the heavenly prosecutor (ἐκβληθήσεται, 12: 31). 'The ruler of this world is judged not to have any just title or claim upon God's people.'[2] Conversely, by winning the lawsuit, Jesus acquires a legal claim upon all men – an idea which becomes clear when the juridical background of ἕλκειν is understood.[3] The first phase of the lawsuit is completed when the first Advocate 'ascends' to the Father (20: 17), to plead, according to I John, the cause of sinful believers in the heavenly lawcourt (I Jn 2: 1; cf. Jn 17: 9ff.). The second phase begins when the Holy Spirit comes to function as the Paraclete on earth (14: 16, 25; 16: 8–11). This post-resurrection phase of the lawsuit will be considered in studying chapters 13 to 21.

THE POST-RESURRECTION LAWSUIT (CHAPTERS 13–17)

In chapters 13 to 17 Jesus looks beyond his death and resurrection and speaks to prepare his disciples for the future. For this reason these events can be treated as if they have already occurred; thus Jesus has overcome the world (16: 33); he has

---

[1] Origen perceived the close relationship between the idea of judgment and the cross, as M. F. Wiles has pointed out, *The Spiritual Gospel* (Cambridge, 1960), p. 80.

[2] P. Borgen, 'God's agent', p. 142; cf. G. B. Caird, 'Judgment and salvation: an exposition of John 12: 31–32', *CJT*, 2 (1956), 231–7.

[3] P. Borgen, 'God's agent', pp. 141–2.

finished the work the Father has given him to do (17: 4). Bearing in mind the fact that Christ often speaks here as one who has already passed through death (e.g., 17: 11f.), it is proper to study these chapters for the light that they shed on the post-resurrection lawsuit over the claims of Christ.

The post-resurrection lawsuit can be understood in this fashion:

The high court has already spoken its verdict [namely, that Jesus' death judges the world, not him], but its decision has still to be applied to individual cases. Trials are still going on; those who do not fulfil the conditions of acquittal are already judged by the sentence passed [12: 31; cf. 3: 19]. Before local courts who do not recognize the supremacy of the high court of heaven, the case must still be pleaded, but the final outcome is only the consequence of the legal victory already won [16: 33].[1]

After Christ's glorification and exaltation to the Father, the lawsuit continues, but Christ is no longer the chief witness who bears witness to the truth through his words and works (5: 36; 10: 38; 14: 10f.; 18: 37). Now the Holy Spirit, the Advocate, pleads Christ's case and calls John and other human witnesses to substantiate it. The apostles, like the witnesses in the Old Testament lawsuit, have a two-fold role; they are both witnesses to the facts of the life of Jesus, for they have been with him 'from the beginning' (15: 27; cf. I Jn 1: 1), and they are also advocates, defending him, commending him and trying to convince his opponents that he is Messiah and Son of God. Each of these witnesses must now be examined more closely.

The Witness of the Apostles

The apostles are the original eye-witnesses of the ministry of Jesus (15: 27). Like witnesses to fact in Greek and Hebrew courts of law, they can give firsthand information on some disputed matter; in their case, they can attest both the words and works of Jesus. They can declare with unflinching conviction: 'We have seen the Lord' (20: 25). To borrow words from the opening of I John, they can speak of 'that which was from the beginning, which we have heard, which we have seen with our eyes, which we have looked upon and touched with our hands'

[1] Dahl, 'The Johannine church and history', p. 140.

(I Jn 1: 1), and therefore their testimony is of the greatest importance. This apostolic witness to facts is also insisted upon in Luke–Acts (Lk. 1: 2; Acts 2: 32; 3: 15; 10: 39), and forms one of several points of contact between the Johannine and Lukan concepts of witness. It is brought very intentionally to the fore in Jn 19: 35 and 21: 24, and may also be suggested by the 'eye-witness touches' in John, possibly reflected in the careful topographical references (e.g., 1: 28; 3: 23; 5: 2; 18: 1).

The importance of apostolic attestation of facts can be seen in John's use of predictive prophecy, to which reference has already been made. In addition to the predictions mentioned at the beginning of this chapter, Eric Lane Titus notes five more

[1] predictions as to the safety of the disciples (10: 28; 17: 12, cf. 18: 9);...[2] predictions concerning the reactions of the disciples to Jesus' death (16: 6, 20–2; 6: 62; 10: 17–18; 16: 20b);...[3] predictions of the disciples' enlightenment attendant on the resurrection faith (13: 7; 16: 13–15, 20–4; cf. 2: 22; 12: 16);...[4] predictions of the Jewish rejection (8: 24; 9: 40–1; 10: 26; 12: 48; 15: 24–5; cf. 2: 23–5; 12: 37–40);...[5] predictions regarding the Gentile ingathering (10: 16; cf. 12: 20–2; 17: 20).[1]

In other words, Christ's predictive prophecies are attested by the apostles who have been with him from the beginning, and who can bear witness both to the prediction and to its fulfilment.

The apostles, like Jesus and the Spirit (7: 7; 16: 8–11), serve as advocates for God against the world, and in this respect they resemble Israel, Yahweh's witness to the world (Isa. 43: 10, 12; 44: 8). Because Christ's witnesses take his side against 'the world', they experience the same hatred and antagonism which 'the world' directed against him.[2] The words at the end of John 15 make this very plain: 'If the world *hates* you, know that it has *hated* me before it *hated* you [note the repeated use of μισεῖν here, and elsewhere in John; e.g., 15: 19, 23, 24, 25; 17: 14]...If they persecuted me, they will persecute you' (15: 18, 20; cf. I Jn 3: 13; Gospel of Thomas, logion 68). Then in the

---

[1] Titus, *The Message of the Fourth Gospel*, p. 19. Cf. W. A. Meeks, 'Galilee and Judea in the Fourth Gospel', *JBL*, 85 (1966), 164, who, following Bultmann, thinks that αὐτὸς γὰρ Ἰησοῦς ἐμαρτύρησεν in 4: 44 is a 'fulfilment formula'.

[2] Cf. G. Johnston, 'ΟΙΚΟΥΜΕΝΗ and ΚΟΣΜΟΣ in the New Testament', *NTS*, 10 (1964), 352–60.

opening verses of chapter 16 Jesus continues: 'They will put you out of the synagogues; indeed, the hour is coming when who- ever kills you will think he is offering service to God' (Jn 16: 2; cf. 16: 33; 21: 18–19; Acts 22: 3–5; 26: 9–11; I Tim. 1: 13). Similarly, in his high priestly prayer Christ mentions the hostility of the world against his witnesses (Jn 17: 14). The world hates, persecutes, ostracizes and even kills. How is it to be brought to acknowledge the claims of Christ? The answer is through the testimony of Christ's disciples witnessing in the convincing power of the Holy Spirit (15: 26f.). It is precisely because of the world's opposition to Christ that the witness of the disciples is needed. God loves the world in spite of its hostility (3: 16; cf. I Jn 4: 9f.), and just as he sent his Son into the world to bear witness to the truth, so the Son sends his apostles on a similar mission (17: 18; 18: 37; 20: 21). As his advocates, they meet the same reception which he met.

As in Greek and Hebrew courts of law, it is possible for a person to be an unwilling witness. The case of the blind man's parents is an illustration of witnesses who are reluctant to tell what they know for personal reasons (9: 18–21). Even the apostles are not exempt from this temptation to conceal what they know about Jesus, for three times Peter denies his Lord (18: 17, 25, 27; in the last two references the legal word ἀρνεῖσ- θαι is used). The supreme example of a witness deserting his Lord and going over to the other side is Judas, one of the Twelve. In the Fourth Gospel he represents those who fail to allow Christ's word to abide in them, who do not belong to the truth and who are not *bona fide* believers (8: 31f.; 15: 6–8; cf. II Jn 9). The apostles, like the other members of the Christian community, are constantly on trial to see whether they are of the truth or not; the vital question is: 'Do you now believe?' (16: 31; cf. 13: 19; 14: 1, 10f., 29; 17: 20f.).

The Witness of the Holy Spirit

The witness of the apostles is linked with the witness of the Holy Spirit (15: 27; 20: 21–3). 'It is as anointed with His Spirit that they are bearers of His commission, and in no other way... Indeed,...the Holy Spirit is Himself the primary and essential witness, and it is only His presence in the disciples which makes it possible for them truly to witness to Him.'[1] John tells his readers several things which illuminate the juridical role of the Holy Spirit in the Fourth Gospel.

First, the Holy Spirit is the Παράκλητος. This is a word meaning literally 'called alongside'. It may be used of the advocate or counsel for the defence in a trial (cf. Pirke Aboth, IV.13). Professor Moule has seen the importance of this insight for the Fourth Gospel:

['Paraclete'] in the Fourth Gospel is best interpreted if we take its primary connotation to be uniformly that of *Advocate*. This is not only a literal rendering (*advocatus*), avoiding the linguistic violence done to the form of the word by other proposed equivalents, but makes, I believe, the *best* sense of the notoriously difficult passage 16: 8–11, makes at least *good* sense of 15.26,27, and does not conflict with the other passages (N.B. – ὀρφανοί, 14.18, are precisely the class for whom a *goel* was proverbially needed); is in exact keeping with the use of the word in I John 2.1...and is illustrable (as Bengel remarked) from the story of Acts.[2]

To clarify what this means it is instructive to recall what was learned from the Old Testament lawsuit. First, consider two examples of advocates, one from the Book of Judges (6: 28–32) and the other from Isaiah (3: 13–15). The former passage occurs immediately after Gideon has torn down the altar of Baal (Judg. 6: 25–7). This action provokes the townsmen, who challenge his father Joash on behalf of (*lᵉ*) Baal. Joash replies in juridical terms (note the frequent reference to 'contend', the root *rîb* being used four times). In other words, this is an Old Testament controversy between Baal and Joash in which the townsmen serve as the advocate of the aggrieved party. Similarly in Isa. 3: 13–15 Yahweh functions as an advocate for his oppressed people against the 'elders and princes' who seek to exploit them.[3] In both of these passages we observe that the

---

[1] L. Newbigin, *The Household of God* (London, 1953), p. 95; cf. Barrett, *St. John*, p. 385.

[2] C. F. D. Moule, *The Phenomenon of the New Testament* (London, 1967), p. 91. He adds a *caveat*, however: 'I am not, of course, suggesting that the Fourth Evangelist is likely to have intended the word in only one sense... he uses a word suggestively, as a poet may, with any number of associational overtones.' Cf. Johnston, *The Spirit–Paraclete*, p. 83.

[3] Cf. J. Limburg, 'The root *rîb* and the prophetic lawsuit speeches', *JBL*, 88 (1969), 303.

CONCEPT OF WITNESS IN THE FOURTH GOSPEL

advocate is a third party who takes the side of one of the parties to the dispute and tries to 'talk round' the other side.

Further light is shed on the meaning of 'Paraclete' when we turn to Isaiah 40–55 and Job. In studying the Old Testament lawsuit we noted that the same person could serve both as witness *and* advocate. This point is especially clear in Isaiah 43, where the nations are challenged to produce evidence that will bring from their opponents the confession: 'That is the truth' (Isa. 43: 9; cf. 41: 21–3, 26–8; 44: 7; 45: 21; 48: 14). Here the would-be witnesses of the false gods are very definitely advocates whose function is to convince their opponents of the truth of their position. Similarly, Job's 'comforters' are really his legal opponents; they serve as advocates, presenting accusations and laying charges against their so-called 'friend', who replies with counter-questions and accusations of his own. The aim in both Job and Isaiah 40–55 is to elicit a surrender from one's legal adversary. These parallels from the Old Testament suggest that the verb ἐλέγχειν should be translated 'to convince', as in the Revised Standard Version.

This suggestion is supported by the actual use of ἐλέγχειν in legal proceedings, both in the Old Testament and in the New.[1] In Gen. 21: 25 it is used of Abraham's attempt to 'convince' Abimelech about a well of water which Abimelech's servants had unjustly seized. In Gen. 31: 42 Jacob speaks of God's 'convincing' Laban of having wronged him. In Lev. 19: 17 the command reads: 'You shall not hate your brother in your heart, but you shall reason [ἐλέγξεις] with your neighbour [that is, try to convince him], lest you bear sin because of him.' Job desires to convince Yahweh of his case [ἐλέγξω, Job 13: 3; cf. 40:2 (39: 22)], and the verb ἐλέγχειν, like the corresponding Hebrew *hôkîaḥ*, is used with reference to the activity of people 'in the gate' (Isa. 29: 21; Amos 5: 10). In the New Testament when a dispute occurs in the Christian community the aggrieved person is told to go to the other party and 'convince him' (ἔλεγξον αὐτόν) of his fault (Mt. 18: 15; cf. Barn. 12: 5). All these parallels, then, point to the conclusion that ἐλέγχειν in Jn 16: 8 should probably be translated 'convince' rather than

[1] Cf. Bernard, *St. John*, II, 506. On other meanings of ἐλέγχειν see B. Lindars, 'ΔΙΚΑΙΟΣΥΝΗ in Jn 16.8 and 10', in *Mélanges Bibliques*, eds. A. Descamps and R. P. André de Halleux (Gembloux, n.d.), p. 280, n.5.

'convict', as it is rendered in most English versions of the Bible. Moreover, this translation agrees with the conclusion of Norman Snaith who, after a detailed study of the linguistic evidence, thinks that the proper rendering of Paraclete is 'Convincer'.[1] John is saying that the Holy Spirit will act as an advocate would act in a Hebrew court of law.

But whose cause does the Holy Spirit plead? The context indicates that primarily it is the cause of Christ; this is why the legal activities of 'witnessing' (15: 26) and 'convincing' (16: 8) are mentioned. However, Jn 14: 16 suggests that the Paraclete is also advocate for the disciples, since their cause is the cause of Christ. As Christ is the advocate of the disciples before the Father in heaven (14: 16; cf. I Jn 2: 1), so the Spirit is the earthly advocate of Christ and his disciples before the world. The apostles are witnesses in court, but the chief responsibility for the defence lies with the Holy Spirit. It is he who must open men's hearts and convince them of the evidence (cf. I Jn 5: 6). Hence the *testimonium Spiritus sancti internum* is a *sine qua non* in John's concept of witness (cf. Calvin, *Institutes*, I.vii.4).[2]

The Holy Spirit will convince the world that the real truth about sin, righteousness and judgment is to be seen in the cross. He will convince 'about sin', making the world conscious not only of its past sin in crucifying Christ, but especially of the one great sin of refusing to accept Christ as Saviour and Lord (16: 9). He will also convince 'about righteousness', that is, the righteousness of Christ (16: 10; cf. the Sinaitic Syriac, which reads 'His righteousness').[3] The crucifixion had seemed to imply that Christ's claim to be sinless was without foundation

---

[1] N. H. Snaith, 'The meaning of "The Paraclete"', *ExpT*, 57 (1945), 47–50. Cf. R. E. Brown, 'The Paraclete in the Fourth Gospel', *NTS*, 13 (1967), 116–17.

[2] Cf. J. R. Pelt, 'Witness', *A Dictionary of Christ and the Gospels*, ed. J. Hastings (2 vols.; Edinburgh, 1908), II, 831. On the close parallels between Jesus and the Spirit in John see G. Bornkamm, *Geschichte und Glaube* (Munich, 1968), I, 69.

[3] J. N. Sanders, *The Gospel according to St. John*, ed. B. A. Mastin (London, 1968), pp. 351–2, noting the legal overtones of this section, has suggested that δικαιοσύνη, 'found here only in the Fourth Gospel, may signify "justification" or "acquittal"'. On this interpretation verse 10 refers to those who exercise faith in Christ, 'who are acquitted because of the new conditions which follow his departure from the earth'. Cf. Lindars, 'ΔΙΚΑΙΟΣΥΝΗ in Jn 16.8 and 10', pp. 275–85.

119

(8: 46), and that he 'ought to die' as an 'evildoer' (18: 30; 19: 7). However, all this is changed by Christ's 'going to the Father' (13: 3; 14: 28; 16: 10, 17, 28; 20: 17). By his resurrection and ascension to the Father his claims are demonstrated; rejected by the world, he is welcomed by the Father and vindicated as 'the Righteous One' (cf. Acts 3: 14; 7: 52; II Cor. 5: 21; I Pet. 3: 18). And finally, the Holy Spirit will convince the world 'about judgment', 'because the ruler of this world is judged' (κέκριται, 16: 11). His judgment took place at the crucifixion, and the whole world shared in his condemnation: 'Now is the judgment of this world, now shall the ruler of this world be cast out' (12: 31).

But the Holy Spirit has a *dual* legal function. Like the legal representatives in the Old Testament lawsuit, he is a witness as well as an advocate, and his activity in this capacity must now be examined. To what does the Holy Spirit bear witness and to whom? Fortunately these questions are not too difficult to consider, because John presents the answers to his readers. The Holy Spirit gives testimony concerning Jesus: 'He shall bear witness to me' (15: 26). His testimony deals with spiritual truth and is given to Christ's disciples: 'When the Spirit of truth comes, he will guide you into all truth' (16: 13). This truth is Christocentric in character: 'He will glorify me, for he will take what is mine and declare it to you' (16: 14f.). The Spirit will bear witness of Christ to the disciples in at least two ways. First, he will bring to their remembrance all that Jesus had said (14: 26; cf. 2: 22; 6: 39; 10: 38; 17: 12; 18: 9). Second, he will point to the correspondence between the Messianic predictions and their fulfilment in Christ (Jn 2: 17; cf. Psa. 69: 9; Jn 12: 13–16, cf. Psa. 118: 26 and Zech. 9: 9; Jn 17: 12, cf. Psa. 41: 9; Jn 19: 23f., cf. Psa. 22: 18).

To sum up, the twofold juridical role is that of witness *and* advocate, as in the Old Testament lawsuit, a point made especially clear in the second section of Isaiah (e.g., Isa. 43: 9). The Holy Spirit bears witness (15: 26), taking of the things of Christ and declaring them to his disciples (16: 13–15); he also convinces the world of sin, righteousness and judgment (16: 8–11). Just as Yahweh pleads the cause of his people (Isa. 51: 22), so the Holy Spirit pleads the cause of Christ. Here is another link between the Fourth Gospel and Isaiah 40–55.

The Importance of Dual Witness

Up to this point the work of the apostles and the work of the Holy Spirit have been treated separately. Is there anything to be deduced from the fact that John links them together (15: 26f.)? In attempting to answer that question three observations can be made.

In the first place, the double witness of the Spirit and the apostles is an example of the truth that 'valid witness must always be plural'.[1] As was noted in connection with the Old Testament use of witnesses, the evidence of a single witness was insufficient for any charge to be sustained (Num. 35: 30; Deut. 17: 6; 19: 15; cf. Heb. 10: 28). This principle was also honoured in rabbinic literature, where it was applied to civil as well as criminal cases.[2] It is carried into the New Testament, where it holds not only in witnessing against someone's misdeeds (Mt. 18: 15–17; II Cor. 13: 1; I Tim. 5: 19) but also in witnessing to the truth (Jn 5: 31f.; 8: 17; 12: 26f.; Acts 5: 32; Heb. 2: 3f.; Rev. 11: 3). Later it appears in the *Pistis Sophia* (chs 42–3), where the three witnesses are Philip, Thomas and Matthew. All this evidence shows the value of corporate witness. Indeed, as we noted at the beginning of this chapter, the whole of John's Gospel conforms to the principle that everything must be confirmed by the testimony of two or three witnesses. This is another point of contact between the Fourth Gospel and Luke–Acts, especially when it is remembered that for both John and Luke the two key witnesses after the resurrection are the apostles and the Holy Spirit (Jn 15: 26f.; Acts 5: 32; cf. 1: 8).

The second point has to do with persecution. When the apostles are witnessing for Christ in the face of antagonism and hostility, they do not witness in their own strength but rather in the convincing power of the Holy Spirit (Jn 15: 26f.). They are reassured that when they bear witness in what seem to be the most unpromising circumstances the Holy Spirit is active in convincing the world of the truth of what they say (16: 8–11). All this reminds one of the Synoptic Gospels, where similar

[1] J. R. W. Stott, *The Preacher's Portrait* (London, 1961), p. 62: cf. T. Maertens, *Bible Themes* (2 vols.; Bruges, 1964), I, 399.
[2] Cf. L. N. Dembitz, 'Evidence', *Jewish Encyclopaedia*, ed. I. Singer, v, 277–80.

references are made to the disciples witnessing against a background of hostility and persecution (Mt. 10: 17–23; Lk. 12: 11f.; 21: 12–17). The Synoptic parallels are very interesting from a juridical point of view, for they show that often persecution took the form of haling Christians before Jewish or secular courts of law where they had opportunity to give their testimony (Mt. 10: 17f.; Lk. 12: 11; 21: 12f.). Under such circumstances Christians were encouraged by the reminder that 'it is not you who speak, but the Holy Spirit speaking through you' (Mt. 10: 19f.; Lk. 12: 11f.). There is also a link here between John and the Book of Acts (cf. Jn 15: 18 – 16: 4; Acts 4: 18–21, 29–31; 7: 54–60; 20: 22–4; 26: 16–18); in both books the witness of the apostles and the witness of the Spirit appear against a background of hostility and persecution, and in both the idea of witness is being used very much as a live metaphor.

The third observation is that Christian witness does not cease with the death of the apostles. 'Although the Apostolate, as such, could have no successors, it remained the quite fundamental task of the Church to carry on the "apostolic" witness to the Word made flesh.'[1] This point is clear in John 17, where Christ's high-priestly intercession includes future disciples (17: 20). So those who believe the apostles' testimony also bear witness; they plead Christ's cause as Saviour and Son of God 'that the world may believe' (17: 21). But in the nature of the case they are dependent upon the eye-witness testimony of the apostles for the basic facts of the life, death and resurrection of their master.[2] In other words, they are competent as advocates, but not as eye-witnesses.

This function was vitally important to the life of the early church, for it was only as the Holy Spirit continued to work through Christ's witnesses that he could convince the world of sin, righteousness and judgment. It was not enough to have the accounts of the apostles' testimony as they came to be written down; it was also necessary to have living advocates to present Christ's case 'so that the world may know that thou hast sent me and hast loved them even as thou hast loved me' (17: 23). By this means the post-resurrection lawsuit over the claims of Christ is perpetuated, and the process of judgment continued.

[1] W. D. Davies, *Christian Origins and Judaism* (London, 1962), p. 241.
[2] Cf. O. Cullmann, *The Early Church* (London, 1956), p. 78.

THE LAWSUIT OF THE LAST DAY

In this study of John's Gospel the lawsuit of the ministry and the post-resurrection lawsuit have been examined, and the idea of witness has been shown to have a prominent part in each. It remains to say a few words about the lawsuit of the Last Day. John's emphasis on realized eschatology leads him to stress the judgment which men incur upon themselves now by their rejection of Christ: 'He who does not believe is condemned already, because he has not believed in the name of the only Son of God...he who does not obey the Son shall not see life, but the wrath of God rests upon him' (3: 18b, 36b). At the same time, John plainly affirms his belief in a judgment at the Last Day: 'Do not marvel at this; for the hour is coming when all who are in the tombs will hear his [the Son of Man's] voice and come forth, those who have done good, to the resurrection of life, and those who have done evil, to the resurrection of judgment' (Jn 5: 28f.; cf. Dan. 12: 2). Here the reader is explicitly informed of Christ's judicial function: the Father has given him 'authority to execute judgment, because he is the Son of Man' (5: 27; cf. Dan. 7: 13; Wisd. 9: 3; Lk. 21: 36). The idea of a day of judgment receives greater emphasis in I John, where the 'last hour' is at hand and where 'the spirit of antichrist' seems to have already come (I Jn 2: 18, 22; 4: 3).

Rudolf Bultmann in his famous *Theology of the New Testament* (II, 39) has argued that these futuristic Johannine references are the work of an ecclesiastical redactor since they do not fit the Christian Gnosticism which he thinks is the nature of the Gospel. However, this view does not do justice to the contents of the Fourth Gospel and in any case rests upon dogmatic presuppositions which are open to serious question. The idea of future judgment is present in the Johannine literature, but in vestigial form. There will be a Last Day 'in which Christ shall return (John 14: 3; 21: 22; I John 2: 28), the dead shall be raised (John 6: 39, 40, 44, 54), and final judgment pronounced (John 5: 29; 12: 48; I John 4: 17)'.[1] But the coming of the Last Day is not thought to bring a new and independent act of judgment;

---

[1] R. H. Mounce, *The Essential Nature of New Testament Preaching* (Grand Rapids, 1960), p. 147. Cf. D. R. Carnegie, 'Kerygma in the Fourth Gospel', *VE* (1971), 52–3.

rather, it will reveal the final outcome of the lawsuit that has been in progress over the claims of Jesus Christ. Men who reject Christ will find his words rising up as accusing witnesses against them in the Last Day (Jn 12: 48; cf. Mt. 12: 41f.; Lk. 11: 31f.). For the Christian the Last Day holds no terrors, for he knows that he 'does not come into judgment, but has passed from death to life'; through Christ's work on his behalf the Last Judgment has been anticipated and the sentence of acquittal has been pronounced (Jn 5: 24). In effect, John agrees with Paul's statement of the Christian's position in Rom. 8: 33f.: 'Who shall bring any charge against God's elect? It is God who justifies; who is to condemn? It is Christ Jesus, who died, yes, who was raised from the dead, who is at the right hand of God, who indeed intercedes for us' (cf. I Jn 2: 1).

THE IDEA OF WITNESS IN THE JOHANNINE EPISTLES

The idea of witness appears in the Johannine Epistles, and from time to time cross references have been made to these writings for the light that they cast upon the Fourth Gospel and its concept of witness. The opening words of the First Epistle have already been mentioned for their emphasis upon the apostles as eye-witnesses of Jesus Christ (I Jn 1: 1); the same passage stresses the apostles' other role as advocates who try to convince people 'concerning the word of life': 'The life was made manifest, and we saw it, and testify [μαρτυροῦμεν] to it, and proclaim to you that eternal life which was with the Father and was made manifest to us...so that you may have fellowship with us' (I Jn 1: 1–3; note the double use of ἀπαγγέλλω here). The apostles are similarly presented in I Jn 4: 14: 'And we have seen and testify that the Father has sent his Son as the Saviour of the world.'[1]

This twofold description of the juridical role of the apostles is in harmony with the twofold function of witnesses in the Old

[1] F. V. Filson, 'First John: purpose and message', *Int*, 23 (1969), 259–76, thinks that the 'we' passages in I John 'need not mean that they are the original apostles and the author is one of the Twelve', but concedes that the 'we' group are 'eyewitnesses whose relation to Jesus Christ goes back to the founding days of the church' (p. 265). However, it is pertinent to observe that it is the *apostles* who are described as eyewitnesses ἀπ' ἀρχῆς (Jn 15: 27).

Testament lawsuit. Moreover, it agrees with both the Fourth Gospel and the Book of Acts, though the controversies of Jesus and the apostles with the Jews are no longer significant at the time this epistle is written. Besides trying to deepen the spiritual life of his readers, the author is writing to refute certain gnostic teachers like Cerinthus who denied the reality of the incarnation (cf. Irenaeus, *Adv. Haer.* 1: 26); this is indicated by his use of the juridical verbs for 'confessing' and 'denying' (ὁμολογεῖν in I Jn 2: 23; 4: 2f., 15; cf. II Jn 7; ἀρνεῖσθαι in I Jn 2: 22 (twice), 23). The opposition of false teachers is explicitly recognized in III John, where Diotrephes is singled out not only as a man who loves the first place, but also as one who brings unjustified charges against John the elder (φλυαρῶν ἡμῶν, III Jn 10).

In contrast to false teachers, godly men like Gaius can be attested as to the integrity of their Christian profession (III Jn 3). Thus III John notes that 'Demetrius has testimony [μεμαρτύρηται] from everyone, and from the truth itself'; the author and those with him add: 'We testify to him too, and you know our testimony is true' (III Jn 11, independent translation). When taken together, these three forms of testimony are considered to provide a reliable rule for commending people; perhaps this is another illustration of Johannine deference to the Jewish rule of evidence (Deut. 19: 15). This last passage is important from another point of view, for it is very similar to Jn 19: 35 and 21: 24, and suggests a close relationship between these epistles and the Fourth Gospel.

Only two other passages in the Johannine Epistles call for special comment. One of these concerns the only Paraclete reference outside of the Fourth Gospel. In I John 2: 1 Christ is mentioned as the believer's Advocate with the Father, occupying a role in heaven comparable to the role of the Holy Spirit on earth (Jn 14: 16; cf. Pirke Aboth 4: 5). As *Fürsprecher* Christ pleads the merits of his own finished work before the heavenly lawcourt (Jn 17: 4; cf. 19: 30), so the believer who has sinned is assured of a favourable verdict if he confesses and acknowledges his sin (I Jn 1: 9). The Paraclete passage of the First Epistle is in full agreement with the Paraclete passages of the Fourth Gospel, and also with the general background of the Old Testament lawsuit sketched in the earlier chapters of this book. It also sheds light on John 17, where Jesus acts as 'Paraclete, advocate and intercessor (cf. Heb. 7: 25; Rom. 8: 34)'.[1]

The last passage to consider is I Jn 5: 6–12, where the word for 'witness' in one form or another appears a total of ten times in six verses. The testimony mentioned here is a threefold one provided by the Spirit, the water and the blood, and therefore satisfies the conditions for legally acceptable evidence (Deut.19: 15; cf. Jn 5: 31f.; 8: 17f.). The Holy Spirit is initially given to Jesus at his baptism, a point made clear by the testimony of the Baptist (Jn 1: 32–4; cf. Mk 1: 8f.; Mt. 3: 16f.; Lk. 3: 21f.); after Jesus is 'glorified' through his crucifixion and resurrection, the Spirit is given to the disciples (Jn 20: 22; cf. 7: 39). Working through them, the Spirit is active in bearing witness to Jesus (Jn 15: 26). This testimony continues to be given (note the use of the present participle τὸ μαρτυροῦν in I Jn 5: 6c), and is fully trustworthy, for 'the Spirit is the truth' (I Jn 5: 7).

The water and the blood also give testimony, but scholars have found it difficult to agree on that to which they refer. Is it to the baptism and crucifixion of Jesus, to the water and blood flowing from Christ's pierced side (cf. Jn 19: 34), or to the two sacraments of baptism and the Lord's Supper (cf. Jn. 3 and 6)? In verse 6 of I Jn 5 the words 'he who came by water and blood' are repeated with polemical insistence and definitely seem to root the testimony in the historical facts of the life of Jesus. Similarly, the use of the aorist participle ἐλθών points in the same direction, and suggests that these historical facts are connected with Christ's mission, for ἦλθον is frequently used in this way in John's Gospel (1: 15, 27, 30; 3: 2, 33; 5: 43; 6: 14; 7: 28; 9: 39; 10: 10; 15: 22; 16: 28; 18: 37).

The most likely historical facts alluded to are Christ's baptism in the waters of Jordan and his death by the shedding of blood on Golgotha; these two events sum up the work of redemption. This interpretation explains the order of the words 'water and blood' (I Jn 5: 6b), without excluding a secondary reference to Jn 19: 34, held by Westcott to be 'beyond question'.[2]

But the author does not restrict the testimony of the water and

---

[1] T. F. Glasson, *Moses in the Fourth Gospel* (London, 1963), p. 104.

[2] B. F. Westcott, *The Epistles of St. John* (London, 1886), p. 182. For a recent monograph on the witness theme in John see Johannes Beutler, *Martyria: Traditionsgeschichtliche Untersuchungen zum Zeugnisthema bei Johannes*

the blood to the past, for he sees them, together with the Spirit, as continuing to bear witness (τρεῖς εἰσιν οἱ μαρτυροῦντες, verse 7; the sentence about the 'three heavenly witnesses' is to be rejected on textual grounds). This concern for a continuing witness suggests that in addition to the historical attestation of Christ's baptism and crucifixion there is also a symbolic reference to the two great sacraments – a suggestion made more plausible by the fact that baptism and the Lord's Supper seem to be alluded to in John 3 and 6. In other words,

the Church possesses a counterpart to the Baptism of Christ, in the sacrament of Baptism, and a counterpart to His sacrificial death, in the sacrament of the Eucharist. Both sacraments attest and confirm to believers the abiding effect of the life and death of Christ. It seems likely that our author is thinking of these two sacraments as providing a continuing witness to the truth of Christ's incarnation and re-demptive death. Their value as evidence lies precisely in their being concrete, overt, 'objective' actions, directly recalling (or 'repre-senting') historical facts of the Gospel, while at the same time they are vehicles of a supra-historical life in the Church.[1]

The apostolic testimony, then, is confirmed and authenticated by a threefold testimony in verse 9: 'In the ordinary affairs of life we are ready to be convinced by the testimony of an honest and competent witness. *A fortiori*, in the highest concerns of all, we must accept the testimony of God himself, and the consen-tient testimony of the Spirit, the water and the blood is His testimony.'[2] In other words, the Father's testimony is pluriform (cf. Jn 5: 32–47), and its essential content of the living testimony is Christocentric: 'And this is the testimony that God gave us eternal life, and this life is in his Son' (verse 11). 'He who believes in the Son of God has the testimony in himself. He who does not believe God, has made him a liar, because he has not believed in the testimony that God has borne to his Son' (verse 10).

(Frankfurt am Main, 1972). Unfortunately this study came to the attention of the author too late for consideration in this book. For a penetrating survey and critique see Wayne A. Meeks's review in *JBL*, 93 (1974), 139–41.

[1] Cf. C. H. Dodd, *The Johannine Epistles*, MNTC (London, 1946), p. 131.

[2] *Ibid.* p. 132; cf. T. Preiss, 'The inner witness of the Holy Spirit', *Int*, (1953), 279, and P. Marcel, 'Le Témoignage en parole et en actes', *Reformed Review*, 9 (1958), 38–40, who stresses the role of the witness's word as a vehicle of the Spirit.

CHAPTER 9

THE CONCEPT OF WITNESS IN THE BOOK OF ACTS

The concept of witness also receives great prominence in the Book of Acts. It is here that one observes 'the greatest reflection on the meaning of "witness" as it applies to the mission of the church'.[1] The purpose of this chapter is to consider the importance of the witness motif in Acts; the Third Gospel will be examined later when the Synoptics are treated.

Μάρτυς and six of its derivatives appear a total of thirty-nine times in the Book of Acts (μάρτυς, thirteen times; μαρτυρεῖν, eleven times; διαμαρτύρεσθαι, nine times; μαρτύρεσθαι and μαρτύριον twice each; μαρτυρία and ἀμάρτυρος, once each. By way of comparison, Luke's Gospel uses μαρτύριον three times (Lk. 5: 14; 9: 5; 21: 13), μάρτυς twice (Lk. 11: 48; 24: 48), and μαρτυρία (Lk. 22: 71), μαρτυρεῖν (4: 22), διαμαρτύρεσθαι (16: 28) and ψευδομαρτυρεῖν (18: 20) once each. This evidence points to the importance of the idea of witness in the thinking of Luke,[2] and this conclusion is abundantly substantiated by other evidence.

The Book of Acts, like the Fourth Gospel, shows a tremendous interest in the idea of witness. This is not surprising, for both Luke and John are concerned that people should believe the claims of Christ and enter into a personal experience of his salvation. For both writers the significance of witness lies in its ability to induce faith. The operative question for Luke as for John is: On what grounds can people believe, or on what evidence ought they to believe?

In other words, the facts of the Christian faith and their significance are being presented in an atmosphere of hostility, contention and debate. Under these conditions it is not strange that Luke should make use of the language of the courtroom.

---

[1] R. V. Moss, Jr, 'The witnessing church in the New Testament', *TaL*, 3 (1960), 264–7; cf. A. Rétif, 'Témoignage et prédication missionaire dans les Actes des Apôtres', *NRT*, 73 (1951), 152–65.

[2] Cf. L. E. Keck, *Mandate to Witness – Studies in the Book of Acts* (Valley Forge, 1964), p. 60.

The claims of Christ are being contested, and Luke by the use of lawcourt scenes and legal terminology intends to draw attention to this fact.[1] The place of Jesus and his claims are in dispute, and Luke seeks to meet the challenge by offering 'many convincing proofs' (Acts 1: 3); perhaps the most striking evidence he introduces concerns the resurrection (πίστιν παρασχὼν πᾶσιν, 17: 31). An important part of his method is the presentation of the courtroom material in such a way that it will bear witness to Christ. It is not surprising, then, to find Paul insisting that the chief magistrates of Philippi should come to release him; they had exposed the Christian cause to public disgrace, so a public vindication was called for (witness the use of the contrasting adverbs δημοσίᾳ and λάθρᾳ, 16: 37).

But to say that Luke gives prominence to actual courtroom procedure is not to imply that he confines himself to it. Rather, he appeals to the wider lawcourt of public opinion where the claims of Christ are being vigorously contested. For this reason the idea of witness becomes very much a live metaphor in the Book of Acts. To see what this means in terms of Luke's concept of witness it is necessary to explore the juridical character of the testimony.[2]

THE JURIDICAL CHARACTER OF THE TESTIMONY

The situation in which the apostles found themselves after the crucifixion and resurrection is worth pondering. Their Master had been 'committed for trial and repudiated in Pilate's court' (παρεδώκατε καὶ ἠρνήσασθε κατὰ πρόσωπον Πιλάτου, Acts 3: 13, N.E.B.). He had been condemned by the Jews as a criminal and sentenced to die on the charge of blasphemy (cf. Mk 14: 63 pars.; Jn 18: 30; 19: 7). After the resurrection the trial of Jesus, in effect, is reopened and fresh evidence is presented by the apostles to get the Jews to change their verdict. Their condemnation and crucifixion of Christ had been done in ignor-

---

[1] A. A. Trites, 'The importance of legal scenes and language in the Book of Acts', NovT, 16 (1974), 278–84. Cf. M. Dibelius, Studies in the Acts of the Apostles (London, 1956), p. 213.

[2] Cf. L. Cerfaux, 'Témoins du Christ d'après le Livre des Actes', Recueil Lucien Cerfaux (3 vols., Gembloux, 1954–62), II, 157–61.

ance (Acts 3: 17; 13: 27); they did not know that the one whom they had despised and rejected had been vindicated by God as 'the Righteous One' (3: 14; 7: 52). By raising Jesus from the dead, God showed the Jews that they had made a grievous mistake; they had crucified him who is 'Lord and Christ' (2: 36).

In other words, the Jews must be given an opportunity to change their mind about the one whom God had vindicated through the resurrection and ascension.[1] Repentance (μετάνοια) is important in Acts, not only for the Gentiles (17: 30; 20: 21; 26: 20), but also for the Jews (2: 38; 3: 19; 5: 31).[2] If they fail to repent, they pass the sentence of judgment on themselves, and the gospel is then offered to the Gentiles. Thus the Jews in the synagogue at Pisidian Antioch are bluntly told by Paul and Barnabas: 'It was necessary that the word of God should be spoken first to you. Since you thrust it from you, and judge yourselves unworthy of eternal life, behold, we turn to the Gentiles' (13: 46; cf. 18: 6; 28: 24–8).

This was precisely the situation which the apostles faced in Jerusalem. The people before whom they bore witness had denied the Messiah and delivered him to the Roman authorities (3: 13f.), and the Sanhedrin before whom they were appearing was the one which had condemned Jesus (4: 5ff.; 5: 27ff.). In these circumstances persecution was to be expected. Peter and John were threatened and later thrown into prison for their testimony to Christ (4: 17f., 21; 5: 17f.). Similarly, Stephen's steps were dogged by persecutors who 'stirred up the people and the elders and the scribes' against him (6: 9–14). Later Herod Agrippa killed James the brother of John to gain favour with the Jews (12: 2f.), and the Jews persecuted Paul, not only in Jerusalem (21: 27ff.; 22: 22; 23: 12ff.), but also frequently in the course of his missionary journeys (13: 45, 50; 14: 2; 17: 5ff.).

These persecutions have both a juridical and a Messianic character. They are perceived in continuity with those that have

[1] On the theme of vindication see C. F. D. Moule, *The Phenomenon of the New Testament* (London, 1967), pp. 82–99.

[2] Repentance is also an important theme in Luke's Gospel, where it is connected with the preaching of Jonah (11: 32), John the Baptist (3: 3, 8; cf. 3: 10–14) and Jesus (10: 13; 13: 3, 5; 17: 3–4). Repentance is presented as a central element in the preaching of Jesus (5: 32; cf. 15: 7, 10), and is included in the Lukan version of the Great Commission (Lk. 24: 47).

brought Jesus before the tribunals and condemned him. As βλασφημία had been the charge levelled against Jesus (Mk 14: 64; Mt. 26: 65; cf. Lk. 5: 21; Jn 10: 33), so Stephen is accused of speaking ῥήματα βλάσφημα against Moses and God (Acts 6: 11). As Jesus had been accused of madness (ἐξέστη, Mk 3: 21; cf. μαίνεται, Jn 10: 20), so Paul is similarly attacked (Acts 26: 24). As the Jews had put to death the Nazarene, so they attempt to deal with Paul (διεχειρίσασθε, 5: 30; διαχειρίσασθαι, 26: 21). Paul himself in his pre-Christian days had striven to make believers 'blaspheme', that is, curse the Lord's name and repudiate the primary Christian confession, 'Jesus is Lord' (Acts 26: 11; cf. Rom. 10: 9; I Cor. 12: 3; Phil. 2: 11); his attacks on believers had been particularly ferocious (Acts 8: 3; 9: 1-2, 21). Later Paul reminds his converts that θλῖψις is part of the divine plan: 'through many tribulations we must (δεῖ) enter into the kingdom of God' (14: 22).

In other words, the Messianic Age continues, and the persecutions which characterize its presence are in evidence (cf. Acts 4: 25-30 with Psa. 2: 1f.). It is to a human judgment seat that the persecutions drive Christians, and it is there that they are forced to speak 'before the synagogues and the rulers and the authorities' (Lk. 12: 11). Under such circumstances Luke sees Christ encouraging his witnesses; they are not to worry, for the Holy Spirit will give them the wisdom and courage needed for their task (Lk. 21: 14f.).

According to Luke, Jesus had explicitly predicted these persecutions to his followers: 'They will lay hands on you and persecute you, delivering you up to the synagogues and prisons, and you will be brought before kings and governors for my name's sake' (Lk. 21: 12; cf. Mt. 10: 17f.). Often the encounter with kings and governors would appear disastrous, for frequently Christians would be condemned in the courts and sentenced to prison. Spiritually, however, it would be a great occasion for Christian witness: 'This will be a time for you to bear testimony' (Lk. 21: 13; cf. Mt. 10: 18). In other words, Christians could look forward to such occasions, confident that if they confessed Christ before men, he would confess them as his disciples in heaven. On the other hand, earthly denial of their Lord and Saviour would entail heavenly rejection by the Son of Man (Lk. 12: 8; Mt. 10: 32f.). Similarly ὁμολογεῖν and ἀρνεῖσθαι are used in Acts in contexts which are both juridical and religious (Acts 3: 13f.; 4: 16; 7: 35; 24: 14).[1]

At these trials generally there are no other witnesses than the accused, and it is for their confession that they are condemned. In this respect Christians resemble their Master who had been condemned, without further testimony, for his confession (Lk. 22: 70; cf. I Tim. 6: 12f.). Luke, like the writer of the Fourth Gospel, sees the human and earthly judgment as having a celestial counterpart. Just as the disciples take the part of Christ on earth, so he will take their part in heaven. A striking illustration of this principle occurs in the words of the dying Stephen, who cries: 'Behold, I see the heavens opened, and the Son of Man standing at the right hand of God' (Acts 7: 56). The Son of Man is viewed here in the light of the legal terminology of the Old Testament (where the judge is described as 'sitting', the witness as 'standing', and the right hand as the place of the vindicating 'witness'). As Stephen had confessed Christ before the unbelieving Jews who took his life, so Christ would confess him publicly in heaven; condemned by the earthly tribunal, Stephen would be vindicated by the heavenly one. Here, as Théo Preiss has noted, 'Faith in the Christ-Paraclete and in the Spirit-Paraclete already underlies the story';[2] this suggests another point of contact between the Lukan and the Johannine concepts of witness.

In the case of Stephen the idea of witness is very much a live metaphor: 'There is nothing to suggest that his death was an essential part of his testimony. Stephen, like Paul, was an eye-witness to the risen Jesus, and the fact that he died in consequence of his testimony made him no more and no less a μάρτυς than Paul.'[3]

To sum up, Luke–Acts presents the claims of Christ against a background of hostility, contention and active persecution. It is this which Peter, John, Stephen and Paul all contend with, and it is this which accounts for the large place given to legal

[1] Cf. H. Riesenfeld, 'The meaning of the verb ἀρνεῖσθαι', CN, 11 (1947), 207–19, and G. W. H. Lampe, 'St. Peter's denial', BJRL, 55 (1973), 353f.

[2] T. Preiss, 'The inner witness of the Holy Spirit', Int, 7 (1953), 268. C. F. D. Moule cites other interpretations in Studies in Luke–Acts (ed. L. E. Keck and J. L. Martyn, New York, 1966), p. 182, n. 15.

[3] R. P. Casey, 'Μάρτυς', BC, v, 33. Cf. P.-H. Menoud, 'Jésus et ses témoins', EeT, 23 (1960), 14ff.

terminology and to ideas drawn from the lawcourt. From the beginning the apostles are concerned not only with the facts of the life, death, resurrection and exaltation of Jesus, but also with the defence of their religious significance. They proclaim Jesus as Lord of all (10: 36; cf. 2: 36), the divinely appointed κριτής of the living and the dead (10: 42). For them and their fellow Christians this involves acting as vindicating witnesses for Christ in the face of hostility and persecution. The Holy Spirit prepares them for this work in several ways. On the one hand, he teaches them what to say and gives them the courage to say it (Lk. 12: 12; 21: 14f.; cf. Mt. 10: 19f.). On the other, the Spirit works to confirm their testimony through external signs and wonders and through the boldness which he inspires in their preaching. All of this deserves to be compared with the Fourth Gospel, where the Spirit also has a juridical role in times of persecution (Jn 15: 18 – 16: 11).

Luke has taken the original notion of bearing witness before a court of law and adapted it to the conditions of the Messianic Age. Accordingly, it is not surprising that he should regard the whole Book of Acts as providing evidence which can be adduced in support of the Christian position.

THE BOOK OF ACTS AS TESTIMONY

Luke is concerned to offer legally acceptable evidence for Christ which will be admitted as valid in the wider lawcourt of life itself. That this is in fact the case is attested by a striking formal characteristic of Acts. Again and again everything is established in accordance with the principle stated in Deut. 19: 15; this is the law of the two or three witnesses which is so important to Luke. He accepts the Old Testament principle that everything must be established at the mouth of two or three witnesses, and formulates his historical material in accordance with it.

Proof of this contention is to be found in R. Morgenthaler's detailed study of the Lukan use of doublets, parallelisms and similar phenomena.[1] The concept to which Dr Morgenthaler draws attention is that of twofoldness. One evidence of this

---

[1] R. Morgenthaler, *Die Lukanische Geschichtsschreibung als Zeugnis* (2 vols.; Zürich, 1949). Cf. V. E. McEachern, 'Dual witness and sabbath motif in Luke', *CJT*, 12 (1966), 267–80.

characteristic is the oft-cited parallelism between Peter and Paul; they preach basically the same message, and even use the same proof texts (e.g., Psa. 16: 10; cf. Acts 2: 30; 13: 35). They both strongly rebuke guile and hypocrisy in the church and speak of the devil or satan as the source of it (5: 3; 13: 10). This parallelism also appears in their conflict with magicians (8: 18–24; 13: 6–11; 19: 13–17), raising people from the dead (9: 36–43; 20: 9–12), healing lame men (3: 2–8; 14: 8–10) and exorcisms (5: 16; 16: 18), not to mention in their defence against the Jews (4: 8–12; 5: 27–32; 22: 1ff.; 23: 1ff.; 28: 21–8) and in their persecution and miraculous release from prison (5: 19; 12: 7–11; 16: 25–7).[1]

This parallelism between the 'Acts of Peter' and the 'Acts of Paul' has long been noted, and it is quite correct to say that 'incidents... seem to be selected by Luke in order to show how Paul's apostleship was confirmed by the same signs as was Peter's'.[2] But to say this is not to exhaust Luke's intention, for the principle of twofoldness is not limited in its application to Peter and Paul. Frequently in Acts the witnesses and preachers of the Christian faith are referred to in pairs. So one reads of 'Peter and John' (3: 1, 3f., 11; 4: 13, 19; 8: 14), 'Barnabas and Saul' (11: 26f.; 12: 25; 13: 2), 'Paul and Barnabas' (13: 43, 46, 50; 15: 2, 12, 22, 35), 'Judas and Silas' (15: 32), 'Barnabas and Mark' (15: 39), 'Paul and Silas' (15: 40; 16: 19, 25; 17: 4, 10) and 'Silas and Timothy' (17: 14f.; 18: 5).

Behind all this pairing stands a principle which goes back to Jesus himself in sending out the Seventy two by two (Lk. 10: 1ff.; cf. also the similar ordering of the lists of the Twelve in Luke 6 and Acts 1). This principle may account for the reference to two figures at the tomb in Luke 24: 4 where Mk 16: 5 has only one; John also mentions two angels at the tomb (Jn 20: 12), probably because he too is interested in the principle of two-foldness (cf. Jn 5: 31f.; 8: 17f.).[3] Similarly, the multiple witness

[1] Cf. F. F. Bruce, *The Acts of the Apostles* (London, 1952), p. 33.
[2] *Ibid.* Cf. J. Fenton, 'The order of the miracles performed by Peter and Paul in Acts', *ExpT*, 77 (1965–6), 381–3.
[3] Cf. J. A. Bailey, *The Traditions Common to the Gospels of Luke and John* (Leiden, 1963), p. 85. Luke, however, uses the phrase 'behold two men' to link together such key events as the transfiguration, resurrection, ascension and the outreach of the gospel to the Gentiles (Lk. 9: 30; 24: 4; Acts 1: 10; 10: 19). On the textual problem in Acts 10: 19 cf. Bruce, *op. cit.*, pp. 219–20.

motif may explain why Acts singles out *two* of the Seven for their preaching (i.e., Stephen (6: 8 – 7: 60) and Philip (8: 4–13)), and Paul works with another man, first taking Barnabas and later Silas on his missionary trips (13: 2; 15: 40).

Now the question must be squarely faced and answered, What was Luke's reason for constructing his work on the principle of twofoldness (varied occasionally by threefoldness)? The answer, C. K. Barrett thinks, is given in Dr Morgenthaler's second volume in the observation that 'Luke intends by means of his work to bear witness'.[1] Dr Morgenthaler aptly sees behind this twofoldness the rule of evidence stated in Deut. 19: 15.[2]

In other words, the only testimony Luke means to offer is that which would satisfy a court of law, and this demands twofold or threefold testimony; this is the significance of his repeated use of the principle of twofoldness. By this device Luke seeks to provide evidence for the truth of the events which have transpired, thereby giving Theophilus 'authentic knowledge' (ἀσφάλεια, Lk. 1: 4, N.E.B.; the same word is used by Thucydides in the preface to his historical work, 1.22) and vindicating his own name as an historian. His whole book is meant as a witness to the truth. He uses the historical material for the Book of Acts according to the standards of his time as they are expressed by such ancient historians as Herodotus, Polybius, Thucydides and Josephus, and certainly intends to offer evidence that will stand the test of the closest scrutiny; after all, he has 'investigated' all the pertinent facts 'carefully' (παρακολουθηκότι πᾶσιν ἀκριβῶς, Lk. 1: 3). Thus when the apostles say: 'We are witnesses to these things, and so is the Holy Spirit' (Acts 5: 32), one can fairly assume that Luke intends his readers to take these two sources of testimony as offering compelling evidence for the historical foundation of the Christian faith. Each of these must now be examined, beginning with the testimony of the apostles.

[1] C. K. Barrett, *Luke the Historian in Recent Study* (London, 1961), pp. 25–6.
[2] Morgenthaler, *Die Lukanische Geschichtsschreibung als Zeugnis*, ii, ch. 1.

THE EYE-WITNESS CHARACTER OF THE
APOSTOLIC TESTIMONY

In the preface to Luke's Gospel special emphasis is laid upon the eye-witnesses and ministers of the word (Lk. 1: 1–4). The eye-witnesses are plainly the apostles who have been with Jesus 'from the beginning' (Lk. 1: 2; cf. Jn 15: 27). They are the ones who know the facts of his public ministry and who can therefore act as witnesses when these facts are called into question. The use of αὐτόπται emphasizes the importance of the apostles as those who can guarantee the major historic events in the life of Jesus of Nazareth (cf. Josephus, *Contra Apion* 1.53–5; *Jewish War* VI.134).[1] They have actually touched and handled the risen Lord (Lk. 24: 39; cf. I Jn 1: 1).

The same stress upon the role of the apostles as eye-witnesses of the public ministry of Jesus appears in the Acts of the Apostles. The apostles are obviously qualified to bear witness to 'all that Jesus began to do and to teach' (1: 1), for they have been eye-witnesses of his mighty deeds. They are also competent to bear witness to the aliveness of Jesus, for he 'presented himself alive to them after his passion by many proofs' (1: 3; cf. 13: 31). These apostles occupy a special place in holy history, for they have been specially commissioned as witnesses of the risen Christ (10: 42; cf. 1: 24). The resurrercted Lord was not revealed indiscriminately, but rather to 'witnesses chosen before by God'; they were hand-picked men (note the force of προκεχει-ροτονημένοις in 10: 41).

In the Book of Acts Luke's first great witness is Peter. It is not surprising, therefore, to observe his constantly repeated appeal to the fact that he was an eye-witness of what he preached concerning Christ, in particular his resurrection from the dead (1: 22; 2: 32; 3: 15; 10: 39–41). In this connection the speech in Acts 1 prior to the election of Matthias is of special importance.[2] Here emphasis is placed upon the apostle-witness in

[1] Cf. N. B. Stonehouse, *The Witness of Luke to Christ* (London, 1951), pp. 34ff.; D. E. Nineham, 'Eye-witness testimony and the gospel tradition, III', *JTS*, N.S., 11 (1960), 254, and J. H. Ropes, 'St. Luke's preface; ἀσφάλεια and παρακολουθεῖν', *JTS*, 25 (1923–4), 67–71.

[2] Cf. K. H. Rengstorf, 'The election of Matthias', *Current Issues in New Testament Interpretation*, ed. W. Klassen and G. F. Snyder (London, 1962), pp. 178–92.

words which clarify the reference to eye-witnesses in Lk. 1: 2: 'So one of the men who accompanied us during all the time that the Lord Jesus went in and out among us, beginning from the baptism of John until the day when he was taken up from us – one of these men must become with us a witness to his resurrection' (1: 21f.). In this speech two points become clear: (1) There were others besides the original band of twelve disciples who could serve as witnesses of the events of Christ's ministry since the baptism of John. As Vincent Taylor has remarked: 'The hundred and twenty did not go into permanent retreat; for at least a generation they moved among the young Palestinian communities, and through preaching and fellowship their recollections were at the disposal of those who sought information.' [1] (2) Notwithstanding this fact, the apostolic witness was of special importance and significance. Judas had been privileged to be numbered with the apostles and to be allotted a part in their ministry (διακονία, 1: 17, 25). Matthias was chosen in Judas's place to 'become' a witness to Christ's resurrection (1: 22; cf. 1: 26). Here emphasis is placed upon having seen Christ as a necessary condition for the apostolic office. This is not to deny that Luke occasionally uses the term 'apostle' in the broader sense of 'missionary' (14: 4, 14), but one must not lose sight of the special place Luke gives to 'the twelve apostles' (1: 26; cf. 2: 14) or 'the apostles in Jerusalem' (8: 14; 15: 2; 16: 4; cf. 2: 37).[2]

The eye-witness character of apostolic testimony is of importance in appreciating the nature and authority of what is said and done in the rest of the Book of Acts. Thus it is no coincidence that this special characteristic of 'being a witness' is constantly mentioned in the speeches of Acts, particularly those attributed to Peter. When he speaks of the resurrection of Christ in his speech on the Day of Pentecost, Peter immediately follows it with the words 'of that we all are witnesses' (2: 32), and in 3: 15 the same words occur in the same connection. In both chapters four and five in the speeches before the Sanhedrin

---

[1] V. Taylor, *The Formation of the Gospel Tradition* (London, 1952), p. 42. Cf. A. Barr, 'The factor of testimony in the gospels', *ExpT*, 49 (1937–8), pp. 401–8.

[2] Cf. Menoud, 'Jésus et ses témoins', p. 19, and K. H. Rengstorf, 'Apostleship', *Bible Key Words*, ed. J. R. Coates (2 vols.; London, 1952), II, 27.

there is this consciousness of being witnesses: 'we cannot but speak of what we have seen and heard' (4: 20) and 'we are witnesses to these things' (5: 32). Peter similarly mentions in his speech before Cornelius that he and his fellow apostles 'are witnesses to all that he [Jesus] did both in the country of the Jews and in Jerusalem' (10: 39).

What is one to conclude from this emphasis upon the eye-witness character of apostolic preaching? With H. N. Ridderbos two obvious points may be noted.[1] In the first place, the greatest possible stress is placed upon the *factual* content of the apostolic preaching. The testimony rests upon the great acts of God in Jesus Christ, and the resurrection constitutes the very heart of this (2: 24; 3: 26; 4: 2, 10, 33; 5: 30; 13: 30, 33, 37; 17: 3, 18, 31). In Luke's view the apostles, in effect, were really saying, 'We did not follow cleverly devised myths when we made known unto you the power and coming of our Lord Jesus Christ, but were eye-witnesses' of his life, death, resurrection and ascension (cf. II Pet. 1: 16). To put it another way, the Christian faith rests upon historical facts, and Luke in both his Gospel preface and Acts stresses the importance of the apostolic witness for this reason.

In the second place, the apostles occupy a special place in the history of salvation because of their witness.[2] All that Jesus 'began to do and to teach' (1: 1) is confirmed by their witness. Since they alone have been 'chosen' by God and Christ as eye-witnesses (cf. 10: 41; 1: 2), they alone are authorized to guarantee both the facts of the Christian faith *and* the authoritative form of its proclamation. Their witness is thus unique and normative, and apostolic succession in the personal sense of the term is both impossible and a contradiction in terms. 'The apostolic witness is much rather the canon of the New Testament Church, the delimited standard of Christian preaching and life. It is this apostolicity – the guarantee of the factual content of salvation and of the authoritative form of its procla-

[1] H. N. Ridderbos, *The Speeches of Peter in the Acts of the Apostles* (London, 1962), p. 18. Cf. Morgenthaler, *Die Lukanische Geschichtsschreibung als Zeugnis*, II, 27f.

[2] Cf. B. Gerhardsson, *Memory and Manuscript* (Lund, 1961), pp. 280ff.; K. Barth, *Evangelical Theology* (London, 1963), pp. 26–36, also his *Church Dogmatics* (Edinburgh, 1936–   ), I, 2, 486.

mation – which comes very emphatically and intentionally to the fore'[1] in the speeches which Luke assigns to Peter in Acts.

The apostles' function in interpreting the message and convincing men of its truthfulness is underlined in the preface to Luke's Gospel by the use of the word ὑπηρέτης. The apostles were the 'servants', divinely commissioned to communicate this 'revelation' (note the use of λόγος in this sense in Lk. 1: 2). To put it in legal terms, they were to plead Christ's case before men in order to convince them of his Messiahship and divine Sonship. They were to be Christ's advocates, serving in much the same way that the witnesses for the defendant served in the Old Testament legal assembly. This interpretation of ὑπηρέτης receives confirmation from the parallel passage in Acts 26: 6, where the words ὑπηρέτης and μάρτυς are linked together as describing Paul's task. Paul is as much concerned with interpreting the message as he is in bearing witness to the resurrection; even his enemies who misunderstand and dismiss him as a mere σπερμολόγος are forced to acknowledge that he has a definite message to communicate – he is a καταγγελεύς (17:18). He is a 'witness' in both senses in which the word is used in secular Greek literature and in the Old Testament: he attests the fact that he has seen the risen one, and he also pleads Christ's case, trying to convince men of its truth and power. In other words, the use of αὐτόπται and ὑπηρέται in Lk. 1: 1–4 corresponds to the two basic elements in the idea of μάρτυς, and sheds light both on the eye-witness character of apostolic testimony and on the juridical manner of its communication.

Attention has been directed to the eye-witness character of the apostolic testimony; it must now be focused on the scope of that testimony.

THE SCOPE OF THE APOSTOLIC TESTIMONY

Early in the first chapter of Acts Luke outlines what he is going to describe in the rest of his book. Here the risen Lord says to his disciples: 'You shall receive power when the Holy Spirit has

[1] Ridderbos, *op. cit.*, p. 19; cf. R. P. C. Hanson, *Tradition in the Early Church* (London, 1962), p. 236.

come upon you; and you shall be my witnesses in Jerusalem and in all Judaea and Samaria and to the end of the earth' (1: 8; cf. Isa. 49: 6). Later, when Luke comes to describe the preaching of the gospel outside Palestine, he gives a new and more detailed sketch of the further contents of the book. The figure who then appears in the foreground is the Apostle Paul, of whom it is said that he must bear the name of Christ 'before the Gentiles and kings and the sons of Israel' (9: 15). The course of the Book of Acts is in agreement with these two statements. It outlines the progress of the witness to Jesus Christ. This witness begins at 'Jerusalem' (chapters 2–7), proceeds further in 'Judaea and Samaria' (chapters 8–11) and finally goes on its way to the 'end of the earth' (chapters 13ff.). In this latter stage one sees first Paul's activity as a witness among the 'Gentiles' (chapters 13–20), then his speaking before 'kings' (chapters 24–6) and finally his witness to 'the sons of Israel' (chapters 22, 28), entirely according to the programme sketched in 1: 8 and 9: 15.[1]

Further, it is very remarkable that the position of the great speeches in Acts completely agrees with this scheme. They are held at exactly those places in the progress of the witness to Christ which are indicated in 1: 8 and 9: 15. The first three speeches are given at Jerusalem where the gospel begins its course, two by Peter (2: 14–40; 3: 12–26) and one by Stephen (7: 2–53); then one at Caesarea, by Peter (10: 34–43), is recorded as evidence of the preaching of the gospel in 'Judaea and Samaria'. Of Paul's speeches three are given among the 'Gentiles' (in Antioch of Pisidia, 13: 16–41; in Athens, 17: 22–31; in Miletus, 20: 18–35), two before 'kings' (Felix, 24: 10–21; Agrippa, 26: 2–23) and two before the 'sons of Israel' (in Jerusalem, 22: 1–21; in Rome, 28: 25–8). On the basis of this analysis of the function of the speeches in Acts one may conclude that they are typical, carefully chosen illustrations of the *geographical* outreach of the apostolic witness. They are also indicative of the *diversity* of persons to whom that witness is addressed.[2]

Both of these considerations are important in evaluating the lengthy account of Paul's trials in Jerusalem, Caesarea and

[1] Ridderbos, *op. cit.*, pp. 5–6.
[2] *Ibid.* p. 10.

Rome (chapters 21–8). While these chapters pay scant attention to the σωτηρία which is of central importance to Luke,[1] they do highlight Paul's activity as a witness. His task is to 'testify both to the Jews, and also to the Greeks, repentance toward God and faith toward our Lord Jesus Christ' (20: 21). This he has been commissioned to do, according to the first conversion story (9: 15, where he is described as a 'chosen vessel', divinely fitted for his task as a witness); in the second account Paul is told: 'You will be a witness for him to all men of what you have seen and heard' (22: 15); the third account notes the words of Jesus to him: 'I have appeared to you for this purpose, to appoint you to serve and bear witness to the things in which you have seen me and to those in which I will appear to you' (26: 16). Paul's testimony is given at Jerusalem (22: 18, σου μαρτυρίαν περὶ ἐμοῦ), before the Jews (18: 5), in the presence of the Roman governors and King Agrippa (Acts 24–6), and before all the people (26: 16f.). He is perpetrating no crime, but simply working at the accomplishment of his God-given task: 'as I stand here testifying [μαρτυρόμενος] both to small and great, saying nothing but what the prophets and Moses said would come to pass' (26: 22). He is divinely summoned to bring this testimony even before the highest court in Rome: 'Take courage', the Lord says to Paul, 'for as you have testified [διεμαρτύρω] about me at Jerusalem, so you must bear witness [μαρτυρῆσαι] also at Rome' (23: 11). The δεῖ here indicates that Paul's witnessing is part of a divinely-ordered plan; indeed, this witnessing is the decisive element, the caption of the whole story.[2]

In view of Luke's tremendous emphasis upon Paul's testimony it seems incredible that any scholar should ever have challenged the idea of Paul's being a *bona fide* witness. Yet this is precisely what Lucien Cerfaux has done. Overworking vocabulary distinctions (e.g., the difference between μάρτυς and ὑπηρέτης in Acts 26: 16), Cerfaux tries to make them the basis for theological distinctions which are not justified by a study of the

[1] Cf. I. H. Marshall, *Luke: Historian and Theologian* (Grand Rapids, 1971), pp. 77–222, who has argued strongly the thesis that 'the idea of salvation supplies the key to the theology of Luke' (p. 92).

[2] Cf. P.-H. Menoud, 'Le Plan des Actes des Apôtres', *NTS*, 1 (1954), 44–51.

internal evidence of Luke–Acts; for this he has been justly criticized by A. Rétif.[1]

Now it is true that there is a slight difference of emphasis between Paul and the Twelve; they had been earthly companions of Jesus throughout his public ministry while Paul had not (cf. 1: 21–2; 10: 39–41). Nevertheless, the important point surely is that Luke presents Paul as a witness to fact as well as a witness to convictions.[2] Paul, like the Twelve, was pre-eminently a witness to the fact of the resurrection (25: 19; cf. I Cor. 9: 1; 15: 8; Gal. 1: 15f.); this point is underscored in the threefold telling of Paul's conversion story and encounter with the risen Christ. Paul was to bear witness to all men of the things which he had actually seen and heard (22: 15). With such importance attached to the idea of witness it is fitting that the last words of Acts are words of witness and that Paul's life, which is introduced by his presence at the martyrdom of a Christian witness (7: 58ff.), is left at the point where he too is witnessing (28: 23).

Thus far the eye-witness character and the scope of apostolic testimony have been considered. Attention must now be directed to the content of that testimony.

THE CONTENT OF THE APOSTOLIC TESTIMONY

The content of the apostolic testimony is most fully revealed in the speeches of Acts, particularly those in chapters 2, 3, 5, 10 and 13. Since this is the case, it is necessary to examine the speeches to do justice to the contents of the apostolic testimony.

This is not the place to consider complicated literary questions about the nature and provenance of these speeches. Rather, the interest of this study is simply in Luke's use of the material in his exposition of the apostolic testimony. The primary question to be answered is a twofold one: What are the main ideas in these speeches, and how do they serve to shed light on the Lukan concept of witness?

---

[1] Cerfaux, 'Témoins du Christ', pp. 161–3; Rétif, 'Témoignage et prédication missionaire', pp. 152–6.

[2] C. F. D. Moule, 'Jesus in the New Testament kerygma', in the Stählin Festschrift, *Verborum Veritas*, ed. O. Böcher and K. Haacker (Wuppertal, 1970), pp. 15–26, has vigorously attacked the idea that Paul was uninterested in the historical Jesus.

To answer this question it is helpful to examine the construction of the speeches in Acts. The first thing to note is the constant repetition of the same elements in these speeches.[1] This is certainly the case with the three speeches attributed to Peter in Acts 2: 14–36, 40; 3: 12–26; 10: 34–43. After the opening statement in which the *Sitz im Leben* is discussed, there follows the testimony concerning Jesus of Nazareth. Reference is made in all three speeches to: (1) his appointment by God; (2) his signs, wonders and mighty works; (3) his death and resurrection; (4) the harmony of all these details with the scriptures; (5) Christ's exaltation in heaven; and (6) the authority of the apostles as his witnesses. All three speeches finish with an exhortation containing: (1) a summons to repentance in view of the judgment; (2) a promise of the forgiveness of sins; (3) an appeal to the Jews first, and then to the Gentiles. With some change in order this pattern is repeated without much alteration in Paul's speech in Acts 13: 16–41, and also governs the main contents of the speeches in chapters 17, 20, 22 and 26.[2]

This analysis suggests several observations. First, the content of the apostolic testimony is thoroughly Christocentric. Luke makes it perfectly clear that the apostles are witnesses who testify to the reality and historicity of Jesus. The apostles declare: that Jesus was a real man (ἄνδρα, 2: 22); that his home town was Nazareth (2: 22); that he was anointed with the Holy Spirit and with power (4: 17; 10: 38); that he went about doing good (10: 38); that he had a number of disciples who accompanied him (1: 21); that he was a prophet (3: 22f.; cf. 7: 37); that he accomplished miracles to which the people of Jerusalem could bear witness (2: 22); and that he was delivered up to Pontius Pilate and rejected by the Jews (2: 22; 3: 13).

In such a recital of the public ministry, it was natural that the death of Jesus should be given great prominence; certainly it figures very prominently in the apostolic testimony (e.g., 2: 23; 3: 15; 5: 30; 10: 39; 13: 29). Luke's vocabulary is very rich and vivid in dealing with the death of Christ: the apostles speak of

[1] Cf. C. H. Dodd, *The Apostolic Preaching* (reprinted, London, 1952), pp. 36ff. and Bo Reicke, 'A synopsis of early Christian preaching', *The Root of the Vine*, ed. A. Fridrichsen (London, 1953), pp. 139–40.

[2] Ridderbos, *The Speeches of Peter*, p. 10; cf. T. F. Glasson, 'The kerygma: is our version correct?', *HJ*, 51 (1953), 129–32.

those who laid murderous hands on Jesus and then hung him on a tree (5: 30; cf. 10: 39; 13: 29). Further, Luke notes the apostle's reference to those who with 'wicked hands have crucified and slain' Jesus (2: 23; note the use of προσπήξαντες), and in other passages reference is made to the crucifixion by a different word (σταυροῦν in 2: 36; 4: 10).

The heart of the apostolic testimony, however, is not the passion but the resurrection, for the apostles are pre-eminently witnesses of the resurrection (Lk. 24: 48; Acts 1: 22; 2: 32; 3: 15; 4: 33; 5: 31f.; 10: 40f.; 13: 30). To borrow words from Alfred Plummer, the function of the apostles was

to keep alive and extend the knowledge of events that were of the utmost importance to mankind – the knowledge that Jesus Christ had died on the Cross, and had risen from the grave. That He had died and been buried was undisputed and undisputable; and all of them could testify that they had repeatedly seen Him alive after His burial. This was the primary function of an apostle – to bear witness of Christ's resurrection (Acts 1: 22; 4: 2, 33), and the influence of the testimony was enormous.[1]

Another point to be observed is the fact that the apostles are witnesses to Christ in at least three senses. First, they are witnesses to the fact, for they can testify to the facts of the public ministry of Jesus, as is clear from the speeches in Acts 1, 2 and 10. Second, they are witnesses to character (cf. III Jn 12), for they can testify to the holiness and righteousness of the life of Jesus (3: 14) and can point to the positive works of healing and benevolence which flowed from it (10: 38). Third, they are witnesses to the Christian faith; their testimony is not simply a testimony of fact, but a testimony to lead the Jews, and later the Gentiles, to faith in Christ. All three senses in which the apostles serve as witnesses are illustrated in Peter's speech to Cornelius in Acts 10: 39–43. What a tremendous weight Luke places upon the idea of witness here, using witness words four times in five verses! Clearly he is taking the witness motif and ringing the changes. Assuming the importance of eye-witness evidence, Luke insists that the apostles: (1) function as eye-witnesses to the facts of the life, death and resurrection of Jesus, and (2)

---

[1] A. Plummer, 'Apostle', *Dictionary of the Apostolic Church*, ed. J. Hastings (2 vols., Edinburgh, 1915), I, 83.

testify that Jesus is proved by their evidence to be such as the prophets had predicted. For Luke this witnessing is closely related to preaching, as the juxtaposition of the two ideas in Acts 10: 42 and Lk. 24: 47f. suggests.

Another observation on the speeches is the similarity which they reveal between the apostles and the plaintiff in the Old Testament lawsuit. Just as the plaintiff in the Old Testament controversy tries to 'talk his opponent round', so the apostles try to convince their opponents. In Acts 11, for instance, the circumcision party dispute with Peter about the baptism of Gentiles, but are reduced to silence by his convincing explanation (διεκρίνοντο, 11 : 2; ἡσύχασαν, 11 : 18). In Athens the Stoic and Epicurean philosophers 'began to debate' with Paul (συνέβαλλον, 17 : 18), who has to stand and speak before them (17: 22). Here he is very definitely in a controversy which produces a division of opinion (17: 32, 34). Nor is this an isolated case, for testimony often has the effect of polarizing the audience; twice Acts bluntly remaks: ἐσχίσθη τὸ πλῆθος (14: 4; 23: 7). Despite the opposition which they encounter, the apostles try to talk their hearers into an admission of the Messiahship of Jesus. A striking instance of this technique appears in Damascus, where Paul 'confounds' his Jewish opponents and demonstrates the claims of Christ (συνέχυννεν, 9: 22). Thus the apostles solemnly testify that what they have seen and heard is the great saving act of God; Peter does this on the day of Pentecost (2: 40), John joins him in this activity in Samaria (8: 25), and Paul does it repeatedly (20: 21, 24; 23: 11). This fact helps to explain the frequent use not only of διαμαρτύρεσθαι (2: 40; 8: 25; 10: 42; 18: 5; 20: 21, 23, 24; 23: 11; 28: 23), but also of πείθειν (13: 43; 18: 4; 19: 8, 26; 26: 28; 28: 23; once, ἀναπείθειν, 18: 13), and διαλέγεσθαι (17: 2, 17; 18: 4, 19; 19: 8, 9; 24: 25), which outside of Acts is found only three times in the New Testament (Mk 9: 34; Heb. 12: 4; Jude 9).[1] It also suggests the reason for Luke's use of the

[1] Cf. G. D. Kilpatrick, 'διαλέγεσθαι and διαλογίζεσθαι in the New Testament', *JTS*, N.S., 11 (1960), 338–40. D. Kemmler, 'An inquiry into faith and reason with respect to Paul's method of preaching', Cambridge University Ph.D. thesis, 1972, p. 184, thinks that the 'use of human reason indicated by words like διαλέγεσθαι, διανοίγειν or παρατίθεσθαι in the apostolic preaching has as its first important function the identification of the Lord who is present in the testimony of his witness and thus to make

hapax legomenon διακατελέγχεσθαι to describe Apollos's detailed refutation of the Jews in Corinth (18: 28).

In other words, the apostles aimed at making their hearers recognize that Jesus is God's Messiah promised in the scriptures of the Old Testament (18: 5, 28). Paul does not testify by giving eye-witness testimony to the events of the public ministry of Jesus, for he is not qualified to do so. Rather, he adduces scriptural evidence: the evidence of the law and the prophets proves that Jesus (the man the apostles describe) is foretold and therefore of divine origin and authority. This is the case which Paul argues in the Jewish synagogues, in the market places of Asia Minor and in the imperial capital (17: 17; 18: 4; 28: 23). In the face of the debate which Christ's claims occasion in the Graeco-Roman world, Paul is to testify solemnly that Jesus is the Messiah promised in the Old Testament scriptures. This is the reason that testimony often takes the form of explanation (e.g., 28: 23).

The same is true for the other apostles; they too, after the fashion of the Old Testament legal assembly, take Christ's side when others have borne witness against him and put him to death. So there is a real antithesis between the denial of the Jewish people and the role of 'witness' assumed by the apostles (5: 30–2; 10: 39–42; 13: 27–31); the former are prone to 'blaspheme' (cf. 13: 45 and 18: 6, where βλασφημεῖν is used to describe the Jewish opposition to Paul's preaching of Jesus' Messiahship), the latter are anxious to 'proclaim' (εὐαγγελίζεσθαι is used some fifteen times in Acts!). Christ's representatives summon men to give heed to what they say (2: 14; 7: 2 and 13: 16). In spite of the threat of persecution they insist on delivering their witness in the name of Jesus (4: 18–20), and the repeated references to the growth of the church indicate that their witness is not without its effect (2: 41, 47; 4: 42; 5: 14; 6: 1–2, 7; 9: 31; 12: 24; 19: 20; 21: 20). The Jews have denied Christ before Pilate; now he has witnesses to affirm that he is the Messiah promised in the Old Testament. This latter element is so important that it deserves special attention.

possible an encounter with him'. He also discusses the importance of πείθειν, both in classical literature (pp. 101ff.) and in Acts (pp. 179ff.).

TESTIMONY ACCORDING TO THE SCRIPTURES

Everything which forms the content of the apostolic witness is 'according to the Scriptures'.[1] That this is the view of the Book of Acts is indicated both by the profuseness of Old Testament quotations and by the impressive use of the formula γέγραπται in introducing such quotations. As evidence of the former point it may be stated that Old Testament quotations occupy over one hundred verses in the Acts, and in support of the latter one may cite Acts 1: 20; 7: 42; 13: 33; 23: 5.

A few illustrations will serve to make the importance of the scriptures clear. Psa. 16: 8–11 is adduced to show that the resurrection of Christ is in keeping with the teaching of the Old Testament (Acts 2: 25–8). Deut. 18: 15–16 is mentioned because of its reference to the promised 'prophet', and this prophet is identified with Jesus (Acts 3: 22, 23; 7: 37). Even the defection of Judas is scripturally interpreted (Acts 1: 15–20; cf. Psa. 69: 25; 109: 8). Similarly, Psa. 2: 1f. is read as a Messianic psalm and quoted to remind the reader that the wicked characters in the passion story are unwittingly fulfilling a divine plan outlined in holy scripture (Acts 4: 25–6). As a final example consider Joel 2: 28–32, which is cited to demonstrate the congruence of the outpouring of the Spirit at Pentecost with biblical prophecy (Acts 2: 17–21).

The Book of Acts, then, is full of citations, allusions and references from the Old Testament which are everywhere interpreted in the light of the life, death and resurrection of Jesus and the advent of the Messianic Age (cf. 10: 43; 15: 15). What significance should be attached to this observation, and what does it say concerning the origin of Christological testimony?

Professor Moule of Cambridge has suggested an approach to this question: 'The Christians began from Jesus – from his known character and mighty deeds and sayings, and his death and resurrection; and with these they went to the scriptures, and

---

[1] Cf. C. H. Dodd, *According to the Scriptures* (London, 1952), who acknowledges some indebtedness to Rendall Harris for the notion of Old Testament 'testimonies', but rejects Harris's hypothesis of single, isolated proof texts. Instead Dodd argues that there are 'some parts of scripture which were early recognized as appropriate sources from which *testimonia* might be drawn' (pp. 59f.).

found that God's dealings with his People and his intentions for them there reflected did, in fact, leap into new significance in the light of these recent happenings.'[1] The apostles, according to Luke, believed that God had a great plan of salvation which he had been unfolding through the centuries to the writers of the Old Testament. That plan looked forward to the coming of Messianic days when the redemption of God's people would be accomplished (2: 23f.; cf. 1: 16, ἔδει πλρωθῆναι τὴν γραφὴν). On the one hand, therefore, the scriptures, like Aristotle's μάρτυρες παλαιοί, are competent to speak about the quality of the Messiah who was to come. On the other, the apostles bear witness that 'the things which God foretold by the mouth of all the prophets...he thus fulfilled' (3: 18); they bring the 'good news that what God promised to the fathers, this he has fulfilled' in the life, death and resurrection of Jesus Christ (13: 32f., ἐκπεπλήρωκεν τοῖς τέκνοις ἡμῖν).

According to Luke, then, the truth of apostolic testimony is confirmed by the testimony of the scriptures; the apostles testify that Jesus is in fact proved by their evidence to fit the description of the Messiah predicted by the prophets. Here again there seems to be a suggestion of the two-witness principle enunciated in Deut. 19: 15; eye-witness testimony is supported by scriptural testimony that at the mouth of two or three witnesses every word should be established. Such evidence would be especially impressive to the Jews or Jewish proselytes who were 'ignorant' (3: 17) of the fulfilment of the biblical prophecies in Christ.

There was corroborative evidence to be found in another direction. Not only are the apostles, like the Old Testament scriptures, witnesses to those things, but 'so also is the Holy Spirit, whom God has given to them that obey him' (5: 32). Several times in Acts the testimony of the Spirit is mentioned in warnings about impending suffering and persecution (e.g., 21: 4). Paul makes mention of the Spirit's solemn testimony 'in

[1] C. F. D. Moule, *The Birth of the New Testament* (London, 1962), p. 57; cf. J. Woods, *The Old Testament in the Church* (London, 1949), pp. 6–19, and B. Lindars, *New Testament Apologetic* ((London, 1961), *passim*. On the use of Old Testament *testimonia* in Acts and the relation of quotations to midrash see E. Earle Ellis, 'Midrashic features in the speeches in Acts', *Mélanges Bibliques*, Rigaux Festschrift, ed. A. Descamps and R. P. André de Halleux (Gembloux, 1970), pp. 303–12.

every city' (20: 23), and Agabus introduces his prophecy at Caesarea with the authoritative rubric, 'This is what the Holy Spirit says' (21: 11). The Spirit's guidance was clearly important to Luke (8: 29; 10: 19; 11: 12; 13: 2; 16: 6, 7), and reminds us of the teaching of the Fourth Gospel, where the inner witness of the Spirit is stressed (Jn 14: 26; 15: 26; 16: 13–15).

THE TESTIMONY OF THE HOLY SPIRIT
IN SIGNS AND WONDERS

According to Luke, the witness of the Spirit frequently takes the form of signs and wonders which are evidence of the Spirit's activity and therefore of the Messianic Age (cf. Jos. *Ant.* xx.168, where signs and wonders are mentioned in connection with Messianic claims). These miracles are termed δυνάμεις because they are manifestations of the power of God among men, and are viewed as evidence that the long-promised Messianic Age has arrived. Thus in the Joel quotation of Acts 2 the appearance of signs and wonders is associated with the outpouring of the Spirit and is a work of the Messianic Age (2: 17–21).

Such signs are obviously present in the earthly ministry of Jesus, who is 'attested by God', as Peter reminds the Jerusalem throng on the Day of Pentecost, 'through mighty works and wonders, and signs which God did through him in your midst' (2: 22). They are also present in the ministry of the apostles and their co-workers (e.g., 4: 22; 8: 6). The δυνάμεις of Jesus are paralleled by those attributed to Stephen, Philip and Paul (6: 8; 8: 13; 19: 11). It is to these mighty works that appeal is made to vindicate the testimony; indeed, in one passage the signs and wonders are the content of the testimony (15: 12). Just as God bore witness to Christ by external signs and miracles (10: 38), so he bears witness to Christ's apostles in similar fashion (5: 32; cf. Mk 16: 20). This point is repeatedly underscored by Luke, as if to remind his readers of the Johannine promise: 'He who believes in me will also do the works that I do' (cf. Jn 14: 12). This is surely the implication of 2: 43, with its explicit statement that 'many wonders and signs were done through the apostles' (cf. also 4: 29ff.).

The stress upon this aspect appears from the fact that the

phrase τέρατα καὶ σημεῖα occurs nine times in Acts, compared with only three times in Paul's writings (Rom. 15: 19; II Cor. 12: 12; II Thess. 2: 9) and four times in the rest of the New Testament (Mk 13: 22; Mt. 24: 24; Jn 4: 48; Heb. 2: 4). While elsewhere the New Testament recognizes that ψευδόχριστοι and ψευδοπροφῆται will arise who will produce 'signs' (Mk 13: 22; Mt. 24: 24; cf. II Thess. 2: 9; Rev. 13: 13f.; 16: 14; 19: 20), the stress in Acts is definitely on the positive side – namely, on the outward and tangible evidence which supports the apostolic testimony. After one such *Heilungswunder* Luke notes the frustration of their stoutest enemies (Acts 4: 16); here the opponents of the Christian movement are confronted by ungainsayable evidence.

In this connection Hebrews 2 is especially interesting, because it summarizes, as van Unnik has observed, the Lukan attitude toward the Holy Spirit's witness.[1] The σωτηρία 'which at the first began to be spoken by the Lord…was confirmed to us by them that heard him' (i.e., by the authorized apostolic witnesses). They in turn received endorsement, 'God also bearing them witness, both with signs and wonders and various kinds of miracles and gifts of the Holy Spirit according to his will' (Heb. 2: 3–4; cf. Acts 15: 8; 10: 44–6).

This powerful confirmatory evidence is particularly clear in Acts 14: 3, where it is said that Paul and Barnabas remained for a long time in Iconium, 'speaking boldly in reliance on the Lord, who bore witness to the word of his grace, granting signs and wonders to be done by their hands'.[2] Similarly when Paul, full of the Spirit, rebukes Elymas and afflicts him with blindness, this remarkable exercise of divine power impresses Sergius Paulus and leads him to Christian faith (13: 12).

It is the Holy Spirit who gives these signs, both to Christ and to those who witness in his name. There is a direct parallel here between God's attesting Jesus (2: 22) and God's attesting the disciples (5: 32); both have their teaching and testimony divinely authenticated by mighty works produced by the Holy Spirit. Professor Lampe has correctly drawn attention to this feature:

[1] W. C. van Unnik, 'The "Book of Acts" – the confirmation of the gospel', *NovT*, 4 (1960), 26–59.
[2] Cf. Moule, *Idiom-Book of NT Greek*, p. 50.

To the spoken word there corresponds the visible manifestation of the gospel in 'mighty works, signs and wonders,' somewhat in the way in which the prophetic signs in ancient Israel were related to the uttered word of the Lord. God works mightily through the name of Jesus the Messiah. This divine activity, in its powerful impact through word and sign, is the Spirit, the witness to Christ who speaks and acts through the missionaries, proclaiming and attesting the gospel (cf. Lk. 12: 12).[1]

The effectiveness of these signs in bringing people to faith in Christ is indicated by Luke at several points (5: 12–14; 9: 35, 42; cf. Jn 11: 45; 12: 11). For him as for the writer of the Fourth Gospel signs were not without apologetic significance. They played a definite part in promoting the witness to Jesus as the Christ.

THE HOLY SPIRIT AND BOLDNESS IN TESTIMONY

The Spirit's witness is also to be observed in the boldness which characterizes apostolic testimony. Jesus had instructed the apostles to stay in Jerusalem until they were 'clothed with power from on high' (Lk. 24: 49), and had promised that they would be filled with the Holy Spirit in a few days (Acts 1: 5). Similarly, just before his ascension the risen Christ had promised, 'You shall receive power when the Holy Spirit has come upon you, and you shall be my witnesses' (Acts 1: 8). In other words, Luke sees the power of the Holy Spirit working through these men, teaching them what to say and giving them the boldness to say it (4: 8; 7: 55f.; cf. Lk. 12: 11f.; 21: 14f.). This power is realized on the Day of Pentecost when there is a remarkable outpouring of the Spirit, enabling the apostles to testify with spiritual authority and boldness (2: 4, 14).

This boldness is an outstanding characteristic of their testimony – a fact attested by a careful study of the words παρρησία and παρρησιάζεσθαι in Acts.[2] It is evident in: (1) Peter on the Day of Pentecost when he speaks to the very men who crucified

---

[1] G. W. H. Lampe, 'Miracles in the Acts of the Apostles', *Miracles – Cambridge Studies*, pp. 170–1.

[2] See Schlier, 'παρρησία', *TDNT*, v, 871–86. Cf. R. M. Pope, 'Studies in Pauline vocabulary; of boldness of speech', *ExpT*, 21 (1909–10), 236–8.

his Master (2: 29; cf. 2: 23); (2) John and Peter when they appear before the Sanhedrin (4: 9f., 13); (3) Barnabas and Paul when they do missionary work in Antioch and Iconium (13: 46; 14: 3); (4) Stephen (7: 2–53); (5) Philip (8: 30–5) and (6) Apollos (18: 26) when they preach Christ; (7) the apostles generally (4: 33; cf. 4: 29f.). Above all, this boldness shines out of (8) the Apostle Paul (e.g., 9: 27f.; 19: 8; 28: 31). What is true of Paul's boldness in speaking to Jews at Jerusalem (22: 3–21; 23: 1–6) and at Rome (28: 16–20, 23–31) is also true of his speeches before Felix, Festus, Agrippa and before the Gentiles generally (13: 10f.; 14: 14ff.; 17: 30f.; 19: 26).

It is the Holy Spirit who gives this fearless quality to the apostolic testimony, for it is the Spirit who directs the whole of the church's mission (cf. 8: 29; 10: 19; 11: 12; 13: 2, 4; 16: 6–7). This Spirit-given boldness has its negative as well as its positive side, for it points out sin and rebukes it. So Peter, filled with the Holy Spirit, can bluntly attribute the death of Jesus to the rulers and elders of the Jewish people (4: 8, 10, 11; cf. 5: 28–30), or to the Jewish people as a whole (2: 23, 36). So too he can plainly declare God's judgment upon Ananias for his failure in 'lying to the Holy Spirit' (5: 3; cf. 5: 9; 8: 18–19). In other words, when the apostles give their testimony, the Spirit testifies with them: his power acts on their hearers, either to confound them if they do not accept, or to convince them; several times the Book of Acts draws attention to this 'piercing' ministry of the Spirit (2: 37; 5: 33; 7: 54; cf. 6: 10). Spirit-given boldness is one of the signs and wonders which give evidence of the presence of the Messianic Age.

If one asks why Luke stresses the evidence which the Spirit gives, the answer comes again, 'Because of Deut. 19: 15'; in fact, Luke has told his readers as much in Acts 5: 32. To estab-lish the truth of the Christian faith it was not enough to have the witness of the apostles; there must also be corroborative witness. That is supplied by the witness of the Holy Spirit in signs and wonders which provide external validation of the oral testi-mony; it is also supplied by the boldness of the apostles, which is itself a sign and likewise the work of the Spirit. Just as God had supported Moses with 'wonders and signs in Egypt and at the Red Sea, and in the wilderness' (7: 36; cf. Exod. 7: 3), so now he was supporting his chosen witnesses with similar 'signs and wonders' as evidence of the Messianic Age. Together with the witness of the Old Testament scriptures, these signs and wonders constitute, in Luke's view, powerful confirmatory evidence in support of the apostolic testimony, and consequently, of the truth of the Christian faith.

SUMMARY

For Luke the idea of witness is a living metaphor. Christians take Christ's side in real courts of law when his claims are in dispute and when their loyalty is tested by persecution. The witness is Messianic, juridical and religious. The fundamental witness to Christ includes two prominent witnesses in accordance with Deut. 19: 15, namely, the witness of the apostles and the witness of the Holy Spirit (Acts 5: 32). The witness of the apostles guarantees both the historic facts of the life, death, resurrection and ascension of Christ, and the authoritative form of their transmission and communication. The witness of the Spirit makes possible the boldness of the apostles and other Christians, and enables them to perform signs and wonders which provide external confirmation of their testimony. The witness of both the apostles and the Spirit is strengthened by a third witness, that of the Old Testament scriptures (10: 43), which serves to confirm and corroborate the evidence presented by the other two sources. When taken together, Luke maintains, the witness of the apostles, the Spirit and the Old Testament constitute a compelling case for the claims of Christ as Lord and Messiah.

6-2

CHAPTER 10

THE CONCEPT OF WITNESS IN THE BOOK OF REVELATION

The idea of witness appears to be very much a live metaphor in the Book of Revelation. Since this point is most fully treated in the Black commentary, it will be necessary from time to time to refer to its treatment of that subject.[1]

THE RELATION TO THE OTHER JOHANNINE WRITINGS

At first sight, the importance of the idea of witness in the Apocalypse is not surprising in view of the striking similarities between this book and the other Johannine writings.[2] Dr Caird has made this point very clear:

The repeated use of the words 'witness' and 'testimony' is one of the many points of resemblance between the Revelation and the Fourth Gospel. In Greek as in English these words could be treated as dead metaphors, without any conscious reference to the lawcourt, which was their primary setting. But both these books use the words in their primary, forensic sense. The author of the Fourth Gospel, perhaps inspired by the example of Second Isaiah, presents his argument in the form of a lawcourt debate, in which one witness after another is summoned, until God's advocate, the Paraclete, has all the evidence he needs to convince the world that Jesus is the Son of God, and so win his case. In the Revelation the courtroom setting is even more realistic; for Jesus had borne his testimony before Pilate's tribunal, and the martyrs must face a Roman judge. What they have to remember as they give their evidence is that the evidence is being heard in a court of more ultimate authority, where judgments which are just and true issue from the great white throne.[3]

Both books, then, treat the idea of witness as a live metaphor.

[1] G. B. Caird, *A Commentary on the Revelation of St. John the Divine* (London, 1966). For a liturgical approach see P. Prigent, *Apocalypse et Liturgie* (Neuchâtel, 1964) and M. H. Shepherd, *The Paschal Liturgy and the Apocalypse* (London, 1960).
[2] Cf. A. Plummer, *The Epistles of St. John* (Cambridge, 1916), p. 17.
[3] Caird, *Revelation*, pp. 17–18. On the semantic question see A. A. Trites, 'Μάρτυς and martyrdom in the Apocalypse – a semantic study', *NovT*, 15 (1973), 72–80.

154

Further investigation, however, indicates that there are some definite points of difference between the Revelation and the Fourth Gospel. Reinier Schippers has drawn attention to a number of philological differences between the two books in his monograph on the idea of witness.[1] (1) In the Apocalypse the phrase μαρτυρεῖν περί is lacking, in contrast to its frequent use in the other Johannine writings (eighteen times in the Gospel, twice in I John). (2) Μαρτυρεῖν governs an accusative in the Revelation (1: 2; 22: 16, 20), but this is not the case in either the Gospel or the Epistles (though cf. Jn 3: 11, 32 and 19: 35, where the Greek can be translated by a relative clause like 'what we have seen' and also I Jn 5: 10, where a cognate accusative occurs). (3) Μαρτυρία in Revelation not only has the matching genitives (11: 7; 12: 11) but it also has the special phrase ἡ μαρτυρία Ἰησοῦ which is not present in either the Gospel or the Epistles. (4) The Apocalypse repeatedly uses the substantive μάρτυς, which is absent from the Gospel and the Epistles (Rev. 1: 5; 2: 13; 3: 14; 11: 3; 17: 6). (5) The phrase ἔχειν τὴν μαρτυρίαν of Rev. 6: 9; 12: 17 and 19: 10 cannot be identified with the same phrase in John 5: 36.

This state of affairs suggests that there is common ground in the language of witness between the Apocalypse on the one hand and the Fourth Gospel and the Johannine Epistles on the other. Nevertheless, there is a difference of emphasis which may be due either to different authorship or to different literary form (apocalyptic as opposed to gospel or epistle).[2]

THE TESTIMONY OF JESUS

The *Sitz im Leben* helps to explain the prominence of the idea of witness in the Revelation. Christians are about to face a time of severe testing and persecution, and John as a faithful pastor seeks to prepare them for it. He directs his campaign at both the enemy within and the enemy without. The churches have many sins and defects, so they are summoned to repentance (2: 5, 16, 21, 22; 3: 3, 19). They have external foes, so they must be given

[1] R. Schippers, *Getuigen van Jezus Christus* (Franeker, 1938), p. 188.
[2] On the question of authorship see D. Guthrie, *New Testament Introduction – Hebrews to Revelation* (London, 1962), pp. 254–69.

reassurance (2: 10); this helps to account for the sevenfold use of μακάριος. They need to be reminded that God is still on the throne, and he is not only ἰσχυρός (18: 8), but παντοκράτωρ (one of John's favourite words). The conflict does not separate them from their Lord, for he is leading them and it is essentially his battle. The demonic forces will indeed 'make war on the Lamb', but he will conquer them; as 'Lord of lords and King of kings' his victory is assured, and they are in vital contact with him – 'called and chosen and faithful' (17: 14). John knows that the Roman proconsul of Asia possesses great judicial power, symbolized by the 'sword' (cf. Rom. 13: 4), but he writes to remind his fellow Christians that it is Christ, not Caesar's representative, who has the 'sharp two-edged sword' (Rev. 2: 12). Soon some of them will be hauled into lawcourts and sentenced to martyrs' deaths (6: 9; 13: 10; cf. Mt. 10: 18; Lk. 21: 12). Already Antipas, Christ's faithful witness, has been slain (Rev. 2: 13), and the seer sees him as the first of many Christians who are about to make the supreme sacrifice for holding 'the testimony of Jesus'. What is this 'testimony of Jesus' which John is so concerned that his fellow Christians should 'hold'?

The Grammatical Problem

To answer this question it is necessary to look at the places where 'the testimony of Jesus' is mentioned. The phrase is absent from the Gospel and the Epistles of John, but appears rather prominently in the Apocalypse. In 1: 2 it may mean 'either the witness which Christ Himself imparts, or the witness of life which John gave to Him. Probably the former is the better interpretation because it makes the grammatical construction similar to that of the phrase preceding.'[1] Similarly in 1: 9 and 12: 17 it makes excellent sense to take the genitives to be subjective genitives. 'The word of God and the testimony of Jesus' would then mean 'the word spoken by God and the testimony borne by Jesus' (1: 9) and 'the commandments of

[1] M. C. Tenney, *Interpreting Revelation* (Grand Rapids, 1957), p. 44; cf. E. Burnier, *La Notion de Témoignage dans le Nouveau Testament* (Lausanne, 1939), p. 55. The subjective genitive interpretation is supported by Strathmann, *TDNT*, IV, 500.

God and the testimony of Jesus' would imply 'the command-ments given by God and the testimony borne by Jesus' (12: 17). The subjective genitive interpretation receives further confir-mation in the explanatory words appended by the seer in 19: 10: 'For the testimony borne by Jesus is the spirit which in-spires the prophets.' In other words, 'it is the word spoken by God and attested by Jesus that the Spirit takes and puts into the mouth of the Christian prophet'.[1]

The same testimony is in view when the fifth seal is opened and John sees the souls of them who have been slain 'for the Word of God and for the testimony which they held' (6: 9). The phrase differs only by the omission of the closing words from that which has been used twice before (1: 2, 9). In spite of the absence of the defining words at the end, the sense here must be the same as in the other passages; the 'word' is the word given by God, the 'testimony' is the testimony borne by Jesus. The objective genitive is impossible here, for the expres-sion 'which they held' (A.V., R.V.) implies a testimony which has already been given to them by Christ and which they have faithfully maintained and preserved. The reference is plainly to the testimony of Christ to God which they 'had' (εἶχον), that is, had received, and for which they were prepared to die.

The subjective genitive interpretation receives additional support from two other passages. It is said of the two witnesses that they are killed 'when they have finished their testimony' (11: 7); and of the conquerors, that 'they overcame him [Satan, their accuser] by the blood of the Lamb, and by the word of their testimony' (12: 11). In both passages one is intended to read 'their testimony' as 'the testimony which they gave'. In the first passage reference is made to the testimony of the wit-nesses; in the second, to that given by the brethren. Similarly, one must understand the testimony of Jesus as that given by him, and not, as many commentators have suggested, as the testimony concerning him. It is this testimony which has been given to the faithful; it is their task to maintain and 'hold' it even in the face of hostility, persecution and death (note the use of τηρεῖν in Revelation with either ἐντολήν (12: 17; 14: 12) or

---

[1] Caird, *Revelation*, p. 238. Cf. R. Luther, *Neutestamentliches Wörterbuch* (Hamburg, 1962), p. 250.

λόγον (3: 8, 10; 22: 7, 9)).[1] Later in the Apocalypse 'the word to which Jesus bore testimony in his life and death is...recognized to be indistinguishable from the person of the witness: he is the Word of God' (19: 13).[2]

The Historical Content

So far attention has been focused on the grammatical problem raised by the phrase 'the testimony of Jesus'. Now a further question must be raised, namely, What is the content of the testimony which Jesus gives? Dr Tenney has attempted to answer this question: 'It is the message which includes all of the work of Christ: His preincarnate purpose, His earthly ministry of teaching, death and resurrection, His present work of intercession, and His future reign and judgments.'[3] The difficulty with this rather comprehensive statement is its tendency to lose sight of the forensic nature of the testimony. But whether this description is accepted or not, the question must still be asked, In what way does Christ attest the purpose of God?

A clue is given in the three titles ascribed to Christ in 1: 5. These begin with the idea of 'faithful witness' (cf. Psa. 89: 37; Prov. 14: 5, 25; Isa. 8: 2), and lead on to two Messianic titles from Psa. 89: 27. Christ is described as the faithful witness in his life and death, 'firstborn in his resurrection and sovereign in his session at God's right hand'.[4] The word 'witness' in this passage is set against the background of the death of Christ, as is clear from the reference to 'the firstborn from the dead' (1: 5). It is because Christ has triumphantly made 'the good confession' (cf. I Tim. 6: 13) that believers in the Seven Churches of Asia are to take heart. T. F. Torrance puts it well:

It is in His death that the Word and Acts of Christ, the teaching and the Person of Christ become absolutely identical. It is there that He is supremely 'The faithful and true witness' (Rev. 1: 5; 3: 14). It is there that the Captain of our salvation is made perfect through

[1] On the idea of martyrdom in Revelation cf. E. Günther, 'Zeuge und Märtyrer', *ZNW*, 47 (1956), 145–61.
[2] Caird, *Revelation*, p. 244. Cf. H. B. Swete, *The Apocalypse of St. John* (London, 1906), p. 246.
[3] Tenney, *Interpreting Revelation*, p. 44.
[4] A. Farrer, *The Revelation of St. John the Divine* (Oxford, 1964), p. 62.

suffering...It is God's own witness in the flesh and blood of Jesus Christ, a witness consummated in His death.[1]

The centrality of the historic testimony which Jesus gave in his passion is underscored by John again and again. Jesus is described as 'the faithful and true witness' (3: 14), who in virtue of his testimony can be said to have 'conquered'; he has won the victory on the cross (3: 21; 5: 5; cf. Jn 12: 31; 14: 30; 16: 33). By his faithful attestation of the redemptive purpose of God he has earned the epithet 'Faithful and True' (19: 11). In fact, 'the true one' serves as a model witness, leaving his disciples an example that they should follow (1: 5; 3: 7, 14; cf. Jn 18: 20, 37; I Pet. 2: 21).

It is 'possible that the author of Revelation sees Jesus as the one who has fulfilled the calling of God's "chosen servant" Israel in his true and faithful testimony to God before the world in his earthly mission'.[2] If this should be the case, then one could establish a parallel between the Apocalypse and Isaiah 40–55, where the servant theme is so prominent. But whether this is true or not, it is clear that the seer mentions Christ's testimony because it is of vital significance to his readers facing possible martyrdom for 'holding the testimony borne by Jesus'.

THE TESTIMONY OF CHRISTIANS

As Jesus bore witness, so the church is also to act in the same capacity (2: 13; 6: 9; 11: 7; 12: 11, 17; 17: 6; 20: 4). As in many of the writings of the Old and New Testaments, the word 'testimony' retains its juridical sense, and means the open confession of the truth (1: 9; 6: 9; 12: 17; 19: 10; 20: 4). On account of this confession, however, persecutions immediately come to those who obey the commandments of God and adhere to the testimony of Jesus (12: 17; note the reference to θλῖψις in 1: 9; 2: 9, 10). They are driven by their accusers before Roman lawcourts and there must serve as faithful witnesses to the pur-

[1] T. F. Torrance, 'A study in New Testament communication', *SJT*, 3 (1950), 308.
[2] R. V. Moss, Jr, 'The witnessing church in the New Testament', *TaL*, 3 (1960), 263.

pose revealed in Christ, 'the Word of God' (2: 9f.; 3: 8f.; 19: 13; cf. 10: 11). For the sake of the revelation given by God and the testimony borne by Jesus the seer himself had suffered separation from his Christian friends, having been banished to the island of Patmos (1: 9). He was their 'brother' and a συγκοινωνός with them 'in the tribulation and kingdom and patience which are in Jesus' (1: 9, R.V.).

John foresaw that the maintenance of the testimony borne by Jesus under these circumstances would result in many Christians experiencing death (6: 9; 20: 4). Just as it was the destiny of the Old Testament prophets to experience persecution, suffering and death for the sake of their message, so it is also the lot of the prophetic witnesses of Jesus (11: 7ff.; 16: 6; 18: 24; cf. Lk. 11: 47–51). This is especially clear in the case of Antipas (2: 13); he is called a 'witness' since he proclaimed the word spoken by God and attested by Christ in the place 'where Satan's throne was', and he is referred to as 'true' since he held to this testimony even unto death.

With this background the promises to the conquerors can now be understood. The 'conquerors' for John are the faithful witnesses who are martyred for holding the testimony borne by Jesus. Significantly, John hears the exalted Christ addressing the Seven Churches and making wonderful promises to the conquerors in each of them. The martyrs are promised the privilege of 'eating of the tree of life' (2: 7), of not being 'hurt by the second death' (2: 11), of eating of 'the hidden manna' (2: 17). They are to be given a 'white stone' (2: 17), possibly suggesting their acquittal as the ψῆφος was used for voting by the judges in the courts of Athens. If they remain faithful to the end, they are to reign with Christ and to receive 'the morning star' (2: 29), which is Christ himself (22: 16). The conquerors 'shall be clad...in white garments...for they are worthy'; since they have confessed Christ before men in earthly law-courts, Christ will confess them before his Father and the angels in heaven (3: 4f.; cf. Mt. 10: 32; Lk. 12: 8). They will become 'pillars' in the temple of God, and God's name will be inscribed upon them (3: 12). All of these great promises are held out by way of encouragement to those who must conquer in the same way that Christ conquered (3: 21).

Nothing in Revelation is more apparent, then, than the seer's conviction that a ruthless, widespread persecution was about to break out against the church.

Not less clear is the form that this persecution would take. The enemy of the Church (symbolized by a Beast), would be 'allowed to wage war on the saints and to conquer them' (13: 7); this attack, moreover, would be made through the priests of the Imperial cult, who would demand universal worship of the Beast on pain of death, the detection of recusants being ensured by economic pressure [13: 17].[1]

Informers doubtlessly would include Jews, anxious to dissociate themselves from what they regarded as the blasphemous claims of Christians for Christ (2: 9; 3: 9). Faced with Jewish and Roman persecution for loyalty to the Name (2: 3, 13; 3: 8), John's fellow believers would be in circumstances practically identical with those envisaged in the Synoptic Gospels (Mk 13: 9–13 par.; cf. Jn 15: 18 – 16: 4). Their job was to 'hold fast' (2: 25; 3: 11), despite the attacks of the Beast whose mouth was uttering blasphemies against God and his people (13: 5–6).

Under these conditions one would expect that words with forensic overtones would be given their full weight in any message of encouragement. The use of nouns such as μάρτυς (1: 5; 2: 13; 3: 14; 11: 3; 17: 6), μαρτυρία (1: 2, 9; 6: 9; 11: 7; 12: 11, 17; 19: 10; 20: 4), σατανᾶς (2: 9; 3: 9; 12: 9), διάβολος (2: 10; 12: 9, 12), κατήγωρ (12: 10), κρίσις (14: 7; 16: 7; 18: 10; 19: 2), κρίμα (17: 1; 18: 20; 20: 4), θρόνος (2: 13; 20: 4, 11f.), υἱὸς (τοῦ) ἀνθρώπου (1: 13; 14: 14; cf. Jn 5: 27), νεφέλη (1: 7; 11: 12; 14: 14–16; cf. Mk 14: 62 par.), βιβλία (used twice in 20: 12 to refer to the 'record books'; cf. Dan. 7: 10); of verbs such as 'bear witness' (μαρτυρεῖν, 1: 2; 22: 16, 18, 20), 'confess' (ὁμολογεῖν, 3: 5), 'deny' (ἀρνεῖσθαι, 2: 13; 3: 8), 'accuse' (κατηγορεῖν, 12: 10), 'judge' (κρίνειν, 6: 10; 11: 18; 16: 5; 18: 18, 20; 19:2, 11; 20: 12f.), 'avenge' or 'vindicate' (ἐκδικεῖν, 6: 10; 19: 2; cf. Lk. 18: 3, 5), 'have against' (ἔχειν with κατά in 2: 4, 14, 20), 'find' (εὑρίσκειν, 3: 2); and of adjectives such as πιστός (1: 5; 2: 10, 13; 3: 14; 17: 14; 19: 11; 21: 5; 22: 6) and ἀληθινός (3: 7, 14; 6: 10; 15: 3; 16: 7; 19: 2,

[1] M. Kiddle and M. K. Ross, *The Revelation of St. John*, MNTC (London and New York, 1940), pp. xxxvi–xxxvii. The rival claims of Christian worship and worship of the Beast are vividly portrayed in the frequent use of προσκυνεῖν in the Apocalypse (24 times).

9, 11; 21: 5; 22: 6) show that this is in fact the case. Metaphors drawn from the lawcourt are never far from the author's mind.

The challenging words to the conquerors come in the Letters to the Seven Churches (Rev. 2–3). The next reference to the martyr-witnesses occurs in 6: 9–11 with the opening of the fifth seal and the description of the prayers of the martyrs in heaven. The seer sees an altar in heaven (cf. 8: 3ff.; 9: 13; 14: 18; 16: 7), at the bottom of which lie the souls of those who have been slain 'for the word of God and the testimony which they held' (6: 9); that is, he sees the martyrs from among the Messianic community (cf. 12: 17). The primary reference here surely is to Christian martyrs like Antipas, but since John does not use the specific phrase 'the testimony of Jesus', it is possible that he refers to 'all the righteous blood shed on earth' (Rev. 18: 24; cf. Mt. 23: 35), whether in the Christian or pre-Christian era. However, this possibility is eliminated when the reasons for which the faithful suffered are examined; the martyrs have been put to death because of the word given by God and the testimony borne by Jesus, so that the clause in 6: 9 corresponds exactly to the fuller clause in 12: 17 and 20: 4. 'The martyrs', as Charles has said, 'are incontestably Christian martyrs, to wit, the martyrs of the Neronic times.'[1] They simply 'hold' the testimony of Jesus, and for it they die. Once again the emphasis is placed upon the historic testimony offered by Christ; the testimony of the martyrs in life and death is valued only in so far as it is a repetition or continuation of the testimony of Christ.

The cry which the souls of the slain witnesses raise in 6: 10 is not to be dismissed merely as a vindictive appeal for vengeance. It is rather to be understood in terms of the legal background of the Old Testament lawsuit or controversy. As in the Psalms, the cry 'How long, O Lord?' is the cry of the persecuted for help in obtaining justice (Psa. 74: 10; 79: 5; cf. Zech. 1: 12). It is the cry of those who place their hope of salvation in the righteousness of God (Rev. 15: 3; 16: 5, 7; 19: 2), and ask therefore that he will soon vindicate his righteousness on earth (Psa. 7: 8; 26: 1; 35: 24; 43: 1; cf. I Kgs 8: 31–3). As G. B. Caird puts it:

The martyrs have been condemned in a human court of law, and that decision stands against them unless it is reversed in a higher

[1] R. H. Charles, *The Revelation of St. John*, ICC (2 vols., Edinburgh, 1920), I, 174.

court. But the heavenly judge cannot declare them to be in the right without at the same time declaring their persecutors to be in the wrong and passing sentence against them. Justice must not only be done; it must be seen to be done...John...cannot avoid legal language when he is dealing with men who have been condemned before a pagan tribunal and writing for the benefit of others who must face a like jeopardy. The point at issue here is not the personal relations of the martyrs with their accusers, but the validity of their faith. They have gone to their death in the confidence that God's word, attested in the life and death of Jesus, is the ultimate truth; but unless in the end tyranny and other forms of wickedness meet with retribution, that faith is an illusion.[1]

The question of the martyrs is answered; they must rest a little longer until the appointed number of those who must suffer as martyrs has been fulfilled. What sufferings as are yet to overtake the church are fixed by God, who as 'Sovereign Lord' (δεσπότης) allows nothing to happen without his consent; the repeated use of ἐδόθη reminds us of the same point (6: 4, 8; 7: 2; 9: 5; 13: 5, 15; 16: 8). How much longer? Only a short time, for God has judged the great city, the harlot Babylon (14: 8; 18: 10, 20) in whom was found the blood of the prophets and saints who had been slain on earth (18: 24). God has judged her for taking the blood of his servants (19: 2), and the punishment of the Lamb's enemies is to take place 'in his presence' (note the forensic sense of ἐνώπιον in 14: 10).[2] The divinely promised Prüfungstunde will indeed come upon the whole world, but it will constitute no threat to the faithful (3: 10). Christ's witnesses are to share with him the exercise of regal and judicial power (20: 4). However, it is necessary to have patience (ὑπομονή is mentioned in 1: 9; 2: 2, 3, 19; 3: 10; 14: 12). The suffering which the church has experienced is not yet finished; it must undergo new persecutions – but only for a short time. To the seer's σύνδουλοι is given the special task of

---

[1] Caird, Revelation, p. 85, and similarly R. Leivestad, Christ the Conqueror (London, 1954), p. 217. Cf. however, C. F. D. Moule, 'Punishment and retribution – an attempt to delimit their scope in New Testament thought', SEA, 30 (1965), 21–36, who thinks that retribution, though present in the Apocalypse and in a number of other places in the NT, is essentially foreign to the NT message.

[2] N. Hillyer, '"The lamb" in the Apocalypse', EQ, 39 (1967), 234; cf. J. A. Bollier, 'Judgment in the Apocalypse', Int, 7 (1953), 14–25.

proclaiming the Christian message (6: 11; 19: 10; 22: 9); the same task belongs to the προφηταί, who in Revelation are always the New Testament prophets (10: 7; 11: 10, 18; 16: 6; 18: 20, 24; 22: 6, 9). In fact all these words, together with δοῦλοι (7: 3; 10: 7; 11: 18; 19: 2, 5; 22: 6), are virtually used as synonyms for the faithful Christian witnesses who are prepared to die for their faith.

THE TWO WITNESSES IN CHAPTER ELEVEN

Special attention must now be paid to the 'two witnesses' mentioned in Rev. 11. This chapter is one of the most difficult in the whole book, and certainly one of the most important for the concept of witness. The difficulty has been to relate verses 3–13 to the material that precedes and follows it. While many commentators concede that John gave symbolic significance to the temple, they are reluctant to admit that he also interpreted the two witnesses in a similar fashion. Yet here as elsewhere in the Revelation John has given his readers sufficient clues to guide them into a clear understanding of what he has to say. The seer intends his readers to deduce the identity of the two witnesses from his brief explanation of them.

To begin with, the two witnesses are obviously intended to be understood symbolically. It is inconsistent to concede an eschatological, figurative and symbolic reference to the temple and to deny a similar treatment of the two witnesses. To regard them as individuals is to ignore John's brilliant 'rebirth of images' and to throw his message into needless confusion.[1]

It is evident that John's explanation of the two witnesses owes something to Zechariah. In Zechariah's fifth vision he sees a golden lampstand and two olive trees (Zech. 4: 1–13). The lampstand has seven lamps on it, and 'these seven are the eyes of the Lord, which range through the whole earth' (4: 10). The two olive trees are 'the two anointed who stand by the Lord of the whole earth' (4: 14), i.e., Joshua, the anointed priest, and Zerubbabel, the anointed king. The question arises, Whom

[1] Cf. A. Satake, *Die Gemeindeordung in der Johannesapokalypse* (Neukirchen–Vluyn, 1966), pp. 119–33, who has argued that the two witnesses are not to be interpreted as individuals, but as a symbolic representation of the church.

does John see fulfilling the functions of the anointed priest and the anointed king? Fortunately, John has told his readers the answer to this question. In the opening chapter it is those whom Christ has freed from their sins by his blood that have been made a 'kingdom, priests to his God and Father' (1: 5f.). In chapter five again it is the redeemed whom Christ has made a 'kingdom and priests to our God, and they shall reign on earth' (5: 10; cf. I Pet. 2: 9, which also makes use of Ex. 19: 6). Finally, in chapter 20 this priest-king motif is repeated with special reference to the martyrs; they are 'priests' in their communion with God and Christ and they 'reign' on earth for a thousand years (20: 6; cf. 20: 4; 22: 5).

All of these passages illumine Rev. 11, for they suggest that the anointed 'kings' and 'priests' refer either to the redeemed generally or to the martyrs specifically. In Rev. 11 it is plainly the martyrs who are in view, for John explicitly notes that the prophetic witnesses are killed 'when they have finished their testimony' (11: 7; cf. Jubilees 1: 12, where the witnesses are the prophets who are slain after they have given their witness). John obviously goes to Zechariah for 'the two anointed', but he reinterprets the anointed priest and king in terms of the faithful martyrs who go to their death for holding the testimony of Jesus.

But the two witnesses are not only described as 'the two olive trees'; they are also called 'the two lampstands' (11: 4), a phrase which at once recalls the explanation of 1: 20 that 'the seven lampstands are the seven churches'. The question now arises, What is the relationship between the two lampstands and the seven? Is this to suggest that only two of the seven churches will experience martyrdom? At first sight this suggestion might appear to fit the churches of Smyrna and Philadelphia, the only two churches which do not have an indictment laid against them by the risen Christ.

At least two considerations militate against this possibility: (1) The number seven is used symbolically to indicate the church at large. There were other churches in Asia, for example those in Colossae (Col. 1: 2), Hierapolis (Col. 4: 13) and Troas (Acts 20: 5–12), but John uses the number seven to point to the fact that his message is addressed to the whole church. If the seven lampstands represent the universal church, then two lampstands would seem to represent a portion of that church.

The two lampstands

provide the clearest possible evidence that John did not expect all loyal Christians to die in the great ordeal. We must not, of course, take the fraction two-sevenths any more literally than John's other numbers. He has good reason for this use of the number two. The evidence of a single witness was not admissible in a Jewish court of law.[1]

(2) John expected every Christian community to furnish faithful people strong enough to face martyrdom; this is why the promises to the conquerors are addressed to members of *each* of the seven churches (2: 7, 11, 17, 26; 3: 5, 12, 21). In other words, the two lampstands represent the martyrs of 'the seven churches', that is, the 'conquerors'.

The conquerors are the ones who stand directly in God's presence 'before the Lord of the earth' (11: 12; cf. Zech. 4: 14). Their task is to proclaim with courage and fidelity a world-wide message of repentance (11: 3, cf. Mt. 11: 21 and Lk. 10: 21 where 'sackcloth' is explicitly linked with repentance; see also I Kgs 21: 27–9; Neh. 9: 1–3; Dan. 9: 3–19; Jon. 3: 4–10). In doing this they 'follow the Lamb wherever he goes' (14: 4), and his way is the way of the cross. Through a voluntary surrender of their lives they conquer 'the accuser' by 'the blood of the Lamb and by the word of their testimony' (12: 10f.). Certainly there is no suggestion in the Apocalypse of denying the 'once-for-all' character of Christ's sacrifice, for this theme is frequently mentioned or suggested (1: 5; 4: 9, 12; 7: 14; 12: 11; 13: 8; cf. Heb. 7: 27; 9: 12; 10: 10); rather, 'here is a call for the endurance of the saints, those who keep the commandments of God and the faith of Jesus' (Rev. 14: 12; cf. 13: 10). It is to prepare Christ's people for this prospective martyrdom that John has written the Revelation.

These witnesses 'prophesy'; indeed they are explicitly described as the two προφῆται (11: 10). An interesting comment on the nature of their prophecy is to be found in two later passages, 19: 10 and 22: 6. The first passage makes it clear that the historic testimony borne by Jesus is the inspiration of all their prophecy. Looking to Jesus, who witnessed a good confes-

[1] Caird, *Revelation*, pp. 134–5. Cf. H. B. Swete, *The Apocalypse of St. John* (London, 1906), p. 132.

sion before Pontius Pilate, they are motivated to a fearless proclamation of the gospel (11: 3; cf. Heb. 12: 1; I Tim. 6: 13; Acts 1: 8). The second passage reminds the reader that basically the Revelation is a prophetic book for prophets, which is another way of saying that it is written to prepare Christians for martyrdom. By their courageous testimony the gospel is to be proclaimed to 'many peoples and nations and tongues and kings' (10: 11; cf. 11: 9; Mk 13: 9f.; Lk. 21: 12f.; Mt. 10: 17). As true witnesses it is significant that 'in their mouth was found no lie' (14: 5); this stands in vivid contrast to their opponents (2: 9; 3: 9; cf. 21: 27; 22: 15).

But how were the prophetic witnesses to survive the onslaught of imperial persecution to fulfil their task? John answers this question by referring to Moses and Elijah, who collectively represented the Law and the Prophets. Elijah had possessed the power both to shut the sky and to call down 'fire' from heaven to consume his foes (I Kgs 17: 1; II Kgs 1: 10), while Moses had been given 'power over the waters to turn them into blood, and to smite the earth with every plague' (Rev. 11: 6; cf. Ex. 7–11). Christ's witnesses, however, have no mighty rod with which to work spectacular feats, and their fire is figurative, like the sword issuing out of Christ's mouth (1: 16; 2: 13, 16; 19: 15; cf. Hos. 6: 5; Eph. 6: 17).[1] Their 'fire' is the actual testimony which they must give in a Roman court of law (Rev. 11: 5; cf. Jer. 20: 9; 23: 29). Just as Jesus had warned his earthly judge that he must stand before the judgment seat of the Son of Man (Mk 14: 62), so

the Christian witnesses must by any means in their power persuade their accusers that they are on trial before a higher tribunal, and on a capital charge sustained on the evidence of two or three witnesses. They are to be a torment to the inhabitants of the earth because their testimony is a searing indictment of the world they live in.[2]

Dr Caird's comment calls attention to the juridical character of the martyr's testimony. It also is a reminder that the seer of Patmos, like many other New Testament writers (Mt. 18: 16; Jn 5: 31; 8: 17; 15: 26f.; Acts 5: 32; II Cor. 13: 1; Heb. 10: 28;

[1] On the forensic significance of the sword in Rev. 2: 11, cf. A. Farrer, *A Rebirth of Images* (London, 1949), p. 191.

[2] Caird, *Revelation*, pp. 136–7.

I Tim. 5: 19), honours the Old Testament rule of evidence; this is the significance of his reference to *two* witnesses (Rev. 11: 3; cf. Num. 35: 30; Deut. 17: 6; 19: 15). By means of dual evidence Christ's witnesses will sustain their case and thwart every accuser, including both the Roman *delator* and the arch-persecutor, Satan himself (12: 7ff., who relentlessly presses the case ἐνώπιον τοῦ θεοῦ, cf. Zech. 3: 1; Lk. 22: 31). Though their testimony in a human lawcourt fails to secure their acquittal, in the heavenly court it secures both the vindication of the martyrs and Babylon's condemnation for rejecting their testimony and putting them to death.

When the gospel has been published to all nations through Christ's witnesses bearing their testimony under supernatural protection, the protection will be taken away, and they will be conquered and killed (11: 7). Just as 'their Lord' died for attesting God's word, so too they must demonstrate by death their complete devotion to the testimony which he bore. Christ bore his testimony before the Roman procurator and became the first 'child' of the Messianic community (12: 5), but the martyrs are also included in 'her offspring' (12: 17), and their fate is to be like his.

The scene of the conflict is the same; the saints are killed 'in the streets of the great city...where their Lord was crucified' (11: 8). This city is called 'Sodom' because it is devoted to evil and destined to destruction (Gen. 19: 1–29; cf. Deut. 29: 23; Isa. 1: 9; Jer. 49: 18; Am. 4: 1), and it is termed 'Egypt' because in it the people of God are persecuted and oppressed (cf. Ex. 1: 11–14; 2: 23; 3: 7–9; 5: 4–18). These allegorical names indicate that it is not the city of Jerusalem that is signified, but rather the Earthly City which is opposed to the Heavenly City and which is now represented by the satanic power of Rome, 'the great city' (16: 19; 17: 18; 18: 10, 16, 18, 19, 21).

The witnesses, in other words, are killed wherever they hold the testimony of Jesus, and 'their dead bodies' lie dishonoured in every town and city in the imperial world (11: 9; cf. Psa. 79: 2–3). Their corpses are ignominiously exposed to the gloating gaze of their opponents, who 'rejoice over them and make merry and exchange presents' (11: 10; cf. Est. 9: 22). Their enemies are derisively termed the 'dwellers of the earth' – a phrase used by John to designate the unregenerate inhabitants of the world (3: 10; 6: 10; 8: 13; 11: 10; 13: 8, 12, 14; 14: 6; 17: 2, 8). However, like their Lord, they too have a resurrection (cf. Ezek. 37: 5, 10), but it comes after three and a half days, for John is influenced by Daniel's mysterious half week (cf. Dan. 7: 25; 9: 27; 12: 7). Like Elijah their prototype (II Kgs 2: 11), the witnesses are miraculously taken up to heaven. This is accomplished 'in the sight of their foes' and 'in a cloud', suggesting their complete and utter vindication (Rev. 11: 12; cf. 1: 7; 14: 14–16; Dan. 7: 13; Mk 14: 62 pars.).

At the same time there is an earthquake which destroys 'a tenth of the city' and seven thousand of its inhabitants (Rev. 11: 13). It is quite likely that the law of malicious witness of Deut. 19: 16–21 is in John's mind at this point.[1] In any case the context plainly indicates that those destroyed come from the foes of the martyred witnesses. The rest of earth's inhabitants definitely react to these events, for they are described as ἔμφοβοι (11: 13). Is this servile, cringing fear in the face of inescapable doom, or is it the 'fear of the Lord' which is 'the beginning of wisdom' (Prov. 9: 10; cf. 1: 7; Job 28: 28; Psa. 111: 10)?

Most commentators have taken the former view, but against it can be urged the following considerations: (1) Except in the phrase μὴ φοβοῦ (1: 17; 2: 10), φοβεῖσθαι in Revelation always has the positive meaning; it expresses the worship which the Creator has a right to expect from his creatures: 'Praise our God, all you his servants, who fear him, small and great' (19: 5; cf. 11: 18; 14: 7; 15: 4). There is no reason to suppose that John had any other meaning in view in 11: 13. (2) The positive interpretation of 'fear' is in harmony with the words which immediately follow ἔμφοβοι ἐγένοντο. This is clear from: (a) The use of the co-ordinate conjunction καί. (b) The content of the idiomatic phrase ἔδωκαν δόξαν τῷ θεῷ, which means 'to pay the honour due to God by changing one's attitude and confessing, speaking, or doing, the truth as the truth of God' (Rev. 16: 9; Jer. 13: 16; I Es. 9: 8; cf. I Pet. 2: 12).[2] (3) The Old Testament not only speaks favourably of those who 'fear the Lord' (Gen. 22: 12; I Kgs 18: 3, 12; Psa. 113: 2; Hag. 1: 12; Mal. 3: 16), but also contains numerous exhortations to 'fear the Lord

---

[1] *Ibid.* p. 140.
[2] I. T. Beckwith, *The Apocalypse of John* (New York, 1919), p. 604.

and serve him faithfully' (I Sam. 12: 24; cf. Deut. 6: 2, 13, 24; Josh. 24: 14; II Kgs 17: 39) – a fact attested by the frequent use of *yārē'* meaning 'to fear, reverence'. John was thoroughly acquainted with this motif, and made use of it. (4) Some of Israel's prophets and psalmists looked forward to a time when the pagan nations would 'fear God' and acknowledge his sovereign power and holiness (Psa. 67: 7; cf. 22: 27–9; 65: 2; 86: 9; Isa. 45: 23; 52: 10; 66: 23). That John was also conscious of this expectation is indicated by his quotation from Psalm 86: 9: 'All nations shall come and worship thee' (Rev. 15: 4). John sees the prophecies mentioned in Isaiah and the Psalms fulfilled through the martyrdom of Christ's witnesses, for their victory entails the conversion of a great host. It is not without significance that the seer pictures the worship of a great multitude in heaven (7: 9; 19: 1, 6). In other words, John is saying that the testimony of the witnesses is not in vain. Despite widespread impenitence in the face of the punitive judgments of God (9: 20–1; 16: 9, 11), their witness in life and death is effective, for through it an innumerable company respond to God by revering his name and paying him homage. Here is a classic illustration of the familiar adage, 'the blood of the martyrs is the seed of the Church'.

OTHER LEGAL SCENES IN REVELATION

In Rev. 12 the seer presents one of his great legal scenes. A battle takes place in heaven between Michael and his angels on the one side and the dragon and his angels on the other. The dragon, 'who is called the Devil and Satan', serves as the κατήγωρ in the heavenly lawcourt, and according to the biblical tradition he has every right to be there (cf. Job 1: 6ff.; Zech. 3: 1ff.).

In the New Testament and the Rabbinic writings Satan still retains his legal duties as prosecutor, frequently with Michael as the counsel for the defence (I Pet. v. 8; Jude 9; I Tim. iii. 6; Ber. 46[a]; Yom. 20[a]). For Michael is the great prince who has charge of the people of God (Dan. x. 21; xii. 1; Yom. 77[a]; Ḥul. 40[a]). To his antinomian opponents who treat with contempt the moral law and its angelic guardians, whom he calls 'the glories', Jude commends the behaviour of Michael, who in a debate over the body of Moses paid the respect due to a fellow barrister (Jude 8–9). As long as there are human sinners to accuse, Satan's presence in heaven must be tolerated, for God himself recognizes the justice of the indictment. Thus, although John depicts the battle between Michael and Satan in military terms, it was essentially a legal battle between opposing counsel, which resulted in one of them being disbarred.[1]

In other words, in Revelation John has revivified the original meaning of 'Satan' by reference to the lawcourt setting. Following the Old Testament, he sees Satan still in his legal capacity as the 'accuser of the brethren', 'who accuses them day and night before...God' (12: 10). Similarly, he twice calls the unbelieving Jews a 'synagogue of Satan' (2: 9; 3: 9), for they are the instruments of the great accuser in bringing Christians before Roman courts of law and acting as accusing witnesses against them.

The earthly part of this legal battle is fully worked out in the Fourth Gospel, as we perceived in our chapter on the Fourth Gospel's concept of witness. This battle may be summarized here for the light which it casts on the Book of Revelation. The archprosecutor Satan, working through such earthly agents as Judas Iscariot (Jn 13: 2), accuses Jesus and demands the death penalty (Jn 18: 31). However, Jesus is innocent of the charges laid against him (Jn 18: 38; 19: 4, 6), and Satan only wins his case in the earthly lawcourt by a gross miscarriage of justice; so Jn 14: 30 may be translated: 'The prince of this world is approaching, but he has no [legal] claim on me.' In the heavenly lawcourt Christ is victorious, for his death spells not only the judgment of the world but also the defeat of Satan and his ejection from heaven (Jn 12: 31–2). In other words, the prosecutor in the heavenly lawcourt has been defeated by the legal victory of Christ on Calvary (Jn 12: 31; 14: 30; 16: 33) and this explains the repeated use of the form ἐβλήθη to refer to his ejection (Rev. 12: 9 (twice), 10, 13). On earth, however, he continues to do legal battle with Christians, hauling into court 'those who keep the commandments of God and the testimony of Jesus' (12: 17; cf. 2: 9; 3: 9). The witness of the martyrs is of value because it is linked with the historic testimony of Christ, 'the faithful and true witness', who 'died and came to life' (1: 5; 2: 8). 'The real victory...may be a forensic one,... but it takes open war to clinch it...If the world is to hear and accept God's amnesty,

---

[1] Caird, *Revelation*, pp. 154–5. Cf. Leivestad, *Christ the Conqueror*, p. 226.

there must be witnesses; and if evil is to burn itself out to the bitter end, their testimony must be the testimony of suffering.'[1] For this reason forensic and military metaphors are very closely related in the Apocalypse.

Now attention may be directed to the second courtroom scene in Revelation, where the legal contest is between the martyrs and their earthly accuser, Babylon (18: 20 – 19: 4). The angel has just sung a dirge over the fallen city (Rome), echoing the taunt songs of Isaiah (chapters 14, 23, 24, 47), Jeremiah (chapters 50, 51) and Ezekiel (chapters 26, 27), and stressing the sudden and irreversible character of the divine judgment (18: 1–19). Babylon 'the great city' is really Rome 'the great harlot', whose judgment the seer has already seen (16: 19; 17: 1). Now in 18: 20 a new paragraph really begins, introduced by a cross-reference to the other courtroom scene (cf. 12: 12, where the imperative of εὐφραίνειν is used as it is in 18: 20). The saints, apostles and prophets are told to rejoice, for 'God has judged your judgment out of her' (literal translation of 18: 20b). But what does this mean? If, as Dr Caird has suggested, the sentence is translated, 'God has imposed on her the sentence she passed on you', then the passage is to be understood in terms of two Old Testament laws, namely, the law of bloodshed and the law of malicious witness (Gen. 9: 5–6; Deut. 19: 16–19; cf. Rev. 11: 13):

John has produced a portmanteau version of these two laws... Babylon has brought a malicious accusation against the martyrs, which has resulted in their death. But the case has been carried 'before the Lord', to the court of final appeal, where judgments are true and just. There Babylon has been found guilty of perjury, and God has therefore required from her the life of her victims, exacting from her the penalty she exacted from them.[2]

In other words John reminds his fellow Christians standing before real courts of law and facing imminent death that Babylon's unjust sentence will be reversed. Babylon's malicious witness recoils on her own head (19: 2). The judgment of the 'great harlot' (Rev. 17: 1–18: 24; cf. Nah. 3: 4ff.) is complete and final.

Mention has already been made of the close relationship

---

[1] Caird, *op. cit.*, p. 157.   [2] *Ibid.* p. 230.

between forensic and military metaphors in the Book of Revelation. Nowhere is this more apparent than in Rev. 19: 11–21, where a magnificent picture is given of the victory of Christ and his heavenly armies over the beast and his cohorts. This feature is not surprising, for the same mixture of legal and military metaphors was encountered in the Book of Joel when all the nations were called to wage war in 'the Valley of the Verdict' (Joel 3: 1–14). Moreover, John has already spoken of the war in heaven between the counsel for the defence and the counsel for the prosecution (Rev. 12: 7–12; cf. Jude 9). While it may seem illogical that the same person should function as a witness *and* judge, the study of the use of witnesses both in the Old Testament legal assembly and in the famous trial scene mentioned in the *Iliad* (XVIII.486–508) has shown that this was perfectly normal judicial procedure in ancient times. This argument is also strengthened by the fact that the verbs κρίνειν and even κατακρίνειν are used elsewhere in the New Testament to denote the part played by a witness in a court of law (Mt. 12: 41f.; Lk. 11: 31f.; Rom. 2: 27; Heb. 11: 7; cf. Lk. 11: 19). Similarly in Rev. 19: 11 the witness 'judges' because he provides the evidence on which the legal victory depends; it is significant that the sharp sword he wields proceeds 'out of his mouth' (19: 15, 21).

Before concluding this section, a word must be said about the Last Judgment – a scene described very graphically in Rev. 20: 11–12 in words borrowed from Dan. 7: 9–10. Here the judgment seat is called a θρόνος, the judge is described as 'sitting' (as in the Old Testament lawsuit), and the evidence is contained in the βιβλία. Judgment is given, for 'the dead were judged (ἐκρίθησαν) by what was written in the books, by what they had done' (Rev. 20: 12; cf. the description of the Last Judgment in Mt. 25: 31–46). This passage is arresting, for while no reference is made to the role of witnesses, the forensic setting is unmistakably clear. The 'great white throne' of Rev. 20: 11 stands in striking contrast to the 'throne' in Pergamum, 'where Satan dwells' (2: 13); it is 'the Satanic judge there enthroned who kills Antipas…by the breath of his lips'.[1]

In summary, one can readily see how important the idea of witness is to the seer of Patmos by looking at the superscription

---

[1] Farrer, *A Rebirth of Images*, p. 191.

in the light of the contents of the book. The Revelation is written to help prospective martyrs see that their suffering is part of the eternal purpose declared by God and attested by Jesus Christ (1: 2). This revelation comes from the eternal God 'who is and was and is coming' (1: 1, 4). It also comes 'from Jesus Christ, the faithful witness, the firstborn of the dead, and the ruler of the kings on earth' (1: 5), who epitomizes the whole purpose of God in his life, death and resurrection. It is communicated to others by those whom Christ has made kings and priests through the shedding of his blood (1: 5–6). These folk are called to share 'the ordeal and the sovereignty and the endurance' (1: 9), to reign in the midst of their martyrdom even as Christ reigned from the cross.

Each is called to be a Conqueror, repeating in his own life the archetypal victory of Christ (ii. 7, 11, 17, 26; iii. 5, 12, 31)...The victory of the martyrs is already included in the victory of the Cross by which Satan is ejected from heaven (xii. 11)...The secret purpose of God is known to John only because it has been revealed in the earthly testimony of Jesus, 'the faithful witness', and...it can be known to the world only if there are men like John prepared to hold to the testimony of Jesus, even at the cost of life or liberty.[1]

[1] Caird, *Revelation*, pp. 297, 300, 291.

CHAPTER II

THE IDEA OF WITNESS ELSEWHERE
IN THE NEW TESTAMENT

The idea of witness is most fully developed in the Johannine and Lukan writings, but it is also present in other parts of the New Testament. It is, therefore, important to examine both the Synoptic Gospels and the New Testament Epistles to see where the idea of witness is used, for what reasons, and against what background.

THE IDEA OF WITNESS IN THE SYNOPTIC GOSPELS

In a general sense, of course, the Gospels themselves are witnesses to Christ, and whole books have been devoted to treating them from that perspective.[1] Redaction criticism in particular has given renewed impetus to the study of the unique witness which each of the Evangelists gives to Jesus.[2] Our purpose here is not to repeat this procedure, but to look specifically at the places where witness themes and courtroom terminology are raised in the Synoptic Gospels.

The idea of witness is present in Mark's Gospel, but nothing like as prominent as it is in the Fourth Gospel. Many of the questions of the scribes and Pharisees look as if they may introduce controversies similar to those in the Old Testament and the Fourth Gospel, but instead they turn out to introduce various sayings of Jesus and the debate is cut short (e.g., Mk 2: 18–22 pars.; 11: 27–33 pars.; 12: 13–17 pars.; 12: 18–27 pars.;

---

[1] E.g., the work of N. B. Stonehouse, *The Witness of Matthew and Mark to Christ* (Philadelphia, 1944) and *The Witness of Luke to Christ* (London, 1951). Note also Martin Kähler's famous book, *Der sogenannte historische Jesus und der geschichtliche biblische Christus* (1892; 3rd ed., Munich, 1961), which treated the Gospels not as historical 'sources' for a life of Christ, but rather as kerygmatic 'witnesses'.

[2] For a useful introduction and annotated bibliography see N. Perrin, *What Is Redaction Criticism?* (London, 1970). On the application of *Redaktionsgeschichte* to John's Gospel see W. Nicol, *The Sēmeia in the Fourth Gospel: Tradition and Redaction* (Leiden, 1972).

12: 28–34 pars.). Debating is by no means an uncommon
feature in the Synoptics (witness the use of συ3ητεῖν in Mk 8:
11; 9: 14, 16; 12: 28 and φιλονεικία in Lk. 22: 24). But while
controversy sayings and controversy dialogues are used (e.g.,
Mk 2: 7ff., 16f.; 7: 5ff.; Lk. 6: 2ff.; Mt. 12: 2ff.; 15: 2ff.), they
are not developed along the lines of Isaiah 40–55 or John
1–12.[1]

Nevertheless, the Synoptic Gospels see Christ's mighty works
performed against a background of hostility in which his opponents are constantly observing him (Mk 3: 2; cf. Lk. 6: 7;
14: 1), sometimes even employing spies (Lk. 20: 20).[2] The
enemies of Jesus are bent on seeking opportunities to accuse him
(Mk 3: 2; Mt. 12: 10; cf. Lk. 6: 7), drawing him out with
questions and laying snares to catch him with his own words
(Lk. 11: 53f.; cf. Mk 12: 13; Mt. 22: 15). On the other hand,
the idea of Jesus winning a debate and reducing his opponents
to silence is not unknown in the Synoptics (e.g., Mt. 22: 34,
ἐφίμωσεν τοὺς Σαδδουκαίους; cf. Mk 12: 34; Mt. 22: 46; Lk.
20: 26; and Mk 3: 4, where a juridical question is met with
silence), and reminds one of the similar enforced silence of the
pagan nations in Isaiah 40–55 and the silence of the false witnesses at the trial of Jesus in the Fourth Gospel (Jn 18: 21, 23).
Sometimes those who debate with Jesus are forced to engage in
lively debates among themselves (διελογί3οντο πρὸς ἑαυτούς,
Mk 11: 31; συνελογίσαντο πρὸς ἑαυτούς, Lk. 20: 5; cf. Acts 23:
7–9). Sometimes the debaters are the disciples (examples of
Schulgespräche: Mk 8: 32 – 9: 1 pars.; 9: 33–7 pars.; 10: 35–45);
'here the opposition of viewpoint is so great as to distinguish
these debates from normal discussions between master and

[1] A. J. Hultgren, 'Jesus and his adversaries', Th.D. dissertation, Union
Theological Seminary, New York, 1971, thinks that Mark uses the conflict
stories to serve two functions: 'first, to link up the earlier ministry of Jesus
with the Passion; second, to show a continuity between the victories of Jesus
over his adversaries in verbal combat and his victories over supernatural
hostile powers (the exorcisms)'. See *Dissertation Abstracts*, 32, No. 3 (Sept.
1971), 1610A.
[2] J. A. Baird, *Audience Criticism and the Historical Jesus* (Philadelphia, 1969),
has argued that 'within both narrative and logia there are four basic
audiences consistently described: the Twelve, the "crowd" of disciples, the
opponent crowd, and the opponents' (p. 33). Note especially his treatment
of the hard-core opponents (pp. 46–9).

disciple, and to bring them into the present context of debates with the Jewish authorities'.[1]

Near the beginning of Mark one meets the first of a series of demoniac 'confessions' (Mk 1: 24), which are paralleled by similar accounts in Matthew and Luke. Now unquestionably these 'confessions' recognize Jesus as the 'Holy One of God' (Mk 1: 24; Lk. 4: 34; this rare title appears in Peter's confession in John's Gospel, 6: 69), 'Son of God' (Mk 3: 11; Mt. 8: 29; Lk. 4: 41), 'Son of the Most High God' (Mk 5: 7; Lk. 8: 28), but are they acceptable testimonies to the Messiahship and divine Sonship of Jesus? The Synoptics answer this question in the negative; indeed, the demons are rebuked, told to be silent and ordered not to make Christ known (Mk 1: 25; 3: 12; cf. Lk. 4: 35, 41). Certainly the demons do not show reverence for Christ, but plainly regard him as an enemy: 'What have you to do with us, Jesus of Nazareth? Have you come to destroy us?' (Mk 1: 24; Lk. 4: 34). The demons see the approach of Jesus as a threat, and cry out to escape torment (μή με βασανίσῃς in Mk 5: 7 and Lk. 8: 28, ἦλθες ὧδε πρὸ καιροῦ βασανίσαι ἡμᾶς in Mt. 8: 29). In other words, the 'confessions' of the demons are clearly hostile in character, as James M. Robinson has shown with special reference to Mark's Gospel.[2]

The Synoptic exorcisms deserve to be compared with Acts 16: 16–18. There, as in the Synoptics, the possessed girl speaks of 'the Most High God', a title commonly used among both Jews and Greeks (cf. Num. 24: 16; Isa. 14: 14; Dan. 4: 2; I Esdras 2: 3; Acts 7: 48) and her ceaseless screaming (ἔκραζεν) 'recalls the shouting demons in the gospels, except that the demon of our passage, where he is not threatened, does not accuse but rather announces the true character of a foreign preacher in a way understandable for Gentiles'.[3] In the Acts account, as in

---

[1] J. M. Robinson, *The Problem of History in Mark* (London, 1957), p. 51. Robinson thinks that 'Mark provides the exorcism as the pattern for interpreting the debates in the synagogues' (p. 44). Debates among disciples occasionally appear in Acts (cf. the *Streitfrage* in Antioch and Jerusalem [15: 1–12] and the 'sharp contention' [παροξυσμός] which separates Paul and Barnabas [15: 39]).

[2] *Ibid.* p 37. Robinson sees Mark in one of its aspects as a divine-human controversy, and interprets the demoniac 'confessions' in the light of this controversy.

[3] E. Haenchen, *The Acts of the Apostles* (Oxford, 1965), p. 495.

the Synoptics, exorcism in the name of Jesus is immediately effective.

In Mk 1: 44 Jesus tells the cleansed leper to 'go, show your-self to the priest, and offer for your cleansing what Moses com-manded *as a testimony to them*' (εἰς μαρτύριον αὐτοῖς; cf. Lev. 13: 49). Mt. 8: 4 and Lk. 5: 14 use the same phrase in their ac-counts of the incident, and are to be considered with Mk 1: 44. While Bengel's suggestion that Mt. 8: 4 may be compared with Jn 5: 36 is interesting,[1] the Synoptic passages themselves must not be forced into a procrustean bed; here an exclusively legal interpretation of the witness concept is clearly too narrow, for though the priest is the legal authority, his authority is not exercised in a lawcourt setting, as Lev. 14: 1ff. shows. A similar instruction is given to ten lepers on another occasion, but no mention is made of the testimony factor (Lk. 17: 11–19); the reference to Levitical laws of purification suggests the purpose of the examination without specifying it.

A valid illustration of Aristotle's distinction between witnesses to facts and witnesses to the meaning or quality of the facts occurs in the story of the healing of the Gerasene demoniac (Mk 5: 1–20; Mt. 8: 28–34; Lk. 8: 26–39). News of the miracle stirs up the curiosity of the people in the town and surrounding countryside, who come to Jesus and observe for themselves the complete transformation in the man's health. Here the people are definitely eye-witnesses who can attest the fact of the cure (*Augenzeugen*, Mk 5: 16; Lk. 8: 36), but they are not thereby competent to speak of the spiritual significance of the event, which arouses in them only feelings of fear and antipathy (Mk 5: 15–17; Lk. 8: 35–7). The reaction of the people who hear the testimony is worth noting. They function as a hostile party by pleading to get rid of Christ (ἤρξαντο παρακαλεῖν, Mk 5: 17).

Similarly in Mark and to a lesser extent in Matthew, the disciples are treated as eye-witnesses of the two feedings of the multitudes (the *Zweite Brotvermehrung*), but are rebuked for their lack of perception into the meaning of evidence which has taken place right before their eyes: 'Having eyes do you not see, and having ears do you not hear?' (Mk 8: 14–21; cf. Mt. 16: 5–12). Eye-witnesses, in other words, can be blinded to the true sig-

---

[1] J. A. Bengel, *Gnomon Novi Testamenti* (2 vols.; David Nutt: London, 1850), I, 65.

nificance of what they see. In this instance, Mark attributes their obtuseness to hardness of heart, while Matthew draws attention to the paucity of their faith.

The raising of Jairus's daughter is reported by all three Synoptists (Mk 5: 21–43; Mt. 9: 18–26; Lk. 8: 40–56). The striking point to observe here is that Jesus, after turning out the professional mourners, approached the bed of the little girl by taking witnesses with him (Mk 5: 40; Lk. 8: 51); these included the grieving father and mother and his own close friends, Peter, James and John. However, his action on this occasion seems to have been prompted more by a desire to avoid undue crowding, noise and idle curiosity than it was to satisfy the principle of multiple witness; this would explain the presence of the parents and the absence of the weeping and wailing crowd. Certainly this event became widely publicized (Mt. 9: 26), but both Mark and Luke stress that this was contrary to the intention of Jesus (Mk 5: 43; Lk. 8: 56). The idea of witness is not prominent here.

However, the adjoining account of the woman with the issue of blood deserves a second glance (Mk 5: 25–33 pars.). In Luke, the woman is clearly presented as an unwilling witness who eventually makes a public confession of her healing. This is clear from: (1) the fact that she, like all other members of the crowd, initially denied touching Jesus (ἀρνουμένων δὲ πάντων, Lk. 8: 45); (2) her hesitating approach when she 'saw that she was not hidden, she came trembling' (Lk. 8: 47; cf. Mk 5: 33 'came in fear and trembling'); and (3) her public testimony to Jesus 'in the presence of all the people' (Lk. 8: 47).

Turning to John the Baptist's emissaries (Mt. 11: 2–6; Lk. 7: 18–23), they are obviously witnesses of what they have seen and heard; but they are not termed μάρτυρες, they have no special insight into the meaning of what they have observed, and their commission is fulfilled when they report back to John. On the other hand, the Jewish elders who request Jesus to heal a highly respected centurion's servant function as advocates who present a man's case and take his side (παρεκάλουν αὐτὸν σπουδαίως, Lk. 7: 4; cf. Mt. 8: 5, where the centurion makes his own appeal).

In Mk 6: 11 reference is made to the idea of witness. The context is the sending out of the Twelve (Mk 6: 7–13 pars.). Jesus instructs them, on leaving a place where their message has not been received, to shake off the dust from their feet εἰς μαρτύριον αὐτοῖς. Interpreting this in the light of the Jewish practice of removing dust from a heathen land before returning to Jewish soil,[1] the significance of the action here commanded is to pronounce the place which rejects them heathen (cf. Mt. 10: 14; Acts 13: 51). At the same time it serves as a warning to the people that the missionaries have fulfilled their responsibility toward that place and that from now on they must shoulder their own responsibility (cf. Acts 18: 6, where the shaking off of the dust is accompanied by the solemn words: 'Your blood be upon your own heads!'). Professor Cranfield is helpful when he says that μαρτύριον in Mk 6: 11 includes the ideas of:

(i) witness to God, to his grace and also to his judgement on those who reject his messengers; (ii) witness addressed to the people concerned – a warning and summons to repentance; (iii) evidence which will lie against them at the Final Judgement – the fact that the warning has been delivered to them and not heeded will be produced against them.[2]

Luke's account is even more explicit, for he represents the action as a threat ('witness against them', 9: 5). 'This is because he regards the coming destruction of the cities of Galilee as a divine judgement on their failure to respond to the Gospel.'[3]

In the Transfiguration story Peter, James and John function as witnesses (ἐπόπται in II Pet. 1: 16). This is stressed in both Mark and Matthew: 'He was transfigured *before* them'; 'There *appeared to them* Elijah and Moses'; 'A cloud overshadowed *them*' (Mk 9: 2, 4, 7; Mt. 17: 2, 3, 5). While Luke notes the drowsiness of the disciples, he too observes that the disciples saw 'the two who stood with him' (Lk. 9: 32). However, the three witnesses are not described as μάρτυρες, and no attempt is made to develop courtroom imagery and terminology. In fact, the

[1] T. W. Manson, *The Sayings of Jesus* (London, 1949), p. 76; cf. Strack–Billerbeck, I, 171. 'Shaking' was sometimes connected with threats of divine judgment if the message went unheeded (Neh. 5: 13).

[2] C. E. B. Cranfield, *The Gospel according to Saint Mark* (Cambridge, 1959), p. 201. Josephus uses a similar formula in describing Samuel's action in laying up the book in the tabernacle of God: ταῖς μετέπειτα γενεαῖς μαρτύριον ὧν προείρηκε (*Ant.* VI. 66).

[3] G. B. Caird, '"Shake off the dust from your feet" (Mk. 6: 11),' *ExpT*, 81 (1969–70), 40–3.

disciples are expressly commanded to tell no one what they have seen 'until the Son of Man should have risen from the dead' (Mk 9: 9; Mt. 17: 9), and Luke notes that 'they kept silence and told no one in those days any thing of what they had seen' (Lk. 9: 36).

There seems to be an application of the idea of witness in Mark 8 and its parallels. Those who are ashamed of Christ and his words in 'this adulterous and sinful generation' will be put to shame by the Son of Man 'when he comes in the glory of his Father with the holy angels' (Mk 8: 38; cf. Lk. 9: 26; Mt. 16: 27). Matthew, in keeping with his general emphasis on judgment, stresses the Son of Man's role as judge by citing Psa. 62: 12.

Mark 8 and its parallels also speak of Peter's *Glaubenbekenntnis* (Mk 8: 27–30; Lk. 9: 18–21; Mt. 16: 13–20; cf. Jn 6: 67–71), which stands in marked contrast with his later denial of Jesus at the time of the trial (Mk 14: 66–72 pars.).

Lk. 12: 2–9 and Mt. 10: 26–33 present a challenging summons to fearless confession. As Canon Browning has remarked on the opening verses: 'All the divine secrets are destined to be disclosed at the Last Day; but before that the halting and timid confessions of faith ([Lk.] 9: 20) of the disciples must become triumphant and public, even though they will bring persecution. But this is far preferable to disobedience to God who has power to cast us into Gehenna.'[1]

The forensic element appears even more clearly at the end of this passage: 'So every one who acknowledges me before men, I also will acknowledge before my Father who is in heaven; but whoever denies me before men, I also will deny before my Father who is in heaven' (Mt. 10: 32f.; Lk. 12: 8f.). In both accounts the juridical verbs ὁμολογεῖν and ἀρνεῖσθαι are used, and reference is made to testimony 'before men' (ἔμπροσθεν here has the sense of appearing before a judge; cf. Mt. 27: 11; Lk. 21: 36; II Cor. 5: 10). In each instance what is confessed or denied is the disciple's solidarity with Christ. Confession in Christ's case (ἐν ἐμοί) results in Christ's confession in the believer's case (ἐν αὐτῷ). In other words, the disciple's witness to Christ on earth ensures Christ's witness to him in heaven (cf. Rev. 3: 5).

[1] W. R. F. Browning, *The Gospel according to Saint Luke* (London, 1960), p. 119, who entitles Lk. 12: 1–12: 'Threatened witnesses'.

In the Lukan parallel the juridical note is strengthened in a number of ways: (1) There is an explicit reference to 'the Son of Man', who is definitely viewed as acting in a judicial role (Lk. 12: 8; cf. 21: 36; Jn 5: 27). (2) The interesting verb ἀπαρνεῖσθαι is used, which appears later in all three Synoptic accounts of Peter's denial (Mk 14: 30, 31, 72 pars.). (3) Luke refers to the actual hauling of believers before courts of law (using the striking verb εἰσφέρειν, Lk. 12: 11); later he cites Jason as an illustration of one subjected to such treatment (ἔσυρον 'Ἰάσονα, Acts 17: 6). (4) The ἄρχαι and the ἐξουσίαι mentioned only by Luke (Lk. 12: 11), 'would include the Sanhedrin and Gentile tribunals'.[1] (5) Note the introduction of ἀπολογεῖσθαι, a verb which is frequently common in juridical contexts, particularly in Luke–Acts (Lk. 12: 11; 21: 14; Acts 19: 33; 24: 10; 25: 8; 26: 1, 2, 24). (6) The juridical role of the ἄγγελοι is recognized here, as elsewhere in the New Testament (Lk. 12: 8f.; cf. Mt. 16: 27; 25: 31; I Tim. 5: 21; Rev. 14: 10). (7) Luke appends here his material on 'the sin against the Holy Spirit' which appears in a different context in Mark and Matthew (Lk. 12: 10; cf. Mk 3: 28–30; Mt. 12: 31–2). Luke sees how apposite this material is to the theme of confession and denial of Christ: accusing witnesses against the Son of Man may be forgiven, but

...it would be blasphemy against the Holy Spirit if believers were brought before the authorities to testify to Christ and then, rejecting the Spirit's help, denied their Lord. Therefore to drive away the Holy Spirit is indeed the unforgivable sin, worse even than blasphemy against the Son of Man by unbelievers, for whom after all there is some excuse.[2]

These special characteristics of the Lukan account, however, do not destroy or nullify the common elements in Lk. 12: 8f. and Mt. 10: 32f. In both Matthew and Luke 'the scene of the judgment will be heaven,...God will be the judge,...and Jesus as the Son of man will be the chief *witness* for men (or "the advocate of the faithful before God")'.[3] In other words, the setting is clearly eschatological, as in Mt. 7: 22f., where the

[1] A. Plummer, *Gospel according to St. Luke*, III (Edinburgh, 1896), 321.
[2] Browning, *op. cit.*, p. 119.
[3] A. M. Hunter, *The Work and Words of Jesus* (London, 1950), p. 106; cf. J. A. T. Robinson, *Twelve New Testament Studies* (London, 1962), p. 81.

Lord declares ἐν τῇ ἡμέρᾳ, 'I never knew you'. The solemn importance of 'confessing' or 'denying' Christ is indicated by the frequent use of these verbs in the New Testament as technical terms 'in the vocabulary of persecution, martyrdom, apostasy and infidelity'.[1]

After the summons to fearless confession (Lk. 12: 2–12), Luke mentions a case which is presented to Christ for arbitration (Lk. 12: 13–15). While Christ on principle refuses to act as umpire or arbitrator in this dispute, the passage is noteworthy because of its reference to the κριτής or δικαστής (there is an apparent allusion to Ex. 2: 14 which would account for the textual variant; cf. Acts 7: 27, 35) who is to decide the case. This legal personage is also termed a μεριστής – an unusual word not found elsewhere in the Greek Bible. Later the chapter speaks of the dissension the coming of Christ gives rise to, even in the family circle (διαμερισμός, 12: 51; διαμερίζειν, 12: 52f.). Matthew similarly draws attention to the conflict theme, making the reference to Micah 7: 6 even more explicit by adding: 'and a man's foes will be those of his own household' (Mt. 10: 35f.).

The next passage calling for treatment is Mk 13: 9–13, where the themes of testimony and confession are further developed, this time in an eschatological setting. Here, as in the parallel passages, the witness is definitely given in a hostile context – a point emphasized by the repeated Synoptic use of: (1) καὶ ἔσεσθε μισούμενοι ὑπὸ πάντων διὰ τὸ ὄνομά μου (Mk 13: 13; Lk. 21: 17; Mt. 24: 9); (2) συναγωγαί and συνέδρια (Mk 13: 9; Mt. 10: 17; Lk. 21: 12; cf. 12: 11) – significant in view of the fact that the elders of the synagogue 'held courts, and could sentence to excommunication ([Lk.] vi.22; Jn. ix.22; xii.42; xvi.2), or scourging (Mt. x.17)';[2] (3) παραδιδόναι meaning 'to hand over into the custody of' the police or courts (Mk 13: 9, 11, 12; Lk. 21: 12, 16; Mt. 10: 17, 19; 24: 10); (4) ἐπί with persons in the context of lawsuits (Mk 13: 9; Lk. 21: 12; Mt. 10: 18) and (5) the use of close relatives as accusing witnesses at the trials of Christians (Mk 13: 12; Mt. 10: 21; Lk. 21: 16). This witness is offered in the face of active persecution (note the use of δαρήσεσθε in Mk 13: 9 and ἄγωσιν ὑμᾶς in 13: 11, μαστιγώ-

---

[1] G. W. H. Lampe, 'St. Peter's denial', *BJRL*, 55 (1973), 353f.
[2] Plummer, *St. Luke*, p. 321. Cf. B. T. D. Smith, *The Gospel according to St. Matthew* (Cambridge, 1927), p. 122.

σουσιν ὑμᾶς in Mt. 10: 17, and ἐπιβαλοῦσιν ἐφ' ὑμᾶς τὰς χεῖρας αὐτῶν καὶ διώξουσιν in Lk. 21: 12) and for Christ's sake (ἕνεκεν ἐμοῦ, Mk 13: 9; Mt. 10: 18; cf. Lk. 21: 12). It may lead to imprisonment (φύλακες are mentioned in Lk. 21: 12).

Now according to Strathmann the phrase εἰς μαρτύριον αὐτοῖς in Mk 13: 9, as in Mt. 10: 18 and 24: 14, means incriminating evidence against them at the Last Judgment rather than a witness to them so that they may believe.[1] But, as Cranfield has said:

it is surely better to allow for the various ideas which are involved in the witness-imagery rather than to insist on choosing between 'witness to' and 'evidence against'. We suggest that the meaning here is threefold: first, that the disciples' profession of Christ before the tribunals of governors and kings will be a piece of evidence for the truth of the gospel...; secondly, it will be a piece of evidence for the truth of the gospel offered to their prosecutors (αὐτοῖς probably including both the governors and kings, who otherwise might not have heard the gospel, and also the disciples' Jewish persecutors); and thirdly, if the evidence for the truth of the gospel which this courageous profession of Christ's name presents is not accepted by the persecutors and judges, then at the final judgment it will be evidence against them.[2]

They will be without excuse, having been recipients of such evidence.

In Mark 13: 9–13 and its parallels, then, as in the Fourth Gospel and the Book of Revelation, witness is very much a live metaphor. Hauled into court by their opponents (οἱ ἀντικεί-μενοι, Lk. 21: 15), Christians will be told what to say 'in that hour' by the Holy Spirit (Mk 13: 11; Mt. 10: 19f.): 'I will give you a mouth' (Lk. 21: 15; cf. Acts 6: 10). As the witnesses in the Old Testament 'stand' before their judges and opponents, so the disciples of Jesus will 'stand' before kings, councils and governors (Mk 13: 9; cf. Deut. 19: 16; Psa. 109: 6; Zech. 3: 1). These occasions will offer unprecedented opportunities for bearing 'testimony before them'; this point is specially under-scored in the Lukan parallel: being brought into court 'will give you an opportunity to testify' (ἀποβήσεται ὑμῖν εἰς

[1] H. Strathmann, 'Μάρτυς', TDNT, IV, 503 and TWNT, IV, 509, followed by J. M. Boice, Witness and Revelation in the Gospel of John (Exeter, 1970), p. 168, n. 3.
[2] Cranfield, Saint Mark, pp. 397–8.

μαρτύριον, Lk. 21: 13). In the Matthean account a universal note is sounded – the gospel is to be proclaimed throughout the whole world εἰς μαρτύριον πᾶσιν τοῖς ἔθνεσιν (Mt. 24: 14).

Under these perilous circumstances Luke sees Christ encouraging his witnesses by saying: 'Settle it therefore in your minds, not to meditate beforehand how to answer; for I will give you a mouth and wisdom, which none of your adversaries will be able to withstand or contradict' (Lk. 21: 14f.). The passage is significant on two counts. In the first place, it contains the verb ἀπολογεῖσθαι, whose importance in juridical contexts in Luke–Acts has already been noted. In the second place, it employs in a forensic context the noun ὁ ἀντικείμενος, which is used in the LXX of 'the accuser' in Zech. 3: 1 (Hebrew, haśśāṭān) and in the New Testament of the antichrist (II Thess. 2: 4) and, possibly, of Satan (I Tim. 5: 14f.; cf. Rev. 12: 9–10).

Christians were not to fear these times of persecution, for the Spirit would give them the wisdom and courage needed to bear witness to their faith (cf. Mt. 10: 19f.; Acts 6: 10). Hated by all men for the sake of the Name (Mk 13: 13; Lk. 21: 17; Mt. 10: 22; cf. Jn 15: 18–19), they would often be condemned in earthly lawcourts, but in the heavenly lawcourt the Son of Man would acknowledge them and reverse the unjust judgments pronounced against them by their earthly judges (Mt. 10: 32; Lk. 12: 8f.). Their main concern was to watch and be faithful, in order that they might stand before the Son of Man (Lk. 21: 36; cf. Psa. 1: 5; Mal. 3: 2; Mk 13: 33–7).

These passages provide real parallels to the Book of Acts, where Christians are actually 'dragged' before the local rulers (17: 6) and where the dying Stephen sees the Son of Man standing as a vindicating witness at the right hand of God (7: 55–6). They also illustrate how the Son of Man may serve in a juridical role as a witness *and* judge – a point previously observed in the story of Susanna and in the Old Testament use of controversy (e.g., Mic. 6: 1f.; Mal. 3: 5).

But how can the Son of Man act in a juridical capacity in view of his own condemnation in an earthly lawcourt? After all, had he not been accused by the leaders of his nation and delivered to the Roman procurator as a criminal deserving death (κατηγορεῖν is used in Mk 15: 3f.; Mt. 27: 12; Lk. 23:

2, 10, 14)? This problem is faced, for Mark tells his readers that Jesus himself had plainly predicted the Son of Man's rejection and condemnation by the Jewish leaders (Mk 8: 31; 9: 31; and esp. 10: 33, where κατακρίνειν is used; cf. Mt. 16: 21; 20: 18; Lk. 9: 22; 17: 25; 18: 31–3): παρρησίᾳ τὸν λόγον ἐλάλει (Mk 8: 32).

Moreover, the Gospels describe Christ's condemnation in considerable detail.[1] He is arrested as a λῃστής (Mk 14: 48; Mt. 26: 55; Lk. 22: 52, cf. Lk. 23: 14, ὡς ἀποστρέφοντα τὸν λαόν) and 'brought before' Caiaphas the high priest (ἀπάγειν πρός in Mk 14: 53 and Mt. 26: 57). He is condemned by the chief priests, scribes and elders meeting in council (Mk 14: 53, 55, 64 pars.); they conclude: ἔνοχος θανάτου ἐστίν (Mt. 26: 66). Significantly, no mention is made of the witnesses for the defence. Instead the high priest and the whole council keep looking for testimony κατὰ τοῦ Ἰησοῦ (Mk 14: 55; Mt. 26: 59), for the Jewish leaders had previously decided that Jesus must be put to death (Mk 14: 1; Mt. 26: 4; Lk. 22: 2; cf. Jn 11: 47–53). An attempt is made to prosecute Jesus – this explains the presence of both καταμαρτυρεῖν (Mk. 14: 60; Mt. 26: 62; 27: 13) and ψευδομαρτυρεῖν (Mk 14: 56–7), and the use of ἀνίστημι to describe the activity of an accuser in court (Mk 14: 57; cf. Mt. 12: 41; Lk. 11: 32). Every effort is made to press the accusation that Jesus had said: 'I will destroy this temple that is made with hands, and in three days I will build another, not made with hands' (Mk 14: 58; cf. Mt. 26: 61; Jn. 2: 19). Matthew obviously thinks that Jesus is innocent (cf. Mt. 27: 2, αἷμα ἀθῷον), and regards the testimony against him as false, for he calls it ψευδομαρτυρία (Mt. 26: 59) and the witnesses ψευδομάρτυρες (Mt. 26: 60; cf. Aristotle, Art of Rhetoric, i.xv; Baba Bathra 31b). Mark twice calls attention to the fact that the μαρτυρία of the witnesses did not agree (Mk 14: 56, 59); according to Jewish criminal procedure, this would mean that their evidence was inadmissible, for the very closest agreement was necessary in such cases (Susanna 54, 58, 61; cf. Tosef. San. v.5b; Pes. 12b). Mark and Matthew both stress the role of the false witnesses, who charge Jesus with saying that he would

---

[1] On the historicity of the trial see P. Winter, On the Trial of Jesus (Berlin, 1961), and A. D. Sherwin-White, Roman Society and Roman Law in the New Testament (Oxford, 1963), pp. 24–47.

destroy the temple and build it in three days (Mk 14: 57f.; Mt. 26: 6of.; cf. Jn 2: 19). Similarly both Evangelists record the taunt of the passers-by, which echoes the accusation of the false witnesses (Mk 15: 29; Mt. 27: 40).

Why, it may be asked, does Luke part company with the other Synoptists at this point and omit explicit reference to the false witnesses (though they are acknowledged rather obliquely in 22: 71)? P. A. Blair has suggested a possible explanation:

Luke omits the false witnesses in the Gospel but introduces them in Acts [See Acts 6: 11, which is expanded in 6: 13–14, where the parallel with Jesus is made explicit], not simply to condemn Stephen for his own assertions, but to condemn him as quoting Jesus' declaration against the Temple and the Law. Surely this is not accidental. I suggest that this is the first implicit declaration by Luke of the understanding of Stephen's death and the expansion recorded in Acts viii. Looking back from beyond Pentecost, after the Church had extended throughout the world, Luke sees that Jesus' words quoted by false witnesses were not substantiated till later – he therefore holds over this part of the narrative because the words were to be re-enacted and fulfilled in Stephen's trial and its sequel. For this, I suggest, is the significance of Acts vii and viii: Luke sees in them the working out of the prophecy which Jesus Himself made, and so the realizing of what was implicit in His death from the start.[1]

Let us return to the trial before Caiaphas. Failing to secure unanimous testimony on the accusation, the high priest 'rises', following the custom of the Old Testament controversy (Isa. 3: 13; Ezek. 44: 24 (R.V.); Psa. 76: 9; 82: 8). He proceeds to question Jesus, suggesting that the nature of the testimony against him demands a reply (Mk 14: 60; Mt. 26: 62). When Jesus remains silent and makes no reply (ἀπεκρίνατο has the force of 'reply in a court of law' in Mk 14: 61; Mt. 27: 12; Lk. 23: 9), the high priest tries to establish the charge of blasphemy by asking: 'Are you the Christ, the Son of the Blessed?' (Mk 14: 61; cf. Lk. 22: 70). Matthew tells us that Caiaphas adjures Jesus, that is, 'charges him under oath' (ἐξορκίζω Mt. 26: 63; cf. I Sam. 14: 24–8; I Kgs 22: 16; II Chron. 18: 15; Acts 19: 13; on the use of the Divine Name to compel an unwilling witness, see Mishnah Shebuoth IV). Jesus boldly replies: 'I am

[1] P. A. Blair, 'The death of Stephen', *TB*, 2 (1956–7), 3.

[ἐγώ εἰμι appears in a forensic setting here as it frequently does in both Isaiah 40–55 and the Fourth Gospel]; and you will see the Son of man sitting at the right hand of Power, and coming with the clouds of heaven' (Mk 14: 62; cf. Mt. 26: 64; Lk. 22: 69). There is obviously here

a tacit identification of the Prisoner with the expected Son of man, whom one day every eye shall see as both Judge and Saviour, and the thought may be similar to that of the Fourth Gospel, where it is made clear that, if the Lord stands before judges, whether the Sanhedrin or Pilate, yet in reality it is He who is judge, not they.[1]

Certainly Caiaphas is quick to grasp the significance of Christ's quotation of Psa. 110: 1 and Dan. 7: 13. He declares the affirmation blasphemous and liable to the death penalty, Jesus' own testimony having made further witnesses unnecessary (Mk 14: 63; Mt. 26: 65). In Luke Christ's opponents emphatically insist that they have heard incriminating evidence ἀπὸ τοῦ στόματος αὐτοῦ (Lk. 22: 71; cf. Job 15: 6; Lk. 19: 22).

The charge of blasphemy is quite striking. If the trial is consciously thought of by Mark as also taking place *sub specie aeternitatis*, in the heavenly court, this is the precise point at which the human judges are judged, or threatened with divine judgment, the decisive point at which the tables are turned. The apparent 'blasphemy' is a pivotal point, and really indicates the divine condemnation of the judges. Later Jesus appears before Pilate sitting on his βῆμα (Mt. 27: 19), is sentenced to die between two insurrectionists, and the αἰτία is placed on the superscription over his cross (Mk 15: 26; Mt. 27: 37). Luke stresses the vehemence of the chief priests and the scribes on this occasion (εὐτόνως, Lk. 23: 10; cf. Acts 18: 28).

It is abundantly clear that the Synoptic accounts of the trial of Jesus have a forensic ring about them. All three accounts mention the denial of Peter, which is described in juridical terms by the use of ἀρνεῖσθαι (Mk 14: 68–71 pars.) and ἀπαρνεῖσθαι (Mk 14: 30f., 72 pars.). Matthew notes the public nature of Peter's betrayal (ἠρνήσατο ἔμπροσθεν πάντων, Mt. 26: 70), in this way linking the denial with the sayings of Jesus concerning

[1] R. H. Lightfoot, *The Gospel Message of St. Mark* (Oxford, 1949), p. 54. Cf. J. A. Kleist, 'The two false witnesses (Mk. 14: 55ff.)', *CBQ*, 9 (1947), 321–3.

confession and denial in time of persecution, which we find in
the Q tradition (Mt. 10: 32–3; Lk. 12: 8–9).[1] Both Mark and
Matthew call attention to Peter's oaths (ἀναθεματίзειν καὶ
ὀμνύναι, Mk 14: 71; ἠρνήσατο μετὰ ὅρκου, Mt. 26: 72; κατα-
θεματίзειν καὶ ὀμνύνειν, Mt. 26: 74). Again, all three accounts
insist that the real cause of the condemnation and death of Jesus
was his claim to be the Messiah (Mk 14: 62f.; Mt. 26: 64f.; Lk.
22: 69f.). It was this claim which made the evidence of the
witnesses unnecessary.

In both Matthew and Mark μάρτυς has its forensic meaning
of 'a witness at a trial who gives evidence'. Both Gospels stress
the falsity of the witness: Mark by his repeated use of ἐψευδομαρτύρουν (Mk 15: 56, 57), Matthew by noting the ψευδο-
μαρτυρίαν of the ψευδομαρτύρων (Mt. 26: 59, 60). Mark draws
attention to the lack of agreement of the witnesses. Matthew,
on the other hand, finds no difficulty in admitting that there
was a charge on which the two witnesses agreed, and for him
this is the turning point in the trial (Mt. 26: 60f.). Nevertheless,
in Matthew's view the fact that the evidence of two witnesses
might be self-consistent did not necessarily mean that it was
true. Despite the emphatic prohibition of false witness (Mt.
19: 18; cf. Ex. 20: 16; Deut. 5: 20; Prov. 24: 28), there was
always the real possibility of malicious witness (cf. Psa. 27:
12; 35: 11; and esp. Mt. 15: 19, ἐκ τῆς καρδίας ἐξέρχεται...
ψευδομαρτυρίαι). In this case Matthew patently thinks that
the false witnesses were guilty of perjury and complicity in
a heinous crime against the true 'King of the Jews' (Mt. 27:
37).

One further point may be mentioned. All three accounts
speak of the Son of Man's sitting at the right hand of power, and
in Mark and Matthew the juridical note is strengthened by
reference to 'the clouds of heaven' – a feature which was also
observed in Dan. 7: 13. Condemned by his earthly judges,
Christ will be fully vindicated, and as υἱὸς τοῦ ἀνθρώπου
will judge Caiaphas and company (cf. Dan. 7: 13, where 'one
like a son of man' is similarly mentioned in connection with
the theme of vindication).[2] To borrow words from John's

[1] Lampe, 'St. Peter's denial', 355.
[2] Cf. C. F. D. Moule, *The Phenomenon of the New Testament* (London, 1967),
pp. 87–8.

Gospel which are relevant here, God 'has given him authority to execute judgment, because he is Son of Man' (Jn 5: 27).

Before leaving Mark's Gospel a few observations should be made on chapter 16. Without attempting to justify the longer ending of Mark, one may note several points raised there which are of interest to this investigation and which have parallels either in the other Gospels or elsewhere in the New Testament. Thus, in the textually suspect Markan *Evangelienschlusse* reference is made to Christ's appearances to Mary Magdalene (Mk 16: 9–11; cf. Jn 20: 14–18) and to the two walking in the country (Mk 16: 12, probably on the road to Emmaus, cf. Lk. 24: 13–35). While Mary and the two walkers give eye-witness reports of their contact with the risen Christ, they are not described as μάρτυρες or αὐτόπται, and their evidence does not convince their friends (Mk 16: 11–12; cf. Lk. 24: 10–11). However, the evidence presented is considered satisfactory, for when the risen Lord appears to the eleven themselves, he rebukes them for their unbelief and hardness of heart (Mk 16: 14; cf. Lk. 24: 38). The longer ending closes with a concise statement of the church's missionary task (Mk 16: 16ff.; cf. Mt. 28: 18–20; Lk. 24: 46–9; Jn 20: 21), of the striking ascension and exaltation of Jesus (Mk 16: 19; cf. Acts 1: 6–11) and of the early church's obedience to its divine commission: 'And they went forth and preached everywhere, while the Lord worked with them and confirmed the message by the signs that attended it. Amen' (Mk 16: 20). While this passage prefers to speak of preaching rather than witnessing, it is significant that the divine corroboration through signs fits precisely the concept of witness suggested in Hebrews 2: 3–4 and developed more fully in the Book of Acts.

Some attention must now be given to those passages in Matthew and Luke which have not been dealt with in considering Mark's use of the idea of witness. Mt. 5: 25f. certainly presupposes a forensic situation: 'Make friends quickly with your accuser, while you are going with him to court, lest your accuser (ὁ ἀντίδικος) hand you over to the judge, and the judge (ὁ κριτής) to the guard (ὁ ὑπηρέτης), and you be put in prison; truly, I say to you, you will never get out till you have paid the last penny.' The Lukan parallel speaks of appearing 'before the magistrate' (ἐπ' ἄρχοντα), employs the verb ἀπαλλάσσεσ-θαι in a legal sense meaning 'to be quit of' and uses the unusual word πράκτωρ to refer to the court officer who is under orders from the judge and in charge of the debtor's prison (Lk. 12: 58f.). It also uses the technical terms ἀντίδικος and κριτής and talks of 'dragging' the accused away by force before the judge (μήποτε κατασύρη σε πρὸς τὸν κριτήν). Similarly, note the pre-ceding verses in Matthew, which speak of those who will be liable (ἔνοχος) before the appropriate legal body, whether that be the local court, the Sanhedrin or the final judgment of God (Mt. 5: 21–2). All this suggests the picture of a formal court with regular officials. Jesus' contemporaries apparently lived under the real threat that someone might take them to court to sue them (τῷ θέλοντί σοι κριθῆναι καὶ τὸν χιτῶνά σου λαβεῖν, Mt. 5: 40), so he advised them to steer clear of lawsuits if at all possible; in this respect, as in so many other matters, the teaching of Jesus is echoed in the apostolic counsel of St Paul (I Cor. 6: 1–7).

Similarly, Mt. 12: 36–7 suggests a forensic situation. An eschatological 'day of judgment' is in view when men must give an 'account' (note the same use of ἐν ἡμέρᾳ κρίσεως in Mt. 10: 15 and 11: 22, 24). The evidence presented will prove sufficient to secure either their vindication or condemnation – a fact indicated by the use of the contrasting verbs δικαιοῦν and καταδικάζειν. No witnesses are called, for the evidence will be supplied by their own 'words' (cf. Job 15: 6; Lk. 19: 22; 22: 71). Elsewhere, Matthew makes it clear that a verbal profession of faith which is unaccompanied by moral transformation ex-pressed in good works will be judged insufficient; on the day of judgment the κύριος will bluntly declare: 'I never knew you' (ὁμολογήσω, Mt. 7: 22f.).

The theme of witness is implied in the Beelzebul controversy, though the word itself is not used (Mk 3: 19b–30; Lk. 11: 14–23; Mt. 12: 22–32). After showing the absurd character of the charge laid against him, Christ casts the accusation back on his Jewish opponents: 'And if I cast out demons by Beelzebul, by whom do your sons cast them out? Therefore they shall be your judges' (Lk. 11: 19; Mt. 12: 27). Here the background is definitely one of controversy – a controversy between Jesus and the Pharisees somewhat comparable to the debates in the first half of the Fourth Gospel though far less developed.[1] In this controversy Jesus clearly makes the co-religionists of the Pharisees their accusers. Here, as in the Old Testament lawsuit, the 'judges' can serve as accusing witnesses; hence the use of κριταί is quite natural and appropriate in Lk. 11: 19 and Mt. 12: 27.

The idea of witness is likewise given a striking application in Mt. 12: 41f. and Lk. 11: 31f., where the men of Nineveh and the Queen of the South are spoken of as 'condemning this generation' (cf. Jon. 3: 5; I Kgs 10: 1–10). As in Heb. 11: 7, the verb κατακρίνειν here does not imply that the persons concerned will occupy a place on the bench, but rather that their evidence will secure a conviction (cf. I Jn 3: 20f., where the heart can function as an accuser: ἐὰν καταγινώσκῃ ἡμῶν ἡ καρδία).[2] After the fashion of accusing witnesses in the Old Testament lawsuit, they will 'rise' to give their evidence against 'an evil and adulterous generation' on the day of judgment; this is clear from the use of ἀνίστασθαι and ἐγείρεσθαι with μετά τινος, meaning 'to appear in court against someone' (cf. ḳûm 'im).[3] These passages are to be compared both with John's Gospel, where Moses is mentioned as an accusing witness (Jn 5: 45ff.), and with The Shepherd of Hermas, where Rhoda acts as a heavenly accuser ἵνα σοῦ τὰς ἁμαρτίας ἐλέγξω πρὸς τὸν κύριον (vision, i.i.5). Note also the stubborn Jewish insistence on a σημεῖον without heeding the God-given 'sign of Jonah' (Mt. 12: 38–40; Lk. 11: 29–30; cf. I Cor. 1: 22). The Son of Man proves indeed to be 'a sign that is debated about', amply fulfilling Simeon's prophecy (σημεῖον ἀντιλεγόμενον, Lk. 2: 34).

The interesting phraseology of Mt. 19: 28 should be cited in passing (cf. Dan. 7: 9–10). The terms 'Son of Man', 'thrones', 'sitting' and 'judging' all point to a celestial court 'in the new world'. While similar eschatological pericopes often speak of the place of the angels in the last judgment (e.g., Mt. 16: 27; 25: 31), this passage stresses the forensic role of the apostles

[1] On the use of 'controversy dialogues' in the Synoptics see R. Bultmann, *The History of the Synoptic Tradition* (Oxford, 1963), pp. 39ff.

[2] G. B. Caird, *A Commentary on the Revelation of St. John* (London, 1966), p. 241.

[3] J. Jeremias, *Jesus' Promise to the Nations* (London, 1958), p. 50, n. 2.

vis-à-vis Israel (ἐπὶ δώδεκα θρόνους κρίνοντες τὰς δώδεκα φυλὰς τοῦ Ἰσραήλ; cf. Lk. 22: 30).

In Mt. 18: 15–17 witnesses appear in connection with a dispute between two members of the Christian community. When such a dispute occurs, a three-fold procedure is suggested to the aggrieved party: (1) Go to the offender alone, and try to reason with him or 'talk him round' after the fashion of the Old Testament lawsuit (Mt. 18: 15; cf. Job 40: 2; Isa. 43: 9; Jn 16: 8). (2) If this measure fails, take one or two with you, 'that every word may be confirmed by the evidence of two or three witnesses', a step prompted by Deut. 19: 15.[1] (3) If the additional people fail to convince the offender of his sin, they will serve as witnesses when the matter is brought before the whole assembly and treated after the manner of the Old Testament lawsuit. Finally, 'if he refuses to listen even to the church', he is to be treated as an outsider (Mt. 18: 17). A similar procedure for settling disputes was adopted by the Qumran community (cf. 1QS v.24 – vi.1 and CD ix.16 – x.3). According to Strack–Billerbeck, the duty of bringing an erring brother to the right way by reproof (ἐλέγχειν = hôkîaḥ) was known to the synagogue (cf. Lev. 19: 17), though no such definite instructions had been developed as Mt. 18: 15–17.[2] Both Paul and Luke show a similar recognition of this obligation (Gal. 6: 1; Lk. 17: 3).

A juridical motif is apparent in Matthew's version of the parable of the wicked husbandmen (Mt. 21: 33–46). Thus Mt. 21: 41 adds the words λέγουσιν αὐτῷ which are absent from the parallel passages (Mk 12: 9; Lk. 20: 15). The point to notice is that Matthew's parable resembles the juridical parables of the Old Testament (e.g., II Sam. 12: 1–14; 14: 1–20); in each case the party concerned is made to pronounce sentence against himself (Mt. 21: 41; II Sam. 12: 5–6; 14: 11). Matthew evidently believed that the hypothetical court case was effective, for by it the chief priests and the Pharisees perceived that Jesus 'was speaking about them' (Mt. 21: 45; cf. Mk 12: 12; Lk. 20: 19).

[1] This principle of evidence has also been advanced as a possible explanation of Matthew's use of *two* blind men in Mt. 20: 30. Cf. Z. C. Hodges, 'The two blind men at Jericho', *BS*, 122 (1965), 319–30.
[2] Strack–Billerbeck, I, 787–9.

Mt. 23: 29–36 and Lk. 11: 47–51 also invite examination. Here Jesus warns his unbelieving contemporaries, the ὄφεις γεννήματα ἐχιδνῶν (Mt. 23: 33; cf. 12: 34) of 'this generation', that unless they dissociate themselves from the past by an act of national repentance they will be held morally responsible for 'all the righteous blood shed on earth from the blood of innocent Abel to the blood of Zechariah' (Mt. 23: 35; cf. Lk. 11: 50f.). Their history is a history of cumulative guilt, a continual rejection and persecution of God's 'prophets and wise men and scribes' (Mt. 23: 34; cf. Lk. 11: 49) – a theme frequently sounded in the New Testament (Mt. 23: 37; Acts 7: 35, 39, 51–3; I Thess. 2: 15; Heb. 11: 36–8). By priding themselves on their supposed superiority to their fathers, they provide evidence (μαρτυρεῖτε) that they are ethically the 'sons of those who murdered the prophets' (Mt. 23: 30f., cf. Eph. 5: 6, υἱοὶ τῆς ἀπειθείας and Jn 8: 44), where their ancestry is traced to the devil who is described as an ἀνθρωποκτόνος).[1] In this way they serve as witnesses 'against' themselves (the dative ἑαυτοῖς here is *dativus incommodi*), and consent to the deeds of their fathers (Lk. 11: 48; cf. 6: 22f.; 13: 33f.; Mt. 6: 12; 21: 35f.). They provide evidence which will lead to their condemnation and judgment by God. As Duncan Derrett has shown from rabbinical parallels, 'the saying attributed to Jesus, not content with drawing out the *witness* element, insists on the objectionable type of witness, i.e., the silent participator who consents by being a passive spectator. But beyond this, the word *boniym* is made to produce independently the *two* ideas, because the word *nefashot* does not mean so much *tombs* as corpses, i.e., murders!'[2]

The eschatological picture of 'the Last Judgment' in Mt. 25: 31–46 is also thoroughly juridical. As in the Book of Enoch, the 'Son of Man' is the judge who sits on God's throne (Mt. 25: 31; cf. I Enoch 51: 3; 62: 3, 5; 69: 29; Mt. 19: 28). The 'angels' are the court officials who come 'with him', the judgment seat where the judge 'sits' is the 'throne' (Mt. 25: 31; cf. I Kgs 7:

---

[1] The fact that Lk. 11: 48 has 'you build' where Mt. 23: 31 has 'you are the sons of' is to be explained in terms of an Aramaic original which could be read either way. See M. Black, *An Aramaic Approach to the Gospels and Acts* (3rd ed., Oxford, 1967), pp. 12–13.

[2] J. D. M. Derrett, '"You build the tombs of the prophets" (Lk. 11, 47–51, Mt. 23, 29–31)', *StudEv*, IV, 187–93.

7; Job 23: 3),[1] and 'all the nations' are assembled for judgment (Mt. 25: 32; cf. Isa. 41: 1). While the pastoral imagery is not forgotten (hence the terms 'shepherd', 'sheep' and 'goats'; cf. Jer. 23: 1-4, Ezek. 34), the phrase συναγεῖν ἔμπροσθεν seems to imply a 'gathering before' the divine judge, and the verb for 'separate' is similarly used of a process of judgment (ἀφορίζειν, Mt. 25: 32; cf. 13: 49, where it describes the forensic task of the angels at the close of the age). There is no trial as such, but simply the pronouncing of the verdicts on the two classes (εὐλογημένοι, 25: 34ff.; κατηραμένοι, 25: 41ff.). All judgment rests in the hands of the Son of Man (cf. I Enoch 61: 9; 69: 27; Jn 5: 22, 27). Matthew here and in 19:28 describes the Son of Man as the judge at the Last Day while in similar passages he is usually depicted as a witness (Mt. 10: 32f.; Mk 8: 38; Lk. 9: 26; 12: 8f.). This difference is not the problem that Jeremias has made it out to be,[2] for in the Old Testament lawsuit the same person could serve as both witness *and* judge (e.g., Ruth 4: 1-11); the same principle is also observed in the New Testament (e.g., Jn 5: 30f.; 8: 18). Luke obviously is no more worried about this ambivalence than Matthew, for he sees the Son of Man 'standing' not only as a witness (Acts 7: 56) but also as a judge (Lk. 21: 36).

Another interesting passage is found in Luke 10. When the disciples return from their mission, rejoicing that even the demons are subject to them, Jesus tells them: 'I saw Satan fall like lightning from heaven' (Lk. 10: 18). G. B. Caird has brought out the juridical significance of this passage:

The vision is prophetic: the exorcisms of Jesus and his disciples were not themselves the decisive victory over Satan, but only tokens of a victory to be won through the Cross. Up to this point, it should be noted, Satan is still in heaven. He owes his place there partly to his original office of prosecuting counsel in the divine lawcourt (Job 1, Zech. 3: 1-5), the ruthless accuser who misrepresents God's purpose by pressing the claims of his justice to the complete exclusion of his mercy; partly to the commonly accepted idea that all earthly

[1] J. A. T. Robinson, *Twelve New Testament Studies* (London, 1962), p. 91, cites as a parallel The Assumption of Moses 10: 3, where God rises to judgment from his *royal* throne.

[2] J. Jeremias, *The Parables of Jesus* (6th ed., London and New York, 1963), pp. 206-8.

realities and events have their counterpart in heaven, so that even the sum total of earthly evil must have its heavenly representative (cf. Heb. 9: 23...). The ejection of Satan means that God's redemptive mercy has delivered men both from the sentence that hung over them and from the guilt and power of sin that held them captive (Rev. 12: 7–12).[1]

In other words, Luke 10: 18 affords a very illuminating cross-reference to the Johannine concept of witness, where Satan loses his case and is banished from the heavenly lawcourt by the victory of Christ on Calvary (cf. Jn 12: 31; Rev. 12: 8f.).

The parable of the unjust steward employs διαβάλλειν, meaning 'to bring charges against' (Lk. 16: 1). This verb is striking for at least two reasons: (1) it appears nowhere else in the New Testament, and (2) διεβλήθη in Lk. 16: 1 deserves to be compared with the repeated use of ἐβλήθη in the Apocalypse (Rev. 12: 9 twice, 10, 13), where it is used of the ejection of the accuser (ὁ διάβολος) from the heavenly court. Though μάρτυρες are not mentioned in the Lukan passage, presumably the charges are brought by accusing witnesses as in the Old Testament lawsuit.

The story of the rich man and Lazarus also calls for a few remarks (Lk. 16: 19–31), for the tormented man begs Abraham to send a witness to his father's house to 'warn' his brothers (the verb διαμαρτύρεσθαι is used; cf. Neh. 9: 26). The appeal, however, is rejected on the grounds that his brothers already have sufficient testimony provided by the scriptures; they should 'hear' the testimony of 'Moses and the prophets' and be persuaded thereby to repent (Lk. 16: 29, 31; cf. Jn 5: 46f.; Acts 15: 21). Their failure to accept the evidence they have been given makes it clear that no additional evidence will convince them, even if a witness were to rise from the dead.

Lk. 18: 1–8 records the parable of the unjust judge, and is of interest to this study for its use of legal terms. The judge's function here, as frequently in the Old Testament, is not to condemn but to help the aggrieved party to justice (Isa. 1: 17; Psa. 7: 8; 26: 1; 35: 24; 43: 1). In this case it is a widow who needs help against her legal opponent (ὁ ἀντίδικος, Lk. 18: 3; cf. Mt. 5: 25; Lk. 12: 58; I Pet. 5: 8), and, according to the Old Testament, she is entitled to special legal aid (Deut. 24: 17;

___
[1] G. B. Caird, *The Gospel of St. Luke* (London, 1963), p. 143.

27: 19; Isa. 1: 17, 23; Zech. 7: 9f.). Consequently, she cries out for the κριτής to 'vindicate' her (ἐκδικεῖν is used in Lk. 18: 3, 5; cf. Rev. 6: 10; 19:2). Although the judge 'neither fears God nor regards man', he decides to grant her vindication to escape 'her continual coming' (Lk. 18: 5; cf. 11: 5–8, where persistence is also stressed); this accounts for the use of ἐκδίκησις with ποιεῖν in Lk. 18: 7, 8. The argument is an *a fortiori* one. If an unjust judge will grant vindication to a needy case for such a selfish reason, how much more will a loving God, the helper of widows and of all in distress (cf. Psa. 10: 14, 18; 68: 5; 146: 9), 'vindicate his elect, who cry to him day and night' (Lk. 18: 7)? Here, as in the Old Testament controversy, the same person can be both judge and witness (cf. Psa. 50: 6–7; Mic. 1: 2–4; Mal. 3:5; Susanna 45ff.); in Lk. 18: 1–8 the 'judge' is the vindicating witness of the aggrieved party, in contrast to Lk. 11: 19, where the 'judges' are the accusing witnesses. Here then is a vivid use of legal language which recalls the Old Testament controversy. It also sheds light upon the concept of witness in the Book of Revelation, where the cries of the martyrs and their answer are similarly described in juridical terms (Rev. 6: 10; 18: 20; 19: 2).

The Lukan parable of the pounds contains a juridical point which deserves a word of explanation (Lk. 19: 11–27). The unfaithful servant is convicted on his own evidence (ἐκ τοῦ στόματός σου, Lk. 19: 22; cf. ἐκ τοῦ στόματος αὐτοῦ, Lk. 11: 54), just as in the juridical parable in the Old Testament: 'So shall your judgment be; you yourself have decided it' (I Kgs 20: 40; cf. Mt. 12: 37). This theme is present in a number of Old Testament passages which shed light on Lk. 19: 22 (II Sam. 1: 16; Job 9: 20; cf. Susanna 61). To borrow words from the Book of Job, one could say: 'Your own lips testify against you' (Job 15: 6).

Several other passages in Luke's Gospel contain interesting juridical words (e.g. ψευδομαρτυρεῖν in 18: 20, κρίμα in 20: 47; 23: 40; 24: 20; αἴτιον in 23: 4; ἀνακρίνειν in 23: 14; ἐπικρίνειν in 23: 24; and possibly συκοφαντεῖν in 3: 14 (see Plummer, *Luke*, p. 93), but a study of their use does not materially advance one's understanding of the Lukan concept of witness.

Before leaving Luke's Gospel, reference should be made to Simeon's encounter with the infant in the temple (Lk. 2: 25–35). Simeon had been promised that he should 'see' the Lord's

Christ before his death (Lk. 2: 26). This was fulfilled when he had the privilege of actually holding the child in his arms. In the beautiful *Nunc Dimittis* Simeon declares, 'Mine eyes have seen thy salvation' (Lk. 2: 30). In other words, the evidence of the senses enables the Spirit-filled old man to make an inference that the child before him is the long-promised Messiah. Clearly Luke intends Simeon to be understood as both an actual eye-witness of the baby Jesus (like the shepherds, Lk. 2: 8–18), *and* a Christian confessor who acknowledges ἐν τῷ πνεύματι God's action in Christ for man's deliverance (cf. Lk. 2: 20, where the pastoral eye-witnesses return 'glorifying and praising God for all the things that they had seen and heard'). This concept of witness Luke has developed at some length in the Book of Acts, where the double role of the apostles as eye-witnesses and advocates receives special attention.

Finally, one passage at the beginning of Luke's Gospel and another at the end call for special comment. In the Prologue Luke makes it clear that his concept of witness places the strongest possible emphasis upon the historical foundations of the gospel (Lk. 1: 1–4); he is deeply interested in the matter of trustworthiness (*Zuverlässigkeit*, Lk. 1: 3). He is not concerned with myths or speculation, but with facts which took place at a definite point in space and time (Lk. 2: 1–2; 3: 1–2; cf. Thucydides II.2). This concern for established facts leads Luke to insist that the fundamental testimony concerning Christ is given by men who are qualified as αὐτόπται as well as ὑπηρέται (Lk. 1: 2).[1] Similarly Lk. 24: 44–9 makes it clear that the apostles are witnesses in a double sense, as in secular Greek and the Old Testament. Consequently, their testimony concerns not only the reality of historical events which they have seen and heard, but also a conviction as to what these events signify, namely, the saving activity of God in history. This testimony is to be given after they are 'clothed with power from on high' (Lk. 24: 49), and is confirmed by the testimony of the scriptures (γέγραπται, Lk. 24: 46).

---

[1] N. B. Stonehouse, *The Witness of Luke to Christ* (London, 1951), pp. 34ff., and I. H. Marshall, *Luke: Historian and Theologian* (Exeter, 1970), p. 41. K. Stendahl, *The School of Matthew* (Lund, 1954), pp. 32–3, has argued that the ὑπηρέται τοῦ λόγου in Lk. 1: 2 are 'the instructors', and thinks this offers 'a most concrete Sitz im Leben for the gospel material, namely the school'.

THE IDEA OF WITNESS IN THE EPISTLES

The Pauline Epistles

The idea of witness is not prominent in the writings of the Apostle Paul. It is true that he uses it a number of times in the asseveration μάρτυς γάρ μού ἐστιν ὁ θεός or its equivalent (Rom. 1:9; II Cor. 1:23; I Thess. 2:5, 10; Phil. 1:8; cf. I Sam. 12:5; Job 16:19; Cicero, *Topica* xx.77); but in these passages the idea of witness is simply 'Paul's characteristic appeal to God in solemn verification of the veracity of a statement'.[1] It is virtually equivalent to saying, 'God...knows that I do not lie' (II Cor. 11:31; cf. Rom. 9:1; Gal. 1:20). Paul is conscious that he is accountable for what he says and therefore speaks as one who is solemnly κατέναντι θεοῦ (II Cor. 2:17; 12:19; cf. II Cor. 4:2, ἐνώπιον τοῦ θεοῦ). The verb μαρτυρεῖν also appears in Paul (e.g., Rom. 3:21, where it refers to the testimony of the law and the prophets in the scriptures and 10:2, where Paul speaks of his knowledge of the religious condition of the non-Christian Jews). However, the witness element is not dominant in Paul, and no attempt is made to develop it, perhaps because Paul thinks the world has passed beyond the stage of the trial and reached a universal persecution stage (cf. I Cor. 4:9; Rom. 1:18 – 3:20).

The Epistle to the Romans has its share of legal words (e.g., βῆμα, 14:10; κρίνειν in 2:1, 3, 12, 16, 27, etc.; κατακρίνειν in 2:1; 8:3; 14:23; διακαίωσις in 4:25; 5:18; δικαίωμα in 5:16, 18; κρίμα in 2:2, 3; 3:8; 5:16; 13:2; δικαιοκρισία in 2:5; ὑπόδικος in 3:19; ἔνδειξις in 3:25f.; διάκρισις in 14:1; κατάκριμα in 5:16, 18; 8:1; ὁμολογεῖν in 10:9f.; παριστάνειν in 14:10; προαιτιᾶσθαι in 3:9; ἀνταποκρίνεσθαι in 9:20),[2] but these do not always occur in forensic contexts, and even when they do, they contribute little to one's understanding of the New Testament concept of witness. The same is true of the verbs δικαῖουν, δικαιοῦσθαι and their famous noun δικαιοσύνη (used

---

[1] J. M. Boice, *Witness and Revelation in the Gospel of John*, p. 19, and see his useful summary of Paul's use of witness terms on p. 163, n. 3. Cf. G. Richter, *Deutsches Wörterbuch zum Neuen Testament* (Regensburg, 1962), p. 1059.

[2] F. W. Danker, 'Under contract', *Festschrift to Honor F. Wilbur Gingrich*, ed. E. H. Barth and R. E. Cocroft (Leiden, 1972), pp. 91–114, stresses the importance of Paul's legal terminology in Rom. 5:16–21 (e.g. καθιστάναι).

about thirty-three times in Romans). As Jeremias has remarked, 'though the forensic aspect is by no means lacking, the soteriological connotation governs his speech'.[1]

There remain a few passages in Romans which should be considered for the light which they shed upon Paul's use of the idea of witness. The first of these is found in Rom. 2: 14f., where the courtroom imagery is given an unusual twist by reference to the 'conscience' (συνείδησις). Here the conscience is a witness; the same is true in 9: 1 (cf. II Cor. 1: 12). C. K. Barrett comments:

It [the word 'conscience'] implies man's ability to detach himself from himself and to view his character and actions independently. He is thus able to act as a witness for or against himself. His conscience is not so much the bar at which his conduct is tried, as a major witness, who can be called on either side as the case may be... All that Paul says [in Rom. 2: 15] is that conscience bears witness with (συμμαρτυρεῖ) – he does not say with what. It suits his argument if we think of the conscience bearing witness with the divine law whose imprint it is; the clause 'their inward thoughts... excuse them' then describes the operation of conscience. The thoughts enter into debate...; some are for acquittal, some for conviction.[2]

An interesting parallel is found in *Pirkē Aboth* iv. 13. In the Romans passage, however, the verbs ἀπολογεῖσθαι and κατηγορεῖν are used, while in *Pirkē Aboth* the nouns *pāraklîṭ* and *kᵉṭîgôr* are employed.

The conscience of a Christian can be a very accurate witness, for it is capable of being illumined by the Holy Spirit (Rom. 9: 1); here συμμαρτυρεῖν is used again in a forensic context of the witness of the conscience, reminding one of a similar usage in Josephus (*Apion* II 218). In both Rom. 2: 14f. and 9: 1, then, the idea of witness is employed by Paul as a living metaphor and given a striking application with reference to the conscience. In 2: 15 the forensic note, we have already suggested, is strengthened by the use of κατηγορεῖν and ἀπολογεῖσθαι –

[1] J. Jeremias, *The Central Message of the New Testament* (London, 1965), pp. 51–70. Cf. W. T. Connor, 'Is Paul's doctrine of justification forensic?', *RE*, 40 (1943), 48–54.
[2] C. K. Barrett, *The Epistle to the Romans* (London, 1957), p. 53. On the origin and use of συνείδησις see C. A. Pierce, *Conscience in the New Testament* (London, 1955) and W. D. Davies, 'Conscience', *IDB*, 1, 671–76.

verbs which elsewhere in the New Testament are frequently
applied to real courts of law, especially in Acts (Mk 15: 3;
Mt. 27: 12; Lk. 23: 2; Acts 24: 2, 8, 10, 13, 19; 25: 5, 8, 11;
26: 1, 2, 24; Rev. 12: 10).

Rom. 2: 27 also calls for some comment. In its use of
κατακρίνειν it resembles a 'Q' passage which speaks of the
evidence furnished by the Queen of Sheba and the population
of Nineveh (Mt. 12: 41–2; Lk. 11: 31–2). Thus

> when Paul says that Gentiles who keep the law will judge Jews who
> possess the law of Moses but break it, he means that they will provide
> the necessary evidence to refute Jewish claims to superiority (Rom.
> ii. 27). This usage probably goes back to the legal practice of the
> small town in ancient Israel, where disputes were settled before an
> assembly of townsfolk in the gate and every speaker was entitled to
> give his verdict.[1]

A passing reference may also be made to Paul's quotation of
Psa. 51: 4 in Rom. 3: 4, for here again lawcourt language is
used, this time to defend the veracity of God, 'that thou mightest
be vindicated when thou speakest and mightest win the case
when thou *enterest into judgment* (κρίνεσθαι should be taken as
middle voice here, not passive)'.[2] This passage thus recalls the
Old Testament lawsuit which was studied in the earlier part of
this inquiry, and also illumines the use of the verb νικᾶν in Rev.
12: 11, where the victory of the martyr-witnesses is really a
forensic victory, though described largely in military imagery
(cf. Psa. 35: 1–6; Joel 3: 1–4).

In Romans 8 there are several passages which invite attention.
In verse 16 Théo Preiss has argued for the translation 'the
Spirit bears witness *to* our spirit', on the ground that nowhere
else in Paul is the certainty of acceptance with God attributed
to the human spirit.[3] However, as J. K. Parratt has recently
pointed out, 'Most commentators opt for the alternative view,
and see two distinct witnesses to adoption – the human spirit

---

[1] G. B. Caird, *A Commentary on the Revelation of St. John the Divine* (London,
1966), p. 241.

[2] F. F. Bruce, *The Epistle of Paul to the Romans* (London, 1963), p. 96. Cf.
W. F. Moulton and G. Milligan, *The Vocabulary of the Greek New Testament*
(London, 1930), p. 427.

[3] T. Preiss, 'The inner witness of the Holy Spirit', *Int*, 7 (1953), 259–80.

and also the Holy Spirit.'[1] That this is likely is suggested by Paul's recognition elsewhere of the formal principle of multiple witness (II Cor. 13: 1; cf. I Tim. 5: 19) – a point overlooked by Parratt. In other words, in Rom. 8: 16 the reader is reminded that the Holy Spirit bears consentient witness with the Christian's own spirit that he is a child of God (the verb συμμαρτυρεῖν being used again, as in 2: 15 and 9: 1). That is, the Spirit not only acts as a Paraclete to convince the world of the claims of Christ (cf. Jn 16: 8–11), but he also acts as a Paraclete in the inner tribunal of the believer to convince him of his adoption into the family of God.

In Rom. 8: 26, 27 the Spirit's role in relation to the believer is further described, again in juridical terms, by the use of the verbs ὑπερεντυγχάνειν and ἐντυγχάνειν: 'The Spirit himself is pleading on our behalf with sighs too deep for words...because he pleads for the saints' (cf. 11: 2, where ἐντυγχάνειν is used of Elijah's pleading against Israel). This passage is similar to the Paraclete passages of the Fourth Gospel; both describe the Holy Spirit's work by means of lawcourt imagery. It is worth noting that the Epistle to the Hebrews similarly employs ἐντυγχάνειν, but there the reference is to Christ's role as advocate and intercessor (Heb. 7: 25; cf. I Jn 2: 1).

Finally, Rom. 8: 33–5 makes ample use of lawcourt imagery and terminology, as is clear in the New English Bible's rendering of the passage: 'Who will be the accuser of [τίς ἐγκαλέσει κατά] God's chosen ones? It is God who pronounces acquittal [θεὸς ὁ δικαιῶν]: then who can condemn [τίς ὁ κατακρινῶν]? It is Christ – Christ who died, and, more than that, was raised from the dead – who is at God's right hand, and indeed pleads our cause [ἐντυγχάνει ὑπὲρ ἡμῶν].' With no judge to condemn and no witness to accuse, the believer's standing in Christ is assured. Rom. 8: 33–5 merits comparison with I Jn 2: 1, for there too Christ is referred to as a Paraclete who pleads the Christian's cause. A striking illustration of Christ acting in this capacity is provided in the vision of the dying Stephen, who sees the Son of Man standing as an advocate at the right hand of God to confess his faithful witness (Acts 7: 56–7; cf. Mt. 10: 32f.; Rev. 3: 5).

[1] J. K. Parratt, 'The witness of the Holy Spirit', EQ, 41 (1969), 166. Cf. the Westminster Confession XVIII.2.

In Rom. 10: 9–10 we see the importance Paul attributes to 'confession' of Christ. This passage presents both faith and confession as essential for justification and salvation. The witness's confession is the primary one: 'Jesus is Lord' (cf. Phil. 2: 11). Elsewhere in Romans Paul speaks of confession in the context of the last judgment (Rom. 14: 10–12, quoting Isa. 45: 23), and in this respect he seems to echo the teaching of Jesus (Lk. 12: 8f.; Mt. 10: 32f.).

A few passages in I Corinthians call for brief comment. In I Cor. 1: 6 and also in I Cor. 2: 1, if μαρτύριον is the correct reading, Paul uses τὸ μαρτύριον to refer to 'the message' concerning Christ or God (both genitives are objective). However, as R. E. Brown has suggested, there are several reasons for accepting μυστήριον as the more probable reading in I Cor. 2: 1; for instance, from 'the point of usage, martyrion is not used with "God" elsewhere; and the New Testament usually says "for a witness of or against"'.[1] I Cor. 1: 20 speaks of a 'disputant' or 'debater' in its use of the hapax legomenon συζητητής, but there is no definite reference to the lawcourt here either. In I Cor. 9: 3 ἀνακρίνειν appears in a juridical sense; Paul is being examined, and must make his ἀπολογία. Elsewhere Paul occasionally uses legal words (e.g., κρίμα and κατακρίνειν in 11: 29, 32), sometimes, as Dieter Kemmler has shown, in contexts involving judgment (e.g., ἔλεγχειν and ἀνακρίνειν in 14: 24).[2] In chapter 15 the apostle refers to ψευδομάρτυρες τοῦ θεοῦ in drawing the consequences if there is no resurrection of the dead (15: 15). Since this passage has already been considered in dealing with the witness terminology of the New Testament, it is not necessary to discuss it again here. Suffice it to say that the passage reflects the Old Testament abhorrence of false witnesses (Ex. 20: 16; cf. Philo, Dec. 138–41), and underscores the almost juridical solemnity (ἐμαρτυρήσαμεν κατὰ τοῦ θεοῦ, 15: 15) with which Paul insists upon the resurrection of Christ as the foundation of Christian faith. This passage is to be compared with others where ψευδαπόστολοι are castigated (II Cor. 11: 13) and Paul's sincerity and truthfulness insisted upon (Rom. 9: 1; II Cor. 2: 17; 11: 10, 31; 12: 19).

[1] R. E. Brown, 'The Semitic background of the New Testament: Mysterion', Bib, 39 (1958), 444f.

[2] Kemmler, 'An inquiry into faith and human reason', pp. 181–2.

Before leaving I Corinthians, it is appropriate that we turn to chapter 6, where Paul is definitely concerned to discourage Christians from going before pagan courts to settle their disputes (I Cor. 6: 1–7). This passage is interesting on several counts. (1) It makes ample use of juridical terms, including nouns such as κρίμα and κριτήριον, and verbs such as κρίνειν, κρίνεσθαι, διακρίνειν and καθίζειν (here 'appoint as judge'). (2) It refers to 'a wise man' – 'a technical term for a judge in the Hebrew courts'.[1] Just as the Jewish elders arbitrated civil disputes in their community, so Paul thought the leaders of the church should resolve civil disputes within the Christian community. Here as in the Old Testament concept of justice in the gate, 'to judge' means 'to arbitrate'. This is the function of the 'wise man'. (3) While this passage makes no direct mention of the use of witnesses, it does afford a partial parallel to Mt. 18: 15–17; in both cases there is a concern to solve disputes within the Christian community by means of established legal procedures. (4) If F. W. Green is right in taking the 'judge not' saying of Mt. 7: 1 as 'a direct prohibition to Christians to use the lawcourts either against one another or against enemies', then 'Paul's stern rebuke of the Corinthians for this kind of thing would, as so often, be an echo of the words of Jesus (I Cor. 6: 1).'[2] (5) Souter is probably right in taking πρᾶγμα in I Cor. 6: 1 to mean *causa*, that is, 'a ground for a lawsuit against someone'.[3] This makes excellent sense, as the German version of the Jerusalem Bible shows in its rendering *Rechtsstreit*.

II Corinthians also employs legal words occasionally. In II Cor. 1: 9 Paul uses the phrase ἀπόκριμα τοῦ θανάτου, which is usually taken to mean 'sentence of death' (AV, RVmg., RSV, NEB). However, secular parallels recently adduced by Dr Colin Hemer of Cambridge strongly suggest that the metaphor is not judicial: '"Verdict" may perhaps be the best verbal rendering of ἀπόκριμα, provided that it is given no forensic connotation.'[4]

[1] M. Dods, 'St. Paul on going to law', *Expositor*, 1st ser., 1 (1875), 148. Cf. D. W. B. Robinson, 'To submit to the judgement of the saints', *TB*, 10 (1962), 1–8.

[2] F. W. Green, *The Gospel according to Saint Matthew* (Oxford, 1947), p. 146.

[3] Alexander Souter, *A Pocket Lexicon to the Greek New Testament* (Oxford, 1916), p. 212.

[4] C. Hemer, 'A note on II Corinthians 1: 9', *TB*, 23 (1972), 103–7.

In II Cor. 1: 12 the testimony of conscience is mentioned, recalling similar passages in the Epistle to the Romans which have already been discussed (Rom. 2: 15; 9: 1). A few verses later Paul calls God to witness against him, but here too the idea of witness is not developed; in fact, the expression is really a solemn affirmation amounting to an oath (II Cor. 1: 23; cf. Rom. 1: 9; I Thess. 2: 5, 10; Phil. 1: 8).

In II Cor. 5: 10 Paul declares that all Christians must appear before the judgment seat of Christ; here the phrase φανερωθῆναι ἔμπροσθεν is probably used technically and βῆμα is clearly a *technicus terminus*, frequently used in the New Testament for a *Richterstuhl* (cf. Mt. 27: 19; Jn 19: 13; Acts 18: 12, 16, 17; Rom. 14: 10). A few verses later the apostle speaks of entreating and beseeching men on Christ's behalf (5: 20); here the task of an ambassador appears to resemble the role of an advocate. Paul takes Christ's side as the apostles do in John's Gospel and the Book of Acts, though he is not, of course, an eye-witness of the whole public ministry of Jesus from the baptism of John onwards (cf. Acts 1: 21f.). In II Cor. 8 and 9 Paul speaks of the generosity of the Macedonian churches to which he can testify (μαρτυρῶ, 8: 3), and begs the Corinthians to furnish tangible 'proof' of their love which will be comparable to their verbal 'confession' (ἔνδειξιν, 8: 24; ὁμολογίας, 9: 13). No effort is made to expand the notion of witness further in his appeal for funds.

In II Cor. 10–13 Paul is dealing with charges levied against his apostleship (e.g., 10: 10; also 12: 19, where the verb ἀπολογεῖσθαι is used); this accounts for his reference to the 'signs, wonders and mighty works' which provide evidence of the validity of his apostleship (12: 12). It is against this background that II Cor. 13: 1ff. must be understood. Paul appeals to the Corinthian church to purify itself in view of his approaching visit, and cites the Jewish law of evidence. Here, as in other New Testament passages connected with church discipline (e.g., Mt. 18: 15–17; I Tim. 5: 19; cf. Heb. 10: 28) Paul reverts to this fundamental principle of Jewish law and announces his intention of acting upon it when he arrives in Corinth. Despite the view of a great many commentators, ancient and modern (e.g., Chrysostom, Theodoret, Stanley, Wordsworth, Godet and Strathmann), three visits are *not* the testimony of three witnesses.

Moreover, the formality with which the principle is announced and the importance of the principle itself elsewhere in the New Testament suggest a perfectly normal use of the Jewish law of evidence. There is no indication that μάρτυς in II Cor. 13: 1 has any but its common meaning of one who can see and testify. Taken in this way, μάρτυς makes good sense in the context and is compatible with similar passages dealing with ecclesiastical disputes both in the New Testament and in the Qumran community.

In Galatians and Ephesians only two or three references require examination. In Gal. 4: 15 Paul uses the verb μαρτυρεῖν to acknowledge the willingness of the Galatians to help him in times past, but there is no suggestion of Paul giving evidence before a real court of law. This observation also applies to Gal. 5: 3: 'I testify (μαρτύρομαι) again to every man who receives circumcision that he is bound to keep the whole law.' Similarly note Eph. 4: 17, where μαρτύρομαι means 'I affirm'.

In Philippians the idea of witness is not obvious, except in the phrase 'God is my witness' (1: 8), which has already been considered in discussing Rom. 1: 9 and similar passages. However, the references to 'defence' (ἀπολογία, 1: 7, 16; cf. Acts 22: 1; 25: 16), 'confirmation' (βεβαίωσις, 1: 7; cf. Heb. 6: 16), 'disputes' (διαλογισμοί, 2: 14; cf. James 2: 4) and 'opponents' (οἱ ἀντικείμενοι, 1: 28; cf. I Cor. 16: 9; Lk. 21: 15) may be mentioned, for they bear comparison with other passages that have a juridical character.

The theme of vindication may be present in Phil. 1: 19 where Paul appears to borrow a phrase from Job 13: 16 (LXX) and make it his own. The use of τοῦτό μοι ἀποβήσεται εἰς σωτηρίαν strongly suggests that Paul no less than Job expects to be vindicated, whether he is released from prison or executed. The next verse speaks of Paul's desire to act ἐν πάσῃ παρρησίᾳ (Phil. 1: 20). 'As Paul is doubtless thinking of his trial, it is possible that he is using the word [παρρησία] in its original sense of boldness of utterance, and boldness of utterance is one of Job's main characteristics...Paul will emulate his boldness of speech as he stands before his judges.'[1] This boldness, which is suggested a number of times in the Pauline Epistles (II Cor. 3: 12; 7: 4;

[1] J. H. Michael, 'Paul and Job: a neglected analogy', *ExpT*, 36 (1925), 67–70.

I Thess. 2: 2; cf. Eph. 3: 12; 6: 19, 20), is also an outstanding characteristic of the apostolic testimony in the Book of Acts.

In Col. 2: 4, however, Christians are warned that even persuasive speech may be deceptive; they must not be talked into error by 'specious argument' (ἐν πιθανολογίᾳ). In Col. 4: 13 Paul pays Epaphras a tribute by saying 'I bear witness that he has worked hard for you and for those in Laodicea and in Hierapolis', but here Paul is certainly not using μαρτυρῶ with any reference to a lawcourt; it is simply a matter of vouching for a faithful colleague. Similarly in his Letter to Philemon Paul twice appeals for Onesimus (παρακαλῶ, verses 9, 10), but there is no hint of Paul actually going to court as an advocate for Onesimus; Paul simply entreats Philemon to do him a favour.

In I and II Thessalonians the idea of witness receives scant attention. It occurs in the familiar Pauline phrase 'God is my witness', where Paul is concerned to defend the integrity of his ministry in the face of criticism (I Thess. 2: 5, 10); both of these passages also appeal to the knowledge of Paul's readers (cf. 2: 1; also Acts 20: 18, 34). Paul warns that God will function as an ἔκδικος in cases of sexual offence against a fellow Christian (I Thess. 4: 6); this is 'the regular term for a legal representative' in *koinē* Greek.[1] The verb μαρτύρεσθαι is used in I Thess. 2: 12, but here the participle μαρτυρόμενοι simply means 'solemnly charging'. The phrase τὸ μαρτύριον ἡμῶν is employed in II Thess. 1: 10 to mean 'the testimony borne by us', and passing reference is made to 'evidence' (ἔνδειγμα, II Thess. 1: 6) and to the demonic adversary (ὁ ἀντικείμενος, II Thess. 2: 4), but no attempt is made to develop the juridical idea. Similarly, the verb διαμαρτύρεσθαι is used in I Thess. 4: 6 (where it has the well-established Old Testament meaning of 'exhorting solemnly', but there is no evidence in Paul's letters that διαμαρτύρεσθαι plays the prominent role in witness-bearing which it plays in the Book of Acts.

The Pastoral Epistles

Turning to the Pastoral Epistles, several passages make use of witness terms. In I Tim. 2: 6, for instance, τὸ μαρτύριον is used with reference to Christ, 'who gave himself as a ransom for all,

---

[1] Moulton and Milligan, p. 193; cf. G. Milligan, *Paul's Epistles to the Thessalonians* (London, 1908), p. 50.

the testimony to which was borne at the proper time' (cf. Tit. 1 :
3). On this difficult passage N. J. D. White has written:

τὸ μαρτύριον, as Ellicott says, 'is an accusative, in apposition to the
preceding sentence,' or rather clause, ὁ δούς...πάντων. So R.V.
Bengel compares ἔνδειγμα, 2 Thess. i. 5, cf. also Rom. xii. 1. The
great act of self-sacrifice is timeless, but as historically apprehended
by us, the testimony concerning it must be made during a particular
and suitable period of history, i.e. from the descent of the Holy
Spirit upon the apostolic company (Acts i. 8) until the Second
Coming (2 Thess. i. 10)...The testimony is of course borne by God
(I Jn. v. 9–11), but He uses human agency, the preachers of the
Gospel...The plural [καιροῖς ἰδίοις] expresses the fact that the
bearing of testimony extends over many seasons...[1]

Notice also the next verse, where the writer insists that he is
a κῆρυξ καὶ ἀπόστολος (1 Tim. 2: 7).

The next passage calling for comment is I Tim. 3: 6, where
the devil functions as the accuser of God's people, whose aim is
to secure their condemnation (κρίμα); later the figure is described as 'Satan' and 'the adversary' (I Tim. 5: 14f.). The
following verse employs a witness term, but μαρτυρία here
simply means 'reputation' (I Tim. 3: 7). It was obviously important for the early church to have leaders who possessed a
'good testimony' (cf. Acts 6: 3; III Jn 12), especially ἀπὸ τῶν
ἔξωθεν (I Tim. 3: 7; cf. the reference to Christians 'walking'
properly πρὸς τοὺς ἔξω in Col. 4: 5 and I Thess. 4: 12); this is
clear from the demand that Timothy and his bishops must be
blameless, 'giving no cause for accusation' (ἀνεπίλημπτος
I Tim. 3: 2; 6: 14; cf. 5: 7, where the same standard is applied
to all sections of the Christian community). The same general
observation applies to I Tim. 5: 10, where the participle
μαρτυρουμένη is used in speaking of widows whose character is
'attested' by good works. In I Tim. 5: 19, however, a real lawcourt setting is in view, for formal charges are contemplated
against an elder of the local church; the preposition ἐπί introduces the basis of the proposed legal action. Here the words
μάρτυς and κατηγορία are used, and the Jewish law of evidence
is invoked to resolve a question of church discipline, as in Mt.

[1] N. J. D. White, 'The First and Second Epistles to Timothy and the
Epistle to Titus', *The Expositor's Greek Testament*, ed. W. R. Nicoll (5 vols.,
London, 1910), IV, 105–6.

18: 16 and II Cor. 13: 1. In I Tim. 5: 21 διαμαρτύρεσθαι is used in solemnly 'charging' Timothy 'in the presence of God and of Christ Jesus and of the elect angels', and the same verb is used in the same way in II Tim. 4: 1. But by far the most important passage on witness in I Timothy is found in chapter 6.

First, Timothy is warned of false teachers who produce strife (ἔρις, 6: 3ff.); this passage is rich in its use of controversy terms (περὶ ζητήσεις καὶ λογομαχίας, 6: 4; διαπαρατριβαί, 6: 5). Then he is reminded that he has made 'the good confession before many witnesses'. The perfect pattern of confession has been given to him by Jesus Christ, who witnessed 'the good confession before Pontius Pilate' (note the use of ἐπί in I Tim. 6: 13 in a juridical sense; cf. Mk 13: 9; Acts 25: 9). Now what was that confession? According to the Gospels Jesus had confessed that he was the Christ (Mk 14: 62) and that he was a king (Jn 18: 36). His confession was before men (cf. Jn 18: 20), over against the false witness of his enemies (Mk 14: 56) and the denial of a disciple (Mk 14: 68, 70), and was very costly (Mk 8: 31; 9: 31; 10: 45). Instead of 'denying the faith' (note the use of ἀρνεῖσθαι in I Tim. 5: 8; II Tim. 2: 12–13), Timothy in his ὁμολογία has identified himself 'before many witnesses' with 'the good confession' of his condemned and crucified Saviour.

It is only natural to raise the question about the occasion when this identification took place. Whether it occurred at his baptism (Kattenbusch, Dibelius, Richardson), his ordination (Jeremias, Käsemann) or before a hostile lawcourt (Baldensperger, Cullmann), it is difficult to say categorically. Probably it took place at Timothy's baptism, 'when he was called, enrolled as a soldier in the army of Jesus Christ (2 Tim. ii. 4; I Cor. ix. 7), and professed fidelity to his new Leader (his response to the divine call) before many witnesses'.[1] This view is supported by the fact that in 'the primitive Church the baptism of an individual was a matter in which the Church generally took an interest and part [cf. *The Didache* 7, Justin Martyr, *Apology* 1.61]...[while] it is not so natural to refer *the good confession* to a crisis of persecution, or to his ordination'.[2] But

---

[1] *Ibid.* p. 145.
[2] *Ibid.* pp. 145–6. Cf. A. Richardson, *An Introduction to the Theology of the New Testament* (London and New York, 1958), p. 337.

even if the confession of Timothy before many witnesses is not a reference to a judicial action, the context of this statement, as well as the general character of the [pastoral] letters, indicates the need for steadfastness and faithfulness in moments of trial and testing. The demeanor of Jesus during his trial is the pattern for Timothy as he 'fights the good fight of faith' (I Tim. 6. 12).[1]

In II Timothy the need for steadfastness and fidelity appears again in relation to the idea of witness. Timothy's task is a solemn one: διαμαρτυρόμενος ἐνώπιον τοῦ θεοῦ μὴ λογομαχεῖν (2: 14; cf. 2: 23). His witness must be gentle and tactful, 'correcting those who are in opposition' and leading them hopefully to repentance and the knowledge of the truth (II Tim. 2: 25). The message of Christ is to be declared in the face of the hostility and persecution of the pagan world. For this reason Timothy is admonished: 'Do not be ashamed then of testifying to our Lord, nor of me his prisoner, but take your share of suffering for the gospel in the power of God' (II Tim. 1: 8). Here τὸ μαρτύριον τοῦ κυρίου ἡμῶν means 'your testimony to our Lord', the genitive being taken objectively, as in the RSV, NEB and Phillips. While διαβολοί are very much in evidence (3: 3), there is no definite indication that Timothy's testimony is to be given before a formal court of law. Nevertheless a 'trial' is in progress all the time as the stage on which the Christian witness is played out, and Timothy must face real opponents (τοὺς ἀντιδιατιθεμένους, 2: 25). So he is advised to commit to others the Christian instruction which he has received 'before many witnesses' (II Tim. 2: 2). Here the reference to witnesses underscores the public character of the teaching given by Timothy which he is charged to communicate to faithful men.

II Tim. 4: 16 seems to suggest a juridical situation. There is a reference to a legal 'defence' made on a former occasion, and παρεγένετο is used in the technical sense of a witness standing forward in a court of law on behalf of the accused. Commentators are divided on the precise meaning of the apostle's 'first defence'. There are three main positions. (1) The apostle has in view an earlier trial in contrast to the present legal proceedings.

---

[1] V. N. Neufeld, *The Earliest Christian Confessions* (Leiden, 1963), p. 133; cf. O. Cullmann, *The Earliest Christian Confessions* (London, 1949), pp. 25–6, and H. von Campenhausen, 'Das Bekenntnis im Urchristentum', *ZNW*, 63 (1972), 210–53.

This view was popular with the church fathers and the majority of commentators prior to the nineteenth century. It can be harmonized with Acts 28 and makes good sense of II Tim. 4: 17, but it is difficult to explain why Timothy would be so completely abandoned by his friends. (2) The advocates of a fragment hypothesis think it is a reference to Paul's appearance before Felix in Caesarea (Acts 24: 1–23) or possibly before the Sanhedrin in Jerusalem (Acts 23: 1–10). The vision of the Lord encouraging Paul is cited to buttress the Jerusalem view (Acts 23: 11). But here too one faces serious difficulties, for at Jerusalem Paul receives marked support from the Pharisaic legal experts, and at Caesarea the tone is far less harsh than it is in II Tim. 4: 16. (3) On the whole, the position of Principal Kelly has much to commend it:

it is preferable, with most present-day supporters of authenticity, to locate Paul's *first defence* in his present, i.e. second Roman captivity, and to understand by it, not the trial proper (which of course was to issue in his condemnation), but what in Roman legal parlance was called the *prima actio*, i.e. the preliminary investigation. This had apparently gone favourably for the accused, at least to the extent of the judge not being able to resolve his doubts and thus pronouncing the verdict '*Non liquet*', of '*Amplius*'. When this happened, Roman legal practice required that a further investigation, or *secunda actio* should take place, and this might involve considerable delay.[1]

On this explanation, Timothy may well have been unaware of the turn events had taken, and may have required updating. It would still remain a mystery why no one should come forward as a witness on Paul's behalf, but perhaps it was simply cowardice or moral weakness which was responsible for their critical absence. On this interpretation the next verse explains how Paul exploited the preliminary investigation in order to make the gospel more widely known (II Tim. 4: 17; cf. Phil. 1: 19–20). 'He had always used his previous trials for this purpose, and he now regards his appearance before the august tribunal of the capital as setting a crown on his career as a preacher.'[2]

In the Letter to Titus such Johannine-like legal words as μαρτυρία (1: 13), κατηγορία (1: 6), ἐλέγχειν (1: 9), ὁμολογεῖν (1: 16) and ἀρνεῖσθαι (1: 16) are used, together with an un-

[1] J. N. D. Kelly, *A Commentary on the Pastoral Epistles* (London, 1963), p. 218.   [2] *Ibid.* p. 219.

usual phrase meaning 'opponent' (ὁ ἐξ ἐναντίας, 2: 8). It is not surprising that such terms should appear, for the Epistle sets forth what is required of bishops or elders in the face of false teachers as well as local shortcomings. In this milieu, some controversy terminology is to be expected. The 'objectors' to the Christian message (οἱ ἀντιλέγοντες, 1: 9) must be silenced (ἐπιστοματίζειν, 1: 11; cf. 1: 13), and 'put to shame' (2: 6–8).

To sum up, the Pastorals illustrate how much the witness metaphor is used, how appropriate and live it is, even by its few references.

The General Epistles

The Epistle of James makes even less use of the idea of witness than the Pastorals, though the nouns κρίσις (2: 13 (twice); 5: 12), κρίμα (3: 1) and κριτής (4: 11, 12; 5: 9) are used, and also the verbs κρίνειν (2: 12; 4: 11–12 (four times); 5:9) and ἐλέγχειν (2: 9). The Epistle roundly condemns the social snobs who function as the self-styled κριταί of the poor (2: 4),[1] and castigates the rich who 'drag' (ἕλκουσιν) their opponents into the 'lawcourts' (κριτήρια, 2: 6; cf. I Cor. 6: 2, 4). There is no room for presumption, since the divine νομοθέτης is able to destroy as well as save (4: 12). In 5: 3 the wicked rich are subjected to a blistering attack: 'Your gold and silver have rusted, and their rust will be evidence against you.' Here, as in the Old Testament, μαρτύριον is used to mean 'evidence' (cf. Gen. 21: 30; Deut. 31: 19, 26; Josh. 24: 27; Ruth 4: 7). In this case the evidence is to be given in the eschatological judgment of 'the last days' (5: 3; cf. Jn 12: 48), when the cries of the exploited labourers will rise as accusing witnesses to 'the ears of the Lord of hosts' (5: 4; cf. Mt. 12: 41f.). The evidence to be presented is obviously hostile in character (ὑμῖν here, as in Lk. 10: 11, being a dative of disadvantage). The threat of judgment is an imminent one, for the judge already 'stands' (note the force of the perfect ἕστηκεν); in terms of Old Testament legal procedure, this means he is about to pronounce his judgment (cf. Isa. 3: 3, Psa. 76: 8f.; 82: 8).

---

[1] R. B. Ward, 'Partiality in the assembly: James 2: 2–4', *HTR*, 62 (1969), 87–97, thinks this passage is to be connected with the rabbinic tradition concerning judicial proceedings and the Old Testament instructions for judging (Lev. 19: 15–18; Ex. 23: 1–3, 6–9; Deut. 1: 16–17; 16: 18–20).

There are a few passages in I Peter which catch the eye from the viewpoint of witness, and there are occasional words which have juridical overtones (e.g., κρίμα, 4: 17; κρίνειν, 1: 17; 2: 24; 4: 5, 6). I Pet. 1: 10–12 describes the work of the Old Testament prophets who searched into the promised salvation, and uses προμαρτυρόμενον to refer to the Spirit of Christ's antecedent testimony to the sufferings of Christ and the subsequent glory. Here the participle means 'predicted', and the passage deserves to be compared with Acts 1: 16, where the Spirit's antecedent testimony in scripture is again in view. A participle is also used in I Pet. 5: 12, where ἐπιμαρτυρῶν has the force of 'declaring'.

I Pet. 2: 15 provides a striking contrast with both Isaiah 40–55 and the Fourth Gospel, where the litigants on one side are reduced to silence by the arguments of their legal opponents. In I Peter it is deeds rather than words which are expected to silence (φιμόω, 'muzzle', cf. I Cor. 9. 9) the believers' opponents. In the larger arena of life, the Christian faith is certainly 'on trial', and here 'actions speak louder than words'.

I Peter 3 contains two passages of real interest. At the beginning of the chapter instructions are given to wives and husbands (3: 1–7). The wives are told to be submissive to their own husbands, providing evidence for their faith by their chaste and reverent lifestyle (ἀναστροφή, 3: 1, 2).[1] Their unbelieving partners will be eye-witnesses (ἐποπτεύσαντες, 3: 2) of this ungainsayable evidence, and some may thereby be 'won' to the Christian faith by this witness 'without a word' (3: 1). Here emphasis is placed upon Christian living rather than on 'techniques of witnessing' (cf. I Cor. 7: 16; Tit. 2: 3–5, where similar instructions are accompanied by the negative reason: 'that the word of God may not be discredited'). As E. G. Selwyn once remarked: 'ἀγαθοποιΐα is as essential as κήρυγμα to the fullness of the Christian μαρτυρία'.[2] I Pet. 3: 15 is also

[1] P. Marcel, 'Le Témoignage en parole et en actes', RR, 9 (1958), 36–47, thinks that deeds rather than words constitute the dominant mode whereby women bear witness to their faith, but concedes it is 'a question of degree not of nature' (pp. 44f.). For examples in Latin literature where the witness of deeds is striking see Cicero, De Natura Deorum III.83 and Demetrius, Epistulae Morales, xx.9.

[2] E. G. Selwyn, 'Image, fact and faith', NTS, 1 (1954), 235–47.

noteworthy, for ἀπολογία is used to describe the defence made in a court of law (cf. Acts 25: 16). 'This is certainly the force here, for the phrase πάντι τῷ αἰτοῦντι λόγον can only apply to a judicial interrogation.'[1] The meaning is that the Christian is to be prepared to give his testimony on behalf of Christ when called upon to do so in a court of law.

In I Pet. 5: 8 the Christian's foe is described at 'the devil' and 'the adversary', words which elsewhere in the Bible are often used in juridical contexts (Job 1: 6; 2: 1; Zech. 3: 1f.; Prov. 18: 17; Mt. 5: 25 = Lk. 12: 58; 18: 3; Rev. 12: 9–12). Once more the world in which the Christian lives is being likened to a lawcourt and the διάβολος or false accuser, taking up the position of ἀντίδικος, is trying through persecution to make Christians recant and so witness against Jesus. Christians at this time are very much 'on trial', perhaps in an actual persecution situation (cf. I Pet. 1: 6–7; 4: 12–19).

The most important passage to be considered in I Peter is 5: 1, where the writer describes himself as a 'fellow elder and witness of the sufferings of Christ as well as a partaker of the glory that is to be revealed'. Here the use of μάρτυς seems to imply an eye-witness of Christ's suffering and death (cf. II Pet. 1: 16ff.).[2] However, μάρτυς need not necessarily mean an eye-witness; it can simply mean 'one who testifies to'. On this explanation 'witness' is said to mean no more than 'preacher'. The argument supposes that as Peter has just used the word συμπρεσβύτερος to put himself on the same plane as the other elders, he does not intend in his next words to elevate himself above them. However, for three reasons this objection cannot be sustained: (1) the climax in this verse is quite natural and in keeping with the context; (2) the writer has already referred to himself as an ἀπόστολος in the salutation (I Pet. 1: 1); (3) the author could have used the word συμμάρτυς if he had merely wished to express the idea of 'fellow-preacher'.

Professor Beare suggests that the author is a witness for Christ by virtue of his personal sufferings on behalf of the

---

[1] F. W. Beare, *The First Epistle of Peter* (2nd ed.; Oxford, 1961), p. 172. On p. 191 Beare attacks the alleged eye-witness touches of the Epistle as 'singularly unconvincing'.

[2] E. G. Selwyn, *The First Epistle of St. Peter* (London, 1947), p. 229.

Saviour.[1] Strathmann agrees with this interpretation, noting that the idea of Christians partaking of the sufferings of Christ is a common theme in the New Testament (Jn 16: 2; II Cor. 1: 5; Phil. 3: 10; Col. 1: 24; I Pet. 1: 6f.; 2: 20; 3: 14; 4: 1, 12f.; Rev. 7: 14).[2] However, a witness generally testifies to a fact or a truth: 'A witness of the sufferings of Christ is one who is in a position to certify that the sufferings actually occurred. There are special and appropriate phrases for those who imitate the patience of their Master; they are said to partake of the sufferings of Christ (I Pet. 4: 13).'[3] In other words, μάρτυς in I Pet. 5: 1 is best taken to mean 'eye-witness' (as in Acts 1: 8, 22; 2: 32; 3: 15; 5: 32; 10: 39, 41; cf. the use of αὐτόπτης in Lk. 1: 2). Thus in the only place where μάρτυς is used in I Peter, it probably refers to an eye-witness of the passion of Christ.[4]

Eye-witnesses are also mentioned in II Peter, where the ἐπόπται of the transfiguration are in view (II Pet. 1: 16–19; cf. Mk 9: 2–8 pars.). Here eye-witness testimony is regarded as making the testimony of the 'prophetic word' (i.e. the Old Testament scriptures) 'more sure'.[5] This passage provides an interesting parallel to the Book of Acts, where eye-witness testimony furnished by the apostles corroborates the scriptural testimony to the promised Messiah (cf. Acts 10: 38–43; 13: 26–41). Perhaps it is not surprising to find the same two kinds of testimony in I Peter as well: in chapter 1 reference is made to the 'prophets' of the Old Testament who through the Spirit 'testified beforehand' of the sufferings of the Messiah and the subsequent glory, and in chapter 5 eye-witness testimony is introduced (I Pet. 1: 10–12; 5: 1). This twofold testimony re-

---

[1] Beare, op. cit., cf. also F. L. Cross, I Peter: A Paschal Liturgy (London, 1954), p. 22. On the question of authorship see D. Guthrie, New Testament Introduction (3rd ed.; London, 1971), pp. 773–90.

[2] Strathmann, TDNT, IV, 494–5 and TWNT, IV, 499. Cf. J. H. B. Mastermann, The First Epistle of S. Peter (London, 1900), p. 159.

[3] C. Bigg, The Epistles of St. Peter and St. Jude, ICC (Edinburgh, 1901), p. 187.

[4] Cf. A. M. Stibbs, The First Epistle General of Peter (London, 1959), pp. 166–7.

[5] M. Rist, 'Pseudepigraphy and the early Christians', Studies in New Testament and Early Christian Literature, ed. D. E. Aune (Leiden, 1972), pp. 75–91, however, thinks that those 'who question the historicity of this purported theophany might consider its conclusion a disproof rather than a proof of Petrine authorship' (p. 76).

minds us of the distinction observed earlier in Aristotle between μαρτυρίαι περὶ τοῦ πράγματος and μαρτυρίαι περὶ τοῦ ἤθους. The Petrine Epistles, like Luke-Acts and the Fourth Gospel, view the apostles as properly qualified witnesses to the facts of the life and ministry of Jesus, and see their witness as corroborated by the biblical προφῆται who wrote τὸν προφητικὸν λόγον (I Pet. 1: 10; II Pet. 1: 19). However, unlike Aristotle's 'recent witnesses', the apostles are considered competent to speak of the divine meaning of that which they have seen and heard.

II Peter speaks of expecting 'the judgment' (εἰς κρίσιν) or 'the day of judgment' (εἰς ἡμέραν κρίσεως) which will involve 'the destruction of ungodly men' and the final doom of the fallen angels (2: 4, 9; 3: 7). However, there is no indication of the place of witnesses in this judgment; even the ἄγγελοι do not bring an abusive judgment κατ' αὐτῶν παρὰ κυρίῳ (2: 11). All the author tells us is that the κρίμα of the ungodly is sure (2: 3); those who 'deny' the Master who bought them will bring upon themselves 'swift destruction' (2: 1). The use of ἀρνεῖσθαι here recalls other passages in the New Testament where confession and denial have strong forensic overtones (Mt. 10: 32–3 = Lk. 12: 8–9; Mk 14: 68f. pars.; I Tim. 6: 12–13; Rev. 3: 8; Jn 1: 20).

Similarly in Jude there are nouns such as κρίμα (4) and κρίσις (6, 9), and verbs such as ἀρνεῖσθαι (4), διαλέγεσθαι (9), ἐπιφέρειν (9) and ἐλέγχειν (15). Verse 9 refers to a juridical dispute over the body of Moses in which the archangel Michael 'did not presume to pronounce a reviling judgment' upon the devil, but paid proper respect to the opposing counsel (ὁ διάβολος; cf. Rev. 12: 9–10; Zech. 3: 1f.). Verse 15 also sounds a forensic note, this time in connection with the Last Judgment: the Lord is coming 'to execute judgment' (ποιῆσαι κρίσιν: cf. κρίσιν ποιεῖν in Jn 5: 27) and this will entail the condemnation of the ungodly for their wicked deeds and words. In certain respects this passage resembles Mal. 3: 5 where Yahweh, the 'swift witness', 'draws near' for 'judgment', though in Jude 15 no mention is made of the Lord as a 'witness'. The idea of witness is not developed in Jude, and μάρτυς and its cognates are not used.

The Epistle to the Hebrews

The idea of witness appears a number of times in the Epistle to the Hebrews, a fact suggested by the use of words drawn from the vocabulary of witness. Thus μάρτυς appears in a reference to the Old Testament law of evidence (10: 28) and also in connection with the 'cloud of witnesses' (12: 1). Similarly, μαρτύριον is used with reference to Moses's testimony to the 'things that were spoken later' (3: 5), and both μαρτυρεῖν (10: 15; 11: 4) and a number of cognate verbs (μαρτυρεῖσθαι (7: 8, 17; 11: 2, 4, 5, 39), συνεπιμαρτυρεῖσθαι (2: 4) and διαμαρτυρεῖσθαι (2: 6)) are used. In addition to all these words, the noun and verb for 'confess', which elsewhere in the New Testament can have a juridical significance (e.g., Lk. 12: 8; Jn 1: 20; Rev. 3: 5), appear several times in the vocabulary of Hebrews (3: 1; 4: 14; 10: 23; 11: 13; 13: 15). Note also the use of ἀρνεῖσθαι (11: 24), which similarly appears at times in juridical contexts (e.g., Mt. 10: 33; Lk. 12: 9; Acts 3: 13f.). All of this information would seem to indicate that witness is a prominent theme in Hebrews. This presumption must now be examined to see if it is indeed borne out by a careful study of the contents of the Epistle.

The first passage calling for examination is Heb. 2: 2–4, to which attention has already been directed in considering the idea of witness in the Book of Acts. There it is said that the divine message of salvation is proclaimed by Jesus in the first instance, and then subsequently by the apostles, the witnesses who have 'heard' him and can therefore testify concerning him. Their testimony is supported by corroborative evidence in the form of 'signs and wonders and various miracles and by gifts of the Holy Spirit distributed according to his will' (2: 4; cf. Mk 16: 20). These mighty works are tangible, concrete means whereby God bears witness to all men of the truth of the proclaimed word. But this is not the only source of supporting evidence for the apostolic testimony; it is also bolstered by the evidence of holy scripture. So Heb. 2: 6–8 both cites Psa. 8: 4–6 and introduces the biblical passage with διεμαρτύρατο. Eyewitness testimony is backed by scriptural testimony as in II Pet. 1: 16–19, and the idea of witness is very similar to that which is unfolded in greater detail in the Book of Acts.

The witness of holy scripture is repeatedly adduced in the Epistle to the Hebrews, where the 'word of God' is said to function as a judge of the thoughts and intents of the heart (κριτικός, 4:12). This fact is indicated in a general way by the importance given to Old Testament citations, e.g., 1: 5 (cf. Psa. 2: 7; II Sam. 7: 14); 2: 12 (cf. Psa. 22: 22); 3: 7–11 (cf. Psa. 95: 7–11), and specifically by introducing some of these citations with participles and verbs drawn from the vocabulary of witness (e.g., μαρτυρούμενος in 7: 8; μαρτυρεῖται in 7: 17; μαρτυρεῖ of the Holy Spirit's witness in 10: 15; ἐμαρτυρήθη in 11 : 4; and μεμαρτύρηται in 11 : 5). Observe also the author's use of Old Testament passages which mention God's swearing (3: 11, 18; 4: 3, 5); these are all solemnized by εἰ or μή which serves to strengthen the declaration: 'They shall assuredly not enter into my rest' (cf. I Kgs 14: 45; Mk 8: 12).[1] For the writer of Hebrews, as for Luke, the truth of one kind of testimony required confirmation by another, in this case, by the testimony of the scriptures. Here again there seems to be a reference to the Old Testament law of evidence mentioned in Deut. 19: 15. That this principle was definitely accepted by the author of Hebrews is clear from his explicit recognition of it in 10: 28. The recognition of the Jewish law of evidence by the author of Hebrews is paralleled in the writings of Luke, the Fourth Evangelist, Paul, the seer of Patmos, and Matthew; indeed, it is fair to say that it is an important general observation for the understanding of the New Testament concept of witness.

The idea of confessing one's faith appears several times in Hebrews. Jesus is 'the high priest of whom our confession speaks' (3: 1, so Arndt–Gingrich). The writer urges his readers to maintain their confession (4: 13) : 'At once this is a testimony before men of our faith in and loyalty to God and also a paean of praise to God for his marvellous acts of redemption.'[2] Finally, to prevent his fellow believers from drifting into apostasy the author cries: 'Let us hold fast the confession of our hope without wavering' (10: 23), supporting his exhortation by appeals to good works and warnings of certain divine judgment against

[1] C. F. D. Moule, *An Idiom-Book of New Testament Greek* (Cambridge, 1953), p. 179.

[2] W. A. Quanbeck, 'Hebrews', *The Interpreter's One-Volume Commentary on the Bible*, ed. C. Laymon (London, 1972), p. 904.

'the adversaries' (τοὺς ὑπεναντίους, 10: 27). While ὁμολογία definitely refers to confession, it would probably be unwise to read too much of a juridical element into these passages.[1] The same observation applies to the verbs ὁμολογεῖν (11: 13; 13: 15) and ἀρνεῖσθαι (11: 24), for it is doubtful if any reference is intended to confession or denial before real courts of law. While Christ is not expressly described as a Paraclete, the work of a priestly advocate is suggested in 9: 24 (cf. I Jn 2: 1).

Other words of apparent interest appear in Hebrews, e.g., κρίμα (6: 2), κρίνειν (10: 30; 13: 4), κρίσις (9: 27; 10: 27), κριτής (12: 23), ἔλεγχος (11: 1), κατακρίνειν (11: 7), but they do not develop the idea of witness. The use of μαρτυρεῖσθαι in chapter 11 (verses 2, 4, 5, 39) has already been discussed in studying the evidential role which the Epistle assigns to the testimony of scripture. That leaves only two more sections to deal with, namely, the oath material of Hebrews 6 and 7 and the famous passage on the cloud of witnesses at the beginning of chapter 12.

Heb. 6: 13ff. is interesting on several counts. A forensic situation is envisaged in which God, having no one greater to swear by, swears by himself (Heb. 6: 13f.; cf. Isa. 45: 23; Jer. 22: 5). The preposition κατά is followed by a noun in the genitive to signify the guarantee of an oath (ὤμοσεν καθ' ἑαυτοῦ; cf. Gen. 22: 16), and the oath itself is introduced by εἰ μήν, which has the effect of intensifying the juridical solemnity of the act.[2] The divine practice on this occasion is then compared to human judicial practice where 'an oath is final for confirmation' (Heb. 6: 16f.; cf. Philo, Plant. 82). In this passage, as in the LXX, ὅρκος is used for 'oath', ἀντιλογία for 'dispute' (cf. Prov. 18: 18; Jos., Ant. xiv.235), ὀμνύειν for 'swear', μεσιτεύειν for 'guarantee', ἐπιδεικνύναι for 'demonstrate' or 'prove' (cf. Acts 18: 28) and βεβαίωσις for 'confirmation' or 'legal guarantee'. No wonder Adolf Deissmann was led to remark that 'the context is permeated with juristic expressions'.[3] In addition there seems to be a hint of the Jewish law of evidence in the

[1] Cf. R. H. Fuller, A Critical Introduction to the New Testament (London 1966), p. 149.
[2] Moule, Idiom-Book, p. 60.
[3] G. A. Deissmann, Bible Studies (Edinburgh, 1901), pp. 106–7. For κοινή parallels to the above words see Moulton and Milligan, pp. 457, 48, 448, 399 and 108.

reference to the 'two unchangeable things' (Heb. 6: 18; cf. Deut. 19: 15; Heb. 10: 28). The writer wants his readers to know that God is as good as his word; the evidence for this is twofold, namely, God's promise and God's oath. This dual witness theme has already been frequently observed in the New Testament.

The divine oath is mentioned again in Heb. 7 in a similar connection. The priesthood of Christ is superior to the Levitical priesthood because it has been inaugurated by an oath taken by God himself (ὁρκωμοσία, 7: 20, 21, 28). The comment of Alan Stibbs brings out the juridical significance of this oath: 'This is witness that the new order of priesthood is a divine undertaking, and one that is thus doubly pledged by God's word and God's oath (cf. vi. 13–18). Therefore it cannot fail like the old ...The divine oath implies something final, eternal and unchangeable.'[1] Here again we are reminded of two themes already suggested in Heb. 6: 13–18, namely, the solemn finality of the divine oath and the two-witness principle enshrined in the Jewish law of evidence. Note also the reference to Jesus as the 'guarantee' of a new covenant (ἔγγυος, 7: 22). Later in the Epistle Jesus is said to be the mediator of this new and better covenant (8: 6; 9: 15; 12: 24); here μεσίτης refers to the arbiter who mediates a dispute and enables the two parties concerned to reach a common goal (cf. Philo, Mos. II.166 and examples cited in Moulton and Milligan).[2]

Turning to Hebrews 12, the question is, Who constitutes the 'cloud of witnesses'? To interpret the opening words of Heb. 12 it is necessary to do justice to the force of its opening connective τοιγαροῦν. According to Arndt and Gingrich, this word is 'a particle introducing an inference' (cf. I Thess. 4: 8; I Clement 57: 4, 6).[3] In other words, the exhortation of chapter 12 is based squarely upon the argument of the preceding chapter, where the author has paraded the heroes of faith before his readers' minds to stimulate them to a similar robust faith (11: 4–38). His closing words in the great 'faith chapter' were words of summary: 'All these won a glowing testimony to their faith,

[1] A. M. Stibbs, 'Hebrews', *The New Bible Commentary Revised*, ed. D. Guthrie and J. A. Motyer (3rd ed., London, 1970), p. 1204.
[2] Moulton and Milligan, p. 399.
[3] Arndt and Gingrich, p. 828.

but they did not then and there receive the fulfilment of the promise. God has something better planned for our day, and it was not his plan that they should reach perfection without us' (11: 39–40, Phillips).

The important question to be answered is, How were these men attested or where is their testimony recorded? The answer is obvious: their testimony is preserved in the pages of holy scripture, and it is this testimony which the author has called upon again and again to provoke his readers to a faith which expresses itself in concrete deeds and actions. The testimony of scripture is the testimony of God, a point made very clear in 10: 15ff. (cf. Acts 13: 22, where God is said to bear witness to David in the words of Psa. 89: 20 and I Sam. 13: 14). Accordingly, the cloud of witnesses in 12: 1 is nothing but the heroes of faith mentioned in chapter 11 who are cited in the pages of the Old Testament. It is they who enjoy the approving testimony of scripture, and consequently of God himself, who speaks by his Spirit through the written word. It is their example which is to inspire heroic Christian discipleship. In other words, the context rules out the thought of spectators in an amphitheatre who watch the contemporary Christian race, and instead speaks of God's testimony to the heroes of faith in the pages of the Old Testament. They are described as witnesses because they 'have an experimental knowledge of that which is required of us, viz. faith, x. 35–37, xi. 6sqq., xii. 2'.[1]

The Epistle to the Hebrews, then, has some valuable things to say about witness. It recognizes the Jewish law of evidence, the importance of signs and wonders as offering confirmatory testimony, and the testimony of God through the scriptures. In all these ways it deserves to be compared with the Book of Acts, where the same themes are developed and expanded. It also makes use of legal language connected with oaths, and in this respect it rests squarely upon the Old Testament's use of oaths.

---

[1] H. Cremer, *Biblico-Theological Lexicon of New Testament Greek* (4th ed., Edinburgh, 1895), p. 413.

CHAPTER 12

CONCLUSION

In bringing this study to a close it is proper to return to the point at which we began. At the outset it was noted that μαρτυρία and its cognates greatly outnumber κήρυγμα and κηρύσσειν. This observation prompted no less a New Testament scholar than E. G. Selwyn to ask 'whether the word μαρτυρία and its cognates would not better describe the primitive and indispensable core of the Christian message'.[1] Without wishing in any way to disparage the importance of the kerygma, this investigation has attempted to show that Selwyn was right in suggesting that 'there is room for another monograph on the apostolic testimony'.[2] His contention proves to be abundantly borne out by the evidence. Indeed, the tenor of the present study indicates, as Théo Preiss once intimated, that the juridical terminology of the Bible is a fruitful field deserving more attention from contemporary scholarship.[3]

It is possible, of course, to overstate or to misinterpret the forensic aspect, and this temptation we have striven to avoid. Certainly one must not imply that litigation and quarrelling are to be treated simply on one level, without consideration of a metaphorical use of witness as 'testimony to'. We have had occasion to note (in the Psalms, for instance) the juxtaposition of juridical and non-juridical metaphors. In fact, our study has uncovered four classes of material where the witness imagery operates: (a) actual trials, where the legal terminology is genuinely forensic; (b) controversy, where there is an extension of the forensic; (c) metaphors where the forensic aspect may be in the background but is not necessarily present; (d) the idea of witness as testimony *to*, in a religious context (or in terms of reputation, etc.). There are clearly several gradations which must be taken into account.

As far as testimony in a religious sense is concerned, J. R. van Pelt long ago perceptively remarked:

[1] E. G. Selwyn, 'Eschatology of I Peter', *The Background of the New Testament and Its Eschatology*, ed. W. D. Davies and D. Daube (Cambridge, 1956), p. 395.   [2] *Ibid.*

[2] See T. Preiss, *Life in Christ*, trans. H. Knight (London, 1954).

The idea of witness as related to Christ and His gospel plays an essential and highly important part in the New Testament writings and in the Christian faith and life universally. Not only in the primitive preaching, but also in all effectual preaching throughout the history of the Church, the gospel is conceived not as a speculative system, but as a witness to Jesus the Christ as being Himself God's Witness to the world.[1]

To enlarge upon the implications of van Pelt's statement, the major results of this work may now be summarized. The New Testament use of witnesses rests squarely on the Old Testament concept of justice in the gate. In the Old Testament the law-suit or controversy theme grows out of the legal assembly and plays an important part. It is evident in the frequency of quarrelling in Israelite life, the juridical terminology of the Old Testament, the controversy in the Book of Job, the use of traditional names, phrases and oaths, the preaching of the prophets, the lawcourt scenes of Isaiah 40–55, and in certain passages in the Apocrypha, the Dead Sea Scrolls, Josephus and Philo. The principal background for the New Testament con-cept of witness, then, is to be found in the Old Testament lawsuit.

Turning to the New Testament, the idea of witness, generally speaking, is a living metaphor, despite its comparative neglect in Paul. It is basically to be understood in terms of the Old Testament legal assembly, though there are points of similarity with Greek lawcourts. The idea can be developed as a sustained metaphor, as in the case of the Fourth Gospel, the Book of Acts and the Apocalypse, and it is also used in the Synoptics, the Pastorals, the Catholic Epistles and Hebrews. In all these books there is no suggestion that witness has anything but its common meanings. It is only in contexts of persecution and opposition that the forensic metaphors tend to be identified with military ones, but semantically they are quite distinct. In New Testa-ment times the idea of witness is not confused with the idea of suffering or of battle, though under certain circumstances they are closely related.

It is fitting to ask in conclusion what is the value or signifi-cance of the witness motif for a sceptical, bewildered, fast-

---

[1] J. R. van Pelt, 'Witness', *Dictionary of Christ and the Gospels*, ed. J. Hastings (2 vols.; Edinburgh, 1908), II, 830.

moving world at the end of the twentieth century. Several points may be advanced in attempting to answer this question.

First, the frequent use of the witness theme stresses the importance of the historical foundations of the Christian religion. As Paul reminded King Agrippa, 'This was not done in a corner.' The principal events of the public ministry of Jesus were wrought in the presence of his chosen companions and apostles. They had been present in Jerusalem during that final week, and were in a position to attest the facts of his trial, crucifixion and burial. Above all, they were competent witnesses to vouch for the fact of his resurrection.

For both Luke and John the Jerusalem apostles occupy a special place in holy history, because they have been with Jesus from the commencement of his public ministry. In

the economy of the gospel dispensation, the word of the original witnesses is manifestly of cardinal importance. The mere fact that they were the first witnesses is itself sufficient to give their testimony a peculiar importance...The primitive witnesses, however, were more than merely the first, as though there by chance. They had been chosen beforehand and specially trained for the work of bearing witness.[1]

Other New Testament writers sound different notes on the historical trumpet. For the Book of Revelation the stress seems to fall on Christ, 'the faithful and true witness' who serves as the archetype for the faithful band of believers who must maintain the same testimony, even at the sacrifice of life itself. A similar note is struck in the Pastorals, where Timothy is reminded of the 'good confession' of his Lord before Pontius Pilate and exhorted to offer the same type of witness in his own day. In Acts the factual content of the apostolic testimony receives particular attention. The testimony rests upon the great acts of God in Jesus Christ, and the resurrection forms the very core of this. But for all the major New Testament writers the historical facts of Christian origins are of paramount importance. This is patently true of the four Evangelists, who felt it necessary to set out the life of Christ in the form of Gospels. It is certainly true of Paul, who declared the basic facts of the gospel to be 'of first importance', and appended a list of witnesses

[1] *Ibid.* II, 832.

to the risen Christ. In fine, it was of supreme significance to the New Testament writers that the apostolic teaching was not based on a collection of myths, but on the experience of eye-witnesses.

In the light of the New Testament's repeated insistence on the role of eye-witnesses and the consequent stress on the historical nature of the events which the witnesses report, one must raise the question, Has historical scholarship taken this factor sufficiently seriously? Certainly current preoccupation with form criticism, redaction criticism, audience criticism and the like must not blind our eyes to the New Testament's unmistakable stress on those who were the actual witnesses of the primary events. Unless the testimony of these eye-witnesses can be impugned as spurious, misrepresented or erroneous, their evidence for Christian origins must be taken seriously. It may be questioned, for instance, whether Bultmann's demythologizing programme has taken sufficient account of the presence of eye-witnesses in the earliest strata of gospel tradition. In fact, the importance attached to eye-witnesses in the New Testament strengthens the case for the life, death and resurrection of Jesus, and hence buttresses the historical foundations of the Christian faith. In a day of widespread scepticism about Christian origins this contribution is both timely and significant.[1]

In the second place, the witness theme is particularly pertinent to a sceptical, questioning age. Ours is unquestionably a time of religious as well as cultural pluralism; to be convinced of this one has only to read the works of Francis Schaeffer, John MacQuarrie and H. R. Rookmaaker.[2] Theological ideas from a wide range of sources have been thrown into the contemporary melting-pot and are being vigorously debated. This is precisely the type of situation in which the New Testament writers make abundant use of witness imagery and terminology. The claims of Christ were being hotly contested, then as now, and in such a

[1] For a penetrating criticism of the historical scepticism of much twentieth-century theology on philosophical rather than exegetical grounds see P. Carnley, 'The poverty of historical scepticism', *Christ, Faith and History*, ed. S. Sykes and J. P. Clayton (Cambridge, 1972), pp. 165–89.

[2] F. A. Schaeffer, *Escape from Reason* (London, 1968) and *The God Who Is There* (London, 1968); J. MacQuarrie, *Twentieth-Century Religious Thought* (London, 1966); H. R. Rookmaaker, *Modern Art and the Death of a Culture* (London, 1970).

milieu the language and thought forms of the Old Testament controversy sprang naturally to mind.

The Fourth Gospel provides the setting for the most sustained controversy in the New Testament. The lawsuit in John seems to be patterned on the controversy material of Isaiah 40–55. There the controversy between Yahweh and the false gods is really a lawsuit between God and the world, God being represented by Israel, and the world by the pagan nations. Similarly in the Fourth Gospel God incarnate in Jesus has a lawsuit with the world. His witnesses include John the Baptist, the scriptures, the words and works of Christ, and later the witness of the apostles and the Holy Spirit. They are opposed by the world, represented in the Fourth Gospel by the unbelieving Jews. In Isaiah 40–55 the debate is over the claims of Yahweh as the Creator, the only true God and the Lord of history; in John it is over the Messiahship and divine Sonship of Jesus. John, like his prophetic counterpart, has a case to present, and for this reason he advances his arguments, asks his juridical questions, and presents his witnesses after the fashion of the Old Testament legal assembly. The same observation is true of the Book of Acts, though Luke develops his case somewhat differently from John.

All of this material is suggestive for twentieth-century Christian apologists. The Messiahship and divine Sonship of Jesus in the present pluralistic theological climate are still very much a contentious issue. The claims for Jesus Christ as the Son of God are currently widely disputed. In such an environment a brief must be presented, arguments advanced and defending witnesses brought forward, if the Christian case is to be given a proper hearing. To fail to present the evidence for the Christian position would be tantamount to conceding defeat to its opponents. That is to say, the controversy theme, so evident in the New Testament, appears to be highly pertinent to the missionary task of the church today.

There is another facet to the controversy theme, and it concerns the real problem of dealing with disputes within the Christian community itself. This is surely as much a contemporary problem as it was an ancient one; indeed the whole of Christian history bears witness to the perennial difficulty of resolving contentious issues within the household of faith. Perhaps this study has highlighted some features which deserve renewed attention in the twentieth century such as the importance of the scriptures, and the need for argument, reasoning and explanation to elucidate their meaning and apply them persuasively to life situations. All of this points to the abiding need for a didactic and intellectual element in the presentation of the Christian message if it is to satisfy the needs of its own adherents as well as to address itself to the missionary task. Christianity's inner tensions can prove constructive, if they are handled, as the Book of Acts indicates the early church attempted to handle them, in a positive manner with an honest facing of the vexatious points in a frank, loving and open-ended dialogue under the Spirit's direction.

In the third place, it is noteworthy that faithful witness often entails suffering and persecution. This is still true in the nuclear age, particularly where Christians live in countries whose leaders are hostile to the Christian church. In the Book of Revelation a similar situation is definitely in view. Christians are about to enter a time of severe persecution, and some of them will be hauled into the courts and sentenced to martyrs' deaths. For this reason the seer of Patmos encourages them to 'hold' to 'the testimony of Jesus'. This phrase is best taken as a subjective genitive in the Apocalypse. It refers to the testimony borne by Jesus on the cross, where his faithful attestation of the redemptive purpose of God earned him the epithet 'Faithful and True'. The seer mentions Christ's testimony because it is of vital importance to his readers facing the great martyrdom.

Under such circumstances words with forensic overtones are naturally given their full weight in John's message of encouragement. Metaphors drawn from the lawcourt are never far from the author's mind, as a study of chapters 11, 12, 18 and 19 illustrates. In other words, John has revivified the idea of witness by reference to the original lawcourt setting. Especially is this true of his treatment of Satan, 'the accuser of the brethren', who 'accuses them day and night before God', and who is ejected from his heavenly post by the legal victory of Christ and his martyr-witnesses.

Thus it is not surprising that wherever Christians have faced persecution and hostile lawcourts for the sake of their testimony to Christ, the Book of Revelation has been a source of inspiration. They have been given new strength to endure, knowing that beyond the injustices of earthly courts there stood the eternal justice of God. As Christ had conquered suffering and death, so too they would conquer and share his victory over the forces of evil. As their Lord had witnessed faithfully even unto death, they also must bear unflinching testimony, assured that if they confessed him before men on earth, he would confess them before his Father in heaven – a theme also found in Matthew, Luke and Acts.

The Synoptic accounts of anticipated persecution are also instructive in this connection. Here the idea of witness is certainly very much a live metaphor. Hauled into courts by their opponents, Christians will be told what to say in the hour of crisis by the Spirit. The very fact of standing before kings, councils and governors will offer unprecedented opportunities for bearing testimony before them. Though often Christians would be condemned in earthly lawcourts, in the heavenly lawcourt the Son of Man would acknowledge them and reverse the unjust judgments pronounced against them by their earthly judges.

All this witness material provides a challenge to faithfulness and a note of encouragement, both of which are as pertinent to persecuted twentieth-century Christians as to their first-century counterparts.

Similarly in the Fourth Gospel and Acts when the apostles are witnessing for Christ in the face of antagonism and hostility they do not witness in their own strength but rather in the convincing power of the Holy Spirit. They are reassured that when they bear witness in what seem to be the most unpromising circumstances the Spirit is active in challenging the world with the truth of what they say. John underscores the inner witness of the Spirit whilst Luke in Acts stresses the outward manifestation of the Spirit's work in signs and wonders which confirm the apostolic testimony. The Spirit's task is well summarized by Pierce Beaver:

It is the Holy Spirit who is the Great Apostle and who leads the Church in its witnessing...He crowns faithful witness with fruitfulness, for he goes before every evangelist and missionary preparing hearts and minds to hear. It is only by him that a man can call Jesus

'Lord' (1 Cor. 12: 13). It is by his power that the Gospel of reconciliation is preached effectively and relevantly and then authentically shown forth in the unity, fellowship and service of the Church.[1]

Finally, something must be said about the importance of the witness motif for contemporary preachers and communicators of the Christian message. In this connection three features may be mentioned.

First, witnesses are passionately involved in the case they seek to present.[2] They have been apprehended by it, and so they have an inner compulsion to plead its merits with others. They echo Jeremiah's words, 'There is in my heart as it were a burning fire shut up in my bones and I am weary with holding it in, and I cannot.' Like the first-century preachers they declare, 'We cannot stop speaking what we have seen and heard.'

Secondly, witnesses are held accountable for the truthfulness of their testimony. Perjury was, and still is, a serious offence punishable by heavy penalties. This solemn sense of being responsible under God appears in Paul, who four times declares, 'God is my witness.' Applied to preachers, this means that they are driven back to the scriptures as the test of their witness. This is not to discount the place of biblical criticism in understanding the true meaning of the scriptures in their original setting. Neither is it an attempt to undervalue the task of translating the Christ-event into contemporary terms in one's actual communication of the message. But having said all this, the criterion of a modern witness to Christ remains its fidelity to, and agreement with, the New Testament witnesses to him.[3]

Third, witnesses must be faithful not only to the bare facts of the Christ-event, but also to their meaning. That is, modern witnesses are summoned to speak of the life, death and resurrection of Christ in such a way that the intrinsic divine significance

[1] R. P. Beaver, 'The apostolate of the church', *The Theology of the Christian Mission*, ed. G. H. Anderson (New York, 1961), p. 268.

[2] N. Alexander, 'The united character of the New Testament witness of the Christ-event', *The New Testament in Historical and Contemporary Perspective*, ed. H. Anderson and W. Barclay (Oxford, 1965), p. 32. Cf. J. R. Stott, *The Preacher's Portrait* (London, 1961), pp. 63–9.

[3] Alexander, *op. cit.*

of these events is brought to light.[1] Through their attestation of the gospel, the process of divine judgment is prolonged. In this way the lawsuit over the claims of Jesus Christ continues, and men judge themselves by their response. The witness to Christ, now as much as in apostolic times, simply functions as a best man at a wedding (cf. Jn 3: 28–30). When he has accomplished the task of bringing the Bride and Groom together, he can retire into obscurity, happy in the knowledge that his testimony has been effective.

[1] *Ibid.* pp. 32–3. Cf. A. M. Hunter, *The Unity of the New Testament* (London, 1943).

THE USE OF WITNESSES AND EVIDENCE IN RABBINICAL LITERATURE

Although much of the material contained in the Jerusalem and Babylonian Talmuds and related literature is of late or uncertain date, it is valuable for the light which it throws on the background of the Old and New Testaments. This is nowhere more true than in the study of the legal background of the New Testament concept of witness. For this reason an Appendix has been added on the use of witnesses and evidence in the Talmud and related rabbinic literature.[1]

CRIMINAL CASES

The Jews were particularly strict in their treatment of evidence; this is clear from a study of Jewish law as developed in the Bible and the Talmud. In criminal cases of the type described in the Mishnah 'every precaution is taken to exclude the possibility that by condemning an innocent man the witnesses and the judges should themselves incur the guilt of judicial murder'.[2] While these rules undoubtedly prevented the conviction of criminals in many cases, they certainly provided the innocent person with almost complete protection. It was felt better to leave the guilty party in the hands of the divine Judge than to risk the possibility of the court shedding innocent blood.[3]

[1] Some of the relevant material has been conveniently collected, translated and arranged by Herbert Danby, *Tractate Sanhedrin, Mishnah and Tosefta, the Judicial Procedure of the Jews as Codified towards the End of the Second Century A.D.* (London, 1919); cf. also Danby's translation and notes on *The Mishnah* (Oxford, 1933). For an excellent bibliography see John Wick Bowman, 'The Rabbinic Writings' in *Tools for Bible Study*, eds. B. H. Kelly and D. G. Miller (Richmond, Va, 1956), pp. 145–59.

[2] G. F. Moore, *Judaism* (2 vols.; Cambridge, 1927), II, 184.

[3] Cf. M. Goldberg, 'Evidence', *The Universal Jewish Encyclopedia*, ed. I. Landman (10 vols.; New York, 1939–43), I, 199, to whom this whole section on criminal cases is heavily indebted.

According to biblical law conviction for a capital crime (e.g., apostasy, Deut. 13) required the eye-witness evidence of at least two witnesses (Num. 35: 30; Deut. 17: 6; cf. 19: 15). So seriously was the principle of multiple witness taken that the Talmud in a case involving immorality declared it to be sinful for a single witness to come forward to testify alone (Pesaḥim 113b). This strict insistence on eye-witness evidence also completely ruled out all circumstantial evidence (Tosefta, Sanhedrin VIII.3). Simeon ben Shaṭaḥ gives a striking instance of this in Sanhedrin 37b:

I saw a man chasing another into a ruin; I ran after him and saw a sword in his hand dripping with the other's blood and the murdered man in his death agony. I said to him, You villain! Who killed this man? Either I or you. But what can I do? Your life is not delivered into my hand, for the law says, At the mouth of two witnesses shall he that is to die be put to death. But He who knows the thought, will requite that man who killed his fellow.[1]

In other words, 'the evidence of witnesses is not regarded as valid unless they have actually seen what they assert' (Tosefta, Sanhedrin v.5b; cf. Midrash, Exodus XLVI.1).[2]

Another restriction on evidence in criminal cases was the fact that the testimony of near relatives was inadmissible. According to one list, ineligible relatives included father, brother, uncle, father-in-law and brother-in-law; another limits them to uncle, first cousin and anyone eligible to be an heir (Mishnah, Sanhedrin III.4). Evidence could not be furnished by persons of bad character (Tosefta, Sanhedrin v.5a), or by persons who had received money to testify (Mishnah, Bekoroth IV.6).

The judges subjected the testimony of the witnesses to rigorous cross-examination (Mishnah, Sanhedrin v.2), particularly about the time and place of the crime. Thus if one witness declared that a murder took place at 11 a.m. and another said it occurred at 1 p.m., the evidence was rejected, for both statements were open to question (Mishnah, Sanhedrin v.3; Tosefta, Sanhedrin IX.1b). Similarly, evidence was rejected if there was discrepancy about the place of a crime (cf. Susanna 54–61).

[1] Moore, *op. cit.*
[2] H. Freedman and M. Simon, eds., *Midrash Rabbah* (10 vols.; London, 1939), III, 526.

Another question in the interrogation of the witnesses was whether they had warned the accused that he was about to commit a crime the penalty of which is death (Mishnah, Sanhedrin v.1; Tosefta, Sanhedrin xi.1–5; Sanhedrin 40b, 41a; and especially Jer. Sanhedrin 22a–b). That such a warning had been given, and that in spite of it the man had rejected it and gone right on to the perpetration of the criminal act, was proof that he had done it with full knowledge of the crime and its consequences, and therefore with complete moral responsibility.[1]

CIVIL CASES[2]

In civil cases a note of loan or a bill of sale signed by both parties was accepted as evidence, as well as direct testimony. The testimony of witnesses, however, was given more weight than that of documents. What follows applies in the main to civil cases.

Witnesses

In order to prove a disputed fact, witnesses must fulfil the following requirements:

1. Two must testify to the same fact.[3] This rule is laid down in Deut. 19: 15 and in other passages apparently from criminal cases only, but it has been extended to civil cases as well.[4] In civil cases, however, it is not necessary that the two witnesses should agree very closely as to time and place; minor discrepancies of this kind are within the limit of fair mistake, and the testimony stands. Even less does a disagreement as to cir-

---

[1] Moore, *op. cit.*, p. 185.

[2] The following section, with slight adaptations, is a condensed version of L. N. Dembitz's article on 'Evidence' in *The Jewish Encyclopedia*, ed. I. Singer (12 vols.; New York, 1901–16), v, 277–80.

[3] According to Marcus Jastrow, *A Dictionary of the Targumim, the Talmud Babli and Yerushalmi, and the Midrashic Literature* (2 vols.; London, 1903), ii, 1042, in matters of ritual the statement of one witness was sufficient (Hullin, 10b).

[4] According to R. J. Z. Werblowsky and G. Wigoder (eds.), *The Encyclopedia of the Jewish Religion* (New York, 1966), p. 136, 'no legal decision can be concluded in capital or civil cases in matters of atonement, sacrifices, or involving flagellation or promotion or demotion in the priesthood, etc., on the evidence of a single witness (cf. Deut. 19: 15 and *Siphrei in loco*).'

cumstances other than time and place affect the testimony. When two witnesses vary only in the matter of quantity, the lesser quantity is sufficiently proved. In criminal cases, a much closer agreement is required (see above).

2. The witness must be an Israelite. The Talmud seems to take this for granted, though it allows some facts to stand proved upon a statement 'made innocently' by a Gentile, that is, not as a witness in court. In damage cases the Mishnah says expressly that the witnesses must be freemen and sons of the covenant (Baba Ḳamma 1.3). Slaves were not competent (Baba Ḳamma 88a).

3. The witness must be a man, not a woman (Mishnah, Rosh Hashanah 1.8; Shebu'oth 30a); of full age, that is, more than thirteen years old; not a deaf-mute or a lunatic, and, according to the better opinion, not a blind man (Baba Bathra 128a). A boy not much over thirteen, and having no understanding of business, must not testify in a cause involving title to land (Baba Bathra 155a). Nor should a person of full age testify as to what he saw or heard as a minor except in matters of frequent observation (Mishnah, Kethuboth 11.10).

4. He must not be a 'wicked' man, for the Law says (Ex. 23: 1): 'Put not thy hand with the wicked, to be an unrighteous witness.' Whereas the Torah disqualified only a malicious witness,[1] the Mishnah names as incompetent professional gamblers, usurers, and traders in the fruits of the Sabbatical year (Sanhedrin III.3; cf. 'Eduyyoth II.7; Jos., Ant. IV.219). 'Among persons disqualified to act as judges or witnesses are also to be included robbers, herdsmen and extortioners, and all suspect concerning property', that is, any one whose honesty has ever been called in question (Tosefta, Sanhedrin v.5a). A baraita in the Gemara on this section (Sanhedrin 25a, b) disqualifies also tax-collectors as presumably dishonest unless their good character is proved, as well as butchers who sell unauthorized meat for 'kosher'; and it provides that they can reinstate themselves only by quitting their unlawful trade and by giving up for charitable purposes all the unlawful gains made therein (cf. Lk.

[1] The law of malicious witness made the accuser in a capital crime liable to the death penalty (Deut. 19: 19; cf. Code of Hammurabi, section 3).

19: 1–10). Maimonides (Yadayim, 'Eduth x.3) draws from the Talmudic passages Sanhedrin 25a, b and Baba Ḳamma 72b the inference that one who purposely commits a sin to which the Law attaches the punishment of death or of forty stripes, or who robs or steals, although these latter offences are not punishable by stripes or death, is 'wicked' in the sense of being an incompetent witness. The same is true of one proved to be a 'plotting witness' (Sanhedrin 27a; this may help to explain why, according to Acts 1: 15–26, the first item of apostolic business after the ascension was the replacing of a 'plotting witness' (Judas) by a *bona fide* witness). But the ground of incompetency must be proved by two other witnesses; the sinning witness cannot become incompetent by his own confession.

Informers, 'Epicureans', and apostates are incompetent (Maimonides, 'Eduth x end, followed by later codes). Also men who show lack of all self-respect – by eating on the street, walking about naked at their work, or living openly on the charity of Gentiles – are incompetent (Maimonides, 'Eduth xi 6, based on Sanhedrin 26b). Where the incompetency arises under rabbinical provisions, the objectionable man must be publicly proclaimed incompetent before his testimony can be excluded (*ibid.*).

Where A and B are called as witnesses, and B knows that A is 'wicked' (for instance, a robber), so as not to give force to the testimony of A, B should not testify (Shebu'oth 30b).

5. The witness must not have any interest in the result of the litigation. The Talmud carries this doctrine so far as to state (Baba Bathra) that where someone raises a claim of title to a public bath house or the square of the city, none of the citizens can testify or act as a judge until he divests himself of all share in the title. Similarly, where the suit is on grounds common to two joint owners of land, one may not testify for his companion until he has sold his own share without warranty. In a suit for a field a tenant on shares may not testify for his landlord, for he is interested in the crop (cf. Baba Bathra 29a, 43a).

6. The witness must not be related to the party that calls him: in criminal cases the witnesses for either side must not be related to the accused. The rule is derived from a rather bold interpretation of Deut. 24: 16, which is rendered, 'Fathers shall not be

put to death on (the testimony of) sons, nor sons on (the testimony of) fathers' (see Sanhedrin 27b); but the principle is extended far from capital cases to civil suits, and far beyond the mere relationship between father and son. Relationship by marriage is at an end when the wife dies. The objection of friendship or hate that applies to judges does not hold against witnesses. The later codes follow the Palestinian Talmud on Sanhedrin III in holding that witnesses akin to each other or to the judges are incompetent (Ḥoshen Mishpaṭ 33, 17).

Mode of Examination

1. As in the Old Testament, witnesses are required to stand when they give evidence (Shebu'oth 30b). They are to be thoroughly interrogated (Pirkē Aboth 1.9), though they do not testify under oath but under the sanction of the ninth commandment (Ex. 20: 16). The presiding judge admonishes the witnesses before they testify. All persons other than the litigants and the witness to be examined are then dismissed from the room; the same procedure applies to all subsequent witnesses (Mishnah, Sanhedrin III.6).

2. He who knows testimony of benefit to his neighbour should, under the Mosaic Law (Lev. 5: 1), make it known to him (Sanhedrin 43a); and an oath may be imposed on him to say whether he knows anything and what he knows (cf. Mt. 26: 63). The Talmud (Baba Ḳamma 56a) points to the words 'he shall bear his iniquity'; hence, he is liable only to heavenly, not earthly, punishment. With a view to the former, the litigant may ask that a ban may be pronounced in the synagogue against those who know anything in his favour and will not come forward to testify. Otherwise he has no remedy, no compulsory process against witnesses, and no means to force them to answer questions. But when the court finds that the witnesses for one party are intimidated by his opponent from appearing, it may compel the latter himself to bring these witnesses into court.

3. From 'the mouth of witnesses', Deut. 19: 15 and Num. 35: 30 declare, a man shall be condemned, not upon their written statement; hence, testimony should be given by word of mouth in open court, not by way of deposition (a method not unknown

in the Book of Job, cf. Job 31: 35). In all criminal cases and in all suits for penalties or damages to the person, this rule is invariably followed; but in actions on contract, especially on behalf of the defendant, depositions are admitted for good reasons, such as that the witnesses are sick or absent from the place of trial, or that one of the parties is sick, so that the trial cannot be held, while the witnesses are about to depart. In all such cases notice must be given to the opposite party, and the deposition, in the nature of minutes of judicial proceedings, must be taken before a court of three judges.

4. As a rule, witnesses may be heard only in the presence of the opposing litigant, so that he may suggest to the court points on which to cross-examine them. For this reason witnesses may not be received against a minor, because he would not know how to direct the cross-examination. Later authorities maintain that the rule, 'No witness without the chance of cross-examination', applies to the plaintiff's witnesses only; but the debtor may be plaintiff, when he sues a minor heir of his creditor for the cancellation of his bond, by presenting his receipt attested by witnesses: it is held (Ḥoshen Mishpaṭ 108, 17) that he must wait till the infant heir comes of age.

5. In civil cases, other than those for personal injury, the court is not bound to go, on its own initiative, through the formal cross-questions as to time and place with a view to finding a contradiction between the two witnesses, for such a contradiction would 'close the door before borrowers'; but where the judges have reason to suspect that the claim or defence is fraudulent (Ḥoshen Mishpaṭ 108, 15), they should take all proper means to break down the testimony on that side.

6. Where the witnesses testify to an admission made by a litigant they should give, as far as they can, the very words, not their general import. Let the court decide whether the words amount to an admission or can be explained away as having been made in jest or for an ulterior purpose. The position is drawn from a section of the Mishnah and a baraita (Sanhedrin 29a).

7. Speaking generally, after a witness has been allowed to depart he may not retract his testimony by saying, 'I was mis-

taken'; 'I did not recollect', etc. Even if he gives a plausible reason he is not listened to. But when other witnesses are called to attack the character of one who has testified, the latter may explain or retract (Sanhedrin 74b; Kethuboth 19b).

Documentary Proof

This is often spoken of as *r'yh*, which is the general term for 'evidence' or 'proof'.

1. It is in general either an instrument written by an adverse party, which has to be proved by witnesses acquainted with his handwriting, or the more formal instrument, known as a 'shetar', or deed, attested by two witnesses. When a deed is the basis of an action or defence, it ought to be regularly proved by the testimony of the attesting witnesses; but if they are absent, or refuse to testify, other men may establish the deed by proving the handwriting of the attesting witnesses (there being, of course, two witnesses to the handwriting of each attester). When this is proved, the attesting witnesses are not allowed to attack the validity of the deed (Kethuboth II 3). But the attesting witnesses are always competent to state that the grantor or obligor made a protest to them by reason of duress, for this is not incompatible with the deed (Ḥoshen Mishpaṭ 46, 37, 38).

2. A method to establish a deed, more especially a bond, at the instance of the holder, is given in the Talmud (Baba Ḳamma 112b, see also Baba Bathra 40a and Kethuboth 21a) and is recognized by the codes (Yadayim, 'Eduth VI; Ḥoshen Mishpaṭ 46, 3-4). The two witnesses, at the instance of the holder, come before an improvised court, made up of any three respectable Israelites; and the latter write at the bottom of the deed 'AB and CD appeared before us this day and testified to their own signatures, whereupon we have approved and established this deed'; and the three 'judges' sign. Being in the nature of a judgment, this must be done in the daytime; but the procedure is wholly *ex parte*. A deed thus established may, without further proof, be presented upon the trial of a case.

Effect of Evidence

1. The sages had very little more confidence in circumstantial evidence given for the purpose of 'taking money out of' the defendant's pocket than in that given for the purpose of inflicting the penalty of death or stripes. In fact, circumstantial evidence was generally rejected (Shebu'oth 46a).

2. Hearsay evidence was barred equally in civil as in criminal cases, no matter how strongly the witness might believe in what he heard, and however worthy and numerous were his informants (Yadayim, 'Eduth XVII.1).

3. The length of time between the observation of a fact and the testimony was no reason for rejecting the latter, even though the witness had to refresh his memory by looking at a written memorandum (Kethuboth 20a).

4. A 'set' of witnesses (consisting of at least two persons) may be convicted 'plotters' by another set or sets proving an alibi on them. But the opposite party may prove an alibi on the convicting set, or in some other way show that the facts testified to by the first set were impossible or untrue. Speaking broadly, the judges considered it their duty to decide the effect of testimony as a question of law, not as one of the greatest probability.

5. The rules of evidence were relaxed in one particular case – that of the proof of death of a husband ('Eduyyoth I.12; VI.1; VII.5; Shabbath 145b; Yeb. 90b). In this instance the rabbis succeeded eventually in passing a rule that his death could be proved by the evidence of one witness, even of a slave, a woman or a minor. This was done to prevent the widow from becoming caught in a predicament in which she could neither marry again nor expect to receive support from a deceased husband.[1]

To sum it all up, it is fair to say that Jewish law, as it is expressed in the Talmud and related rabbinical literature, was particularly strict in its treatment of evidence. It was felt better to permit the guilty party to escape than to inflict punishment upon an innocent man.

---

[1] Cf. I. Epstein, *Judaism – A Historical Presentation* (London, 1959), p. 87: 'Another example is their relaxation of the law of evidence to establish a husband's death, the testimony of a single witness, even based on hearsay, being declared sufficient to enable the wife to re-marry.'

BIBLIOGRAPHY

A. BOOKS

Abbot-Smith, G. *A Manual Greek Lexicon of the New Testament*, Edinburgh, 1922.
Aland, K., Black, M., Metzger, B. and Wikgren, A. (eds.). *The Greek New Testament*, Stuttgart, 1966.
Anderson, B. W. and Harrelson, W. (eds.). *Israel's Prophetic Heritage*, New York, 1962.
Anderson, G. H. (ed.). *The Theology of the Christian Mission*, New York, 1961.
Aristotle. *The 'Art' of Rhetoric* (tr. J. H. Freese), LCL, London, 1926.
Works (ed. W. D. Ross *et al.*), 11 vols., Oxford, 1924.
Asting, R. *Die Verkündigung des Wortes im Urchristentum*, Stuttgart, 1939.
Augustin, C. *De Martelaar en zijn Getuigenis*, Kampen, 1966.
Bailey, J. A. *The Traditions Common to the Gospels of Luke and John*, Leiden, 1963.
Baird, J. A. *The Justice of God in the Teaching of Jesus*, London, 1963.
Barrett, C. K. *The Epistle to the Romans*, London, 1957.
The Gospel according to St. John, London, 1962.
Luke the Historian in Recent Study, London, 1961.
Barth, K. *Der Christ als Zeuge*, Munich, 1934.
Evangelical Theology: An Introduction, London, 1963.
Barth, M. *Der Augenzeuge*, Zürich, 1946.
Bavinck, J. H. *An Introduction to the Science of Missions* (tr. D. H. Freeman), Philadelphia, 1961.
Beare, F. W. *The First Epistle of Peter*, Oxford, 1958; 2nd ed. 1961.
Begrich, J. *Studien zu Deuterojesaja* (1938), reprinted, Munich, 1963.
Bernard, J. H. *A Critical and Exegetical Commentary on the Gospel of St. John*, ICC, 2 vols., New York, 1929.
Betz, O. *Der Paraklet*, Leiden, 1963.
Bigg, C. *A Critical and Exegetical Commentary on the Epistles of St. Peter and St. Jude*, ICC, Edinburgh, 1901.
Black, M. *An Aramaic Approach to the Gospels and Acts*, 3rd ed., Oxford 1967.
Boecker, H. J. *Redeformen des Rechtslebens im Alten Testament*, Neukirchen-Vluyn, 1964.
Boice, J. M. *Witness and Revelation in the Gospel of John*, Grand Rapids, 1970.

Bonner, R. J. and Smith, G. E. *The Administration of Justice from Homer to Aristotle*, 2 vols., Chicago, 1938.
Bonsirven, J. *Theology of the New Testament*, London, 1963.
Borgen, P. *Bread from Heaven – An Exegetical Study of the Concept of Manna in the Gospel of John and the Writings of Philo*, Leiden, 1965.
Bouquet, A. C. *Everyday Life in New Testament Times*, London, 1953.
Bousset, W. *Die Offenbarung Johannis*, Göttingen, 1906.
Brown, F., Driver, S. R. and Briggs, C. A. *A Hebrew and English Lexicon of the Old Testament*, Oxford, 1955.
Brown, R. E. *The Gospel according to John*, 2 vols., Garden City, N.Y., 1966–70.
Brox, N. *Zeuge und Märtyrer*, Munich, 1961.
Bruce, F. F. *The Acts of the Apostles*, London, 1952.
The Epistle of Paul to the Romans, London, 1963.
Bultmann, R. *The Gospel of John: A Commentary*, Oxford, 1971.
Theology of the New Testament (tr. K. Groebel), 2 vols., London and New York, 1955.
Burkitt, F. C. *The Gospel History and its Transmission*, Edinburgh, 1911.
Burnier, E. *La Notion de Témoignage dans le Nouveau Testament*, Lausanne, 1939.
Burrows, M. *The Dead Sea Scrolls*, London, 1956.
Caird, G. B. *The Apostolic Age*, London, 1955.
A Commentary on the Revelation of St. John the Divine, London, 1966.
The Gospel according to Saint Luke, London, 1963.
Principalities and Powers, Oxford, 1956.
Campenhausen, H. von. *Die Idee des Martyriums in der alten Kirche*, Göttingen, 1936.
Castelli, E. *et al. La Testimonianza*, Padua, 1972.
Cerfaux, L. *Recueil Lucien Cerfaux*, 3 vols., Gembloux, 1954–62.
Chamberlain, W. D. *An Exegetical Grammar of the Greek New Testament*, New York, 1941.
Charles, R. H. (ed.). *The Apocrypha and Pseudepigrapha of the Old Testament in English*, 2 vols., Oxford, 1913.
A Critical and Exegetical Commentary on the Revelation of St. John, ICC, 2 vols., Edinburgh, 1920.
Cicero. *De Oratore* (tr. E. W. Sutton and H. Rackham), 2 vols., LCL, London, 1949.
Topica (tr. H. M. Hubbell), LCL, London, 1949.
Conzelmann, H. *An Outline of the Theology of the New Testament*, London, 1969.
Coppens, J., Descamps, A. and Massaux, É. (eds.). *Sacra Pagina*, 2 vols., Paris, 1959.
Cranfield, C. E. B. *The Gospel according to Saint Mark*, CGT, Cambridge, 1959.

Creed, J. M. *The Gospel according to St. Luke*, London, 1930.

Cross, F. L. *I Peter: A Paschal Liturgy*, London, 1954.

(ed.). *The Gospels Reconsidered*, Oxford, 1960.

Cullmann, O. *Christ and Time* (tr. F. V. Filson), London, 1951.

The Earliest Christian Confessions (tr. J. K. S. Reid), London, 1949.

Early Christian Worship (tr. A. S. Todd and J. B. Torrance), London, 1953.

The Early Church (ed. A. J. B. Higgins), London, 1956.

Dana, H. E. and Mantey, J. R. *A Manual Grammar of the Greek New Testament*, London, 1928.

Danby, H. *The Mishnah*, Oxford, 1933.

Tractate Sanhedrin, Mishnah and Tosefta, the Judicial Procedure of the Jews as Codified towards the End of the Second Century A.D., London, 1919.

Daube, D. *Studies in Biblical Law*, Cambridge, 1947.

Davies, W. D. *Christian Origins and Judaism*, London, 1962.

Davies, W. D. and Daube, D. (eds.). *The Background of the NT and Its Eschatology*, Cambridge, 1956.

Dibelius, M. *Studies in the Acts of the Apostles* (ed. H. Greeven, tr. M. Ling and P. Schubert), London, 1956.

Dodd, C. H. *According to the Scriptures: the Sub-Structure of New Testament Theology*, London, 1952.

The Apostolic Preaching and its Developments, London, 1936, reprinted, 1952.

Historical Tradition in the Fourth Gospel, Cambridge, 1963.

The Interpretation of the Fourth Gospel, Cambridge, 1954.

The Johannine Epistles, MNTC, London, 1946.

Dunn, J. D. G. *Baptism in the Holy Spirit*, SBT 2nd ser., 15, London, 1970.

Edwards, C. *The Hammurabi Code: and the Sinaitic Legislation*, London, 1921.

Epictetus. *The Discourses as reported by Arrian, the Manual and Fragment* (tr. W. A. Oldfather), 2 vols., LCL, London, 1926–8.

Epstein, I. *Judaism – A Historical Presentation*, London, 1959.

Evans, C. F. *Resurrection and the New Testament*, SBT 2nd ser., 12, London, 1970.

Farrer, A. *The Rebirth of Images*, London, 1949.

The Revelation of St. John the Divine, Oxford, 1964.

Fischer, J. *Das Buch Isaias*, 2 vols., Bonn, 1939.

Freed, E. D. *Old Testament Quotations in the Gospel of John*, Leiden, 1965.

Freedman, H. and Simon, M. (eds.). *Midrash Rabbah*, 10 vols., London, 1939.

Frend, W. H. C. *Martyrdom and Persecution in the Early Church*, Oxford, 1965.

Fridrichsen, A. (ed.). *The Root of the Vine*, London, 1953.

Fuller, R. H. *A Critical Introduction to the New Testament*, London, 1966.
The New Testament in Current Study, New York, 1962.
Gaster, T. H. *The Scriptures of the Dead Sea Sect*, London, 1957.
Gerhardsson, B. *Memory and Manuscript*, Lund, 1961.
Glasson, T. F. *Moses in the Fourth Gospel*, London, 1963.
Green, F. W. *The Gospel according to Saint Matthew*, Oxford, 1947.
Guthrie, D. *New Testament Introduction*, 3rd ed., London, 1971.
Guthrie, D. and Motyer, J. A. (eds.). *The New Bible Commentary*, 3rd ed., London, 1970.
Haenchen, E. *The Acts of the Apostles*, Oxford, 1965.
Harrelson, W. *Interpreting the Old Testament*, New York, 1964.
Hastings, A. *Prophet and Witness in Jerusalem*, Baltimore, 1958.
Hatch, E. and Redpath, H. A. *A Concordance to the Septuagint*, 2 vols., Oxford, 1906.
Heaton, E. W. *Everyday Life in Old Testament Times*, London and New York, 1956.
Higgins, A. J. B. (ed.). *New Testament Essays*, Manchester, 1959.
Holy Bible and Apocrypha. Revised Standard Version, New York, 1952.
Hooker, M. D. *The Son of Man in Mark*, London, 1967.
Hort, F. J. A. *The Apocalypse of St. John I–III*, London, 1908.
Hoskyns, E. C. *The Fourth Gospel* (ed. F. N. Davey), London, 1947.
Hoskyns, E. C. and Davey, F. N. *The Riddle of the New Testament*, London, 1947.
How, W. W. and Wells, J. *A Commentary on Herodotus*, 2 vols., Oxford, 1912.
Hultgren, A. J. 'Jesus and his adversaries: a study of the form and function of the conflict stories in the Synoptic tradition', New York, Union Seminary Th.D. thesis, 1971.
Hunter, A. M. *Introducing New Testament Theology*, London, 1957.
The Work and Words of Jesus, London, 1950.
Jastrow, M. *A Dictionary of the Targumim, the Talmud Babli and Yerushalmi and the Midrashic Literature*, 2 vols., London, 1903.
Jebb, R. C. *Selections from the Attic Orators*, London, 1888.
Jeremias, J. *The Central Message of the New Testament*, London, 1965.
Jesus' Promise to the Nations, London, 1958.
The Parables of Jesus, 6th ed., London and New York, 1963.
The Prayers of Jesus, London, 1967.
Johnston, G. *The Spirit–Paraclete in the Gospel of John*, Cambridge, 1970.
Josephus. *Works* (tr. H. St. J. Thackeray), 8 vols., LCL, London, 1926–34.
Judge, E. A. *The Social Pattern of Christian Groups in the First Century*, London, 1960.

Keck, L. E. *Mandate to Witness – Studies in the Book of Acts*, Valley Forge, 1964.

Kee, H. C., Young, F. W. and Froehlich, K. *Understanding the New Testament*, 2nd ed., Englewood Cliffs, N.J., 1965.

Kelly, B. H. and Miller, D. G. (eds.). *Tools for Bible Study*, Richmond, Va., 1956.

Kelly, J. M. *Roman Litigation*, Oxford, 1966.

Kemmler, D. 'An Inquiry into Faith and Human Reason with respect to Paul's method of preaching as illustrated by I and II Thessalonians and Acts 17, 2–4', Cambridge Ph.D. thesis, 1972.

Kennett, R. H. *Ancient Hebrew Social Life and Custom as Indicated in Law Narrative and Metaphor*, London, 1933.

Kiddle, M. and Ross, M. K. *The Revelation of St. John*, MNTC, London and New York, 1940.

Kilpatrick, G. D. (ed.). H KAINH ΔIAΘHKH, 2nd ed., London, 1962.

The Trial of Jesus, London, 1953.

Kittel, R. (ed.). *Biblia Hebraica*, 7th ed., Stuttgart, 1951.

Klassen, W. and Snyder, G. F. (eds.). *Current Issues in New Testament Interpretation*, London, 1962.

Köhler, L. *Deuterojesaja Stilkritisch Untersucht*, Giessen, 1923.

Hebrew Man (tr. P. R. Ackroyd), London, 1956.

Köhler, L. and Baumgartner, W. *Lexicon in Veteris Testamenti Libros*, Leiden, 1958.

Ladd, G. E. *The Pattern of New Testament Truth*, Grand Rapids, 1968.

Leaf, W. (ed.). *The Iliad*, 2 vols., London, 1902.

Leisi, E. *Der Zeuge im Attischen Recht*, Frauenfeld, 1908.

Leivestad, R. *Christ the Conqueror*, London, 1954.

Lévi, I. (ed.). *The Hebrew Text of the Book of Ecclesiasticus*, Leiden, 1951.

Lightfoot, J. B. *The Apostolic Fathers* (ed. J. R. Harmer), London, 1926.

The Apostolic Fathers, 2nd ed., London, 1890.

Lightfoot, R. H. *St. John's Gospel*, Oxford, 1956.

Lipsius, J. H., Meier, M. H. and Schömann, G. F. *Das Attische Recht und Rechtsverfahren*, Leipzig, 1905–15.

Loos, H. van der. *The Miracles of Jesus*, Leiden, 1965.

McCasland, S. V. *By the Finger of God*, New York, 1951.

Maertens, T. *Bible Themes – A Source Book*, 2 vols., Bruges, 1964.

Mahaffy, J. P. *Cunningham Memoirs, No. 8, The Flinders Petrie Papyri*, Dublin, 1891.

Maine, H. S. *Ancient Law*, London, 1907.

Mandelkern, S. *Veteris Testamenti Concordiantiae Hebraicae atque Chaldaicae*, Graz, 1955.

Marshall, I. H. *Luke: Historian and Theologian*, Grand Rapids, 1971.
Masterman, J. H. B. *The First Epistle of S. Peter*, London, 1900.
May, H. G. and Metzger, B. M. (eds.). *The Oxford Annotated Bible*, *R.S.V.*, New York, 1962.
Minear, P. S. *Images of the Church in the New Testament*, Philadelphia, 1960.
Moore, G. F. *Judaism*, 2 vols., Cambridge, 1927.
Morgenthaler, R. *Die Lukanische Geschichtsschreibung als Zeugnis: Gestalt und Gehalt der Kunst des Lukas*, 2 vols., Zürich, 1949.
Statistik des Neutestamentlichen Wortschatzes, Zürich, 1958.
Morris, L. *The Apostolic Preaching of the Cross*, 3rd ed., London, 1965.
The Biblical Doctrine of Judgment, London, 1960.
Moule, C. F. D. *The Birth of the New Testament*, London, 1962.
An Idiom-Book of New Testament Greek, Cambridge, 1953, 2nd ed. 1968.
(ed.). *Miracles – Cambridge Studies in their Philosophy and History*, London, 1965.
The Phenomenon of the New Testament, London, 1967.
Moulton, W. F. and Geden, A. S. *A Concordance to the Greek New Testament*, Edinburgh, 1953.
Mounce, R. H. *The Essential Nature of New Testament Preaching*, Grand Rapids, 1960.
Muffs, Y. *Studies in the Aramaic Legal Papyri*, Leiden, 1969.
Nestle, Eberhard, Nestle, Erwin and Aland, K. *Novum Testamentum Graece*, Stuttgart, 1943; 25th ed., 1963.
Neufeld, V. N. *The Earliest Christian Confessions*, Leiden, 1963.
New English Bible, Oxford and Cambridge, 1970.
Newbigin, L. *The Household of God*, London, 1953.
Nicoll, W. R. (ed.). *The Expositor's Greek Testament*, 5 vols., London, 1897–1910.
Niles, D. T. *Whereof We Are Witnesses*, London, 1965.
Nineham, D. E. (ed.). *Studies in the Gospels*, Oxford, 1955.
North, C. R. *The Second Isaiah*, Oxford, 1964.
Noth, M. and Thomas, D. W. (eds.). *Wisdom in Israel and in the Ancient Near East*, Leiden, 1960.
Nunn, H. P. V. *The Authorship of the Fourth Gospel*, Oxford, 1952.
O'Neill, J. C. *The Theology of Acts in its Historical Setting*, London, 1961.
Overholt, T. W. *The Threat of Falsehood*, SBT 2nd ser., 16, London, 1970.
Perrin, N. *Rediscovering the Teaching of Jesus*, London, 1967.
Philo. *Works* (tr. F. H. Colson, G. H. Whitaker *et al.*), 10 vols., LCL, London, 1929–42.
Pierce, C. A. *Conscience in the New Testament*, London, 1955.

Plato. *Works* (tr. W. R. M. Lamb *et al.*), 10 vols., LCL, London, 1925.

Plummer, A. *The Epistles of St. John*, CGT, Cambridge, 1916.

Preisige, F. and Bilabel, F. *Sammelbuch griechischer Urkunden aus Ägypten*, 5 vols., Berlin, 1915–50.

Preiss, T. *Life in Christ* (tr. H. Knight), London, 1954.

Quasten, J. *Patrology*, 3 vols., Utrecht, 1950.

Quintilian. *Works* (tr. H. E. Butler), 4 vols., LCL, London, 1926–34.

Rad, G. von. *Old Testament Theology* (tr. D. M. G. Stalker), 2 vols., London, 1962–9.

Rahlfs, A. (ed.). *Septuaginta*, 2 vols., Stuttgart, 1943.

Richardson, A. *Christian Apologetics*, New York, 1947.
An Introduction to the Theology of the New Testament, London and New York, 1958.
A Theological Word Book of the Bible, London, 1950.

Ridderbos, H. N. *The Speeches of Peter in the Acts of the Apostles*, London, 1962.

Riesenfeld, H. *The Gospel Tradition and Its Beginnings*, Oxford, 1970.

Robertson, A. T. *A Grammar of the Greek New Testament in the Light of Historical Research*, 3rd ed., New York, 1919.

Robinson, J. A. T. *Twelve New Testament Studies*, SBT 1st ser., 34, London, 1962.

Roth, L. *Judaism: A Portrait*, New York, 1961.
(ed.). *The Standard Jewish Encyclopedia*, London, 1959.

Rowley, H. H. (ed.). *Studies in Old Testament Prophecy*, Edinburgh, 1950.

Russell, D. S. *The Method and Message of Jewish Apocalyptic*, Philadelphia, 1964.

Sanders, J. N. *The Gospel according to St. John*, ed. B. A. Mastin, London, 1968.

Schippers, R. *Getuigen van Jezus Christus*, Franeker, 1938.

Schmidt, H. *Das Gebet der Angeklagten im Alten Testament*, Berlin, 1928.

Schmoller, A. *Handkonkordanz zum Griechischen Neuen Testament*, Stuttgart, 1960.

Schnackenburg, R. *New Testament Theology Today* (tr. D. Askew), London, 1963.

Selwyn, E. G. *The First Epistle of St. Peter*, London, 1947.

Sherwin-White, A. N. *Roman Society and Roman Law in the New Testament* (*The Sarum Lectures*, 1960–61), Oxford, 1963.

Sidebottom, E. M. *The Christ of the Fourth Gospel*, London, 1961.

Skinner, J. *The Book of the Prophet Isaiah, Chapters XL–LXVI*, CBSC, Cambridge, 1898, rev. 1917.

Sparks, H. F. D. *The Formation of the New Testament*, London, 1952.

Stauffer, E. *Jesus and His Story* (tr. D. M. Barton), London, 1960.
New Testament Theology (tr. J. Marsh), London, 1955.
Stendahl, K. (ed.). *The Scrolls and the New Testament*, New York, 1957; London, 1958.
Stibbs, A. M. *The First Epistle General of Peter*, London, 1959.
Stonehouse, N. B. *The Witness of Luke to Christ*, London, 1951.
Stott, J. R. W. *The Preacher's Portrait*, London, 1961.
Surkau, H.-W. *Martyrien in jüdischer und frühchristlicher Zeit*, Göttingen, 1938.
Swete, H. B. *The Apocalypse of St. John*, London, 1906.
Tasker, R. V. G. (ed.). *The Greek New Testament*, Oxford and Cambridge, 1964.
Taylor, C. *Sayings of the Jewish Fathers*, 2nd ed., Cambridge, 1897.
Taylor, V. *The Formation of the Gospel Tradition*, London, 1952.
The Gospel according to St. Mark, London, 1952.
Tcherikover, V. A. and Fuks, A. *Corpus Papyrorum Judaicarum*, 3 vols., Cambridge, Mass., 1957ff.
Tenney, M. C. *John: The Gospel of Belief*, Grand Rapids, 1948.
Interpreting Revelation, Grand Rapids, 1957.
Til, C. van. *Common Grace and Witness-Bearing*. Phillipsburg, N.J., 1955.
Titus, E. L. *The Message of the Fourth Gospel*, New York, 1957.
Toynbee, A. J. *Greek Historical Thought*, London, 1952.
Turner, G. A. and Mantey, J. R. *The Gospel according to John*, Grand Rapids, n.d.
Ullmann, S. *Semantics. An Introduction to the Science of Meaning*, Oxford, 1962.
Vaux, R. de. *Ancient Israel*, London, 1961.
Vermes, G. *The Dead Sea Scrolls in English*, London, 1963.
Vliet, H. van. *No Single Testimony: A study in the adoption of the law of Deut. 19: 15 par. into the New Testament*, STRT, IV, Utrecht, 1958.
Westcott, B. F. *The Epistles of St. John*, London, 1886.
The Gospel according to St. John, 2 vols., London, 1908.
Westermann, C. *Basic Forms of Prophetic Speech*, trans. H. C. White, London, 1967.
Whiteley, D. E. H. *The Theology of St. Paul*, Oxford, 1964.
Wiles, M. F. *The Spiritual Gospel – The Interpretation of the Fourth Gospel in the Early Church*, Cambridge, 1960.
Winter, P. *On the Trial of Jesus*, Berlin, 1961.
Woods, J. *The Old Testament in the Church*, London, 1949.

B. ARTICLES

Allen, E. L. 'Controversy in the New Testament', *NTS*, 1 (1944), 143–9.

Anderson, F. I. 'The socio-juridical background of the Naboth incident', *JBL*, 85 (1966), 46–57.

Andrew, M. E. 'Falsehood and truth', *Int*, 17 (1963), 425–38.

Anonymous. 'A lawyer looks at Hebrews 9: 15–17', *EQ*, 40 (1968), 151–6.

Barr, A. 'The factor of testimony in the gospels', *ExpT*, 49 (1937–8), 401–8.

Barrett, C. K. 'The Holy Spirit in the Fourth Gospel', *JTS*, N.S., 1 (1950), 1–15.

'The Old Testament in the Fourth Gospel', *JTS*, 48 (1947), 155–69.

Barth, M. 'Jews and Gentiles: the social character of justification in Paul', *JES*, 5 (1968), 241–67.

Bartsch, H.-W. 'The concept of faith in Paul's letter to the Romans', *BR*, 13 (1968), 41–53.

Berrouard, M.-F. 'Le Paraclet, défenseur du Christ devant la conscience du croyant', *RSPT*, 33 (1949), 361–89.

Blair, P. A. 'The Death of Stephen', *TB*, 2 (1956–7), 2–3.

Bollier, J. A. 'Judgment in the Apocalypse', *Int*, 7 (1953), 14–25.

Borgen, P. 'Observations on the Midrashic character of John 6', *ZNW*, 54 (1963), 232–40.

Bowker, J. W. 'The origin and purpose of St. John's Gospel', *NTS*, 11 (1965), 398–408.

Broome, E. C. 'The sources of the Fourth Gospel', *JBL*, 63 (1944), 107–21.

Brown, R. E. 'The Paraclete in the Fourth Gospel', *NTS*, 13 (1967), 113–32.

Brown, R. M. 'True and false witness: architecture and the church', *TT*, 23 (1967), 521–37.

'The "Paraclete" in the light of modern research', *StudEv*, 4 (1968), 158–65.

Bultmann, R. 'Bekenntnis – und Liedfragmente im ersten Petrusbrief', *CN*, 11 (1947), 1ff.

Cadbury, H. J. 'Roman law and the trial of Paul', *BC*, v, 297–355.

Caird, G. B. 'Judgment and salvation: an exposition of John 12: 31–32', *CJT*, 2 (1956), 231–7.

'"Shake off the dust from your feet" (Mk. 6: 11)', *ExpT*, 81 (1969–70), 40–3.

'The transfiguration', *ExpT*, 67 (1956), 291–4.

Campenhausen, H. von. 'Das Bekenntnis im Urchristentum', *ZNW*, 63 (1972), 210–53.

Casey, R. P. 'Appended note on *martys*', *BC*, v, 30–7.

Catchpole, D. '"You have heard his blasphemy"', *TB*, 16 (1965), 10–18.

Chapman, J. 'We know that his testimony is true', *JTS*, 31 (1930), 379–87.

Charlier, J. P. 'L'exégèse johannique d'un précepte légal: Jean VIII 17', *RB*, 67 (1960), 503–15.

Clark, W. M. 'A legal background to the Yahwist's use of "good and evil" in Genesis 2–3', *JBL*, 88 (1969), 266–78.

Connor, W. T. 'Is Paul's doctrine of justification forensic?' *RE*, 40 (1943), 48–54.

Cox, L. G. 'John's witness to the historical Jesus', *BETS*, 9 (1966), 173–8.

Danby, H. 'The bearing of the Rabbinical code on the Jewish trial narratives in the Gospels', *JTS*, 21 (1920), 51–76.

Daube, D. 'Ego eimi', *JTS*, 50 (1949), 56–7.

Davies, J. G. 'The primary meaning of ΠΑΡΑΚΛΗΤΟΣ', *JTS*, N.S., 4 (1953), 35–8.

Deeks, D. 'The structure of the Fourth Gospel', *NTS*, 15 (1968), 107–29.

Dietrich, S. de. '"You are my witnesses" – a study of the church's witness', *Int*, 8 (1954), 273–9.

Dodd, C. H. 'The framework of the gospel narrative', *ExpT*, 43 (1931–2), 396–400.

'The prophecy of Caiaphas (Jn. xi. 47–53)', *Neotestamentica et Patristica* (1962), pp. 134–43.

Downing, J. 'Jesus and martyrdom', *JTS*, N.S. 14 (1963), 279–93.

Eaton, J. H. 'The king as God's witness', *ASTI*, 7 (1968–9), 24–40.

Fairweather, E. R. 'The Christian humanism of Thomas Aquinas', *CJT*, 12 (1966), 194–210.

Farrer, A. 'An examination of Mk. 13: 10', *JTS*, N.S., 7 (1956), 75–9.

Fenton, J. 'The order of the miracles performed by Peter and Paul in Acts', *ExpT*, 77 (1965–6), 381–3.

Filson, F. V. 'First John: purpose and message', *Int*, 23 (1969), 259–76.

Findlay, G. G. 'Christ's name for the Holy Spirit', *ExpT*, 12 (1900–1), 445–9.

Fischer, J. A. 'Notes on the literary form and message of Malachi', *CBQ*, 34 (1972), 315–20.

Fjelstad, O. J. 'The purpose of John's Gospel', *TF*, 1 (1929), 161–214.

Flowers, H. J. 'The convicting power of the Spirit', *ExpT*, 33 (1921–2), 247–50.

Formesyn, R. 'Le Sèmeion johannique et le sèmeion hellénistique', *ETL*, 38 (1962), 856–94.

Gelston, A. 'The missionary message of Second Isaiah', *SJT*, 18 (1965), 308–18.

Gershfield, E. M. 'Questio Quid Juris? – some thoughts on Jewish law', *HTR*, 61 (1968), 60–7.

Gilchrist, J. M. 'On what charge was St. Paul brought to Rome?', *ExpT*, 78 (1967), 264–6.

Glasson, T. F. 'The kerygma: is our version correct?', *HJ*, 51 (1953), 129–32.

Griffiths, D. R. 'Deutero–Isaiah and the Fourth Gospel', *ExpT*, 65 (1953–4), 355–60.

Günther, E. 'Zeuge und Märtyrer', *ZNW*, 47 (1956), 145–61.

Guthrie, D. 'The importance of signs in the Fourth Gospel', *VE* (1967), 72–83.

Halladay, W. L. 'Jeremiah's lawsuit with God', *Int*, 17 (1963), 280–7.

Hanson, A. 'John's citation of Psalm LXXXII reconsidered', *NTS*, 13 (1967), 363–7.

Harris, B. F. 'ΣΥΝΕΙΔΗΣΙΣ (Conscience) in the Pauline writings', *WTJ*, 24 (1961–2), 173–86.

Harrison, E. F. 'Jesus and the woman taken in adultery', *BS*, 103 (1946), 431–9.

'The testimony of Christian conduct', *BS*, 98 (1941), 459–68.

Harvey, J. 'Le "Rîb-Pattern", réquisitoire prophétique sur la rupture de l'Alliance', *Bib*, 43 (1962), 172–96.

Hastings, J. 'Paraclete – a Bible word study', *ExpT*, 10 (1898–9), 169–71.

Hemer, C. 'A note on II Corinthians 1: 9', *TB*, 23 (1972), 103–7.

Higgins, A. J. B. 'The words of Jesus according to St. John', *BJRL*, 49 (1967), 363–86.

Hill, D. 'Δίκαιοι as a quasi-technical term', *NTS*, 11 (1964–5), 296–302.

Hillyer, N. '"The Lamb" in the Apocalypse', *EQ*, 39 (1967), 228–36.

Hilmer, M. R. 'Major themes in the Fourth Gospel', *MTB*, 6 (1969), 1–14.

Hindley, J. C. 'Witness in the Fourth Gospel', *SJT*, 18 (1965), 319–37.

Hodges, Z. C. 'The two blind men at Jericho', *BS*, 122 (1965), 319–30.

Holdsworth, W. W. 'The informing spirit', *ExpT*, 21 (1909–10), 310–12.

Holladay, W. L. 'Jeremiah's lawsuit with God', *Int*, 17 (1963), 280–7.

Huffmon, H. B. 'The covenant lawsuit of the prophets', *JBL*, 78 (1959), 285–95.

Jansen, E. E. 'The first century controversy over Jesus as a revolutionary figure', *JBL*, 60 (1941), 261–72.

Jervell, J. 'The Law in Luke–Acts', *HTR*, 64 (1971), 21–36.

Jocz, J. 'The Jewish-Christian dialogue: a theological assessment', *GR*, 10 (1967), 187–203.

Johnson, A. F. 'A stylistic trait of the Fourth Gospel in the *Pericope Adulterae*?', *BETS*, 9 (1966), 91–6.

Johnston, G. 'OIKOYMENH and KOΣMOΣ in the New Testament', *NTS*, 10 (1964), 352–60.

Judge, E. A. 'The Decrees of Caesar at Thessalonica', *RTR*, 30 (1971), 1–7.

Kattenbusch, F. 'Die Märtyrtitel', *ZNW*, 4 (1903), 111–27.

Kennard, J. S. 'The Jewish provincial assembly', *ZNW*, 53 (1962), 25–51.

Kilpatrick, G. D. 'διαλέγεσθαι and διαλογίζεσθαι in the New Testament', *JTS*, N.S., 11 (1960), 338–40.

Kingsbury, E. C. 'The prophets and the Council of Yahweh', *JBL*, 83 (1964), 279–86.

Kleist, J. A. 'The two false witnesses (Mk. 14. 55ff.)', *CBQ*, 9 (1947), 321–3.

Lampe, G. W. H. 'The Lucan portrait of Christ', *NTS*, 2 (1956), 160–75.

'St. Peter's Denial', *BJRL*, 55 (1973), 346–68.

Langford, T. A. 'Giovanni Miegge on Jesus as a martyr', *Int*, 18 (1964), 183–90.

Lawton, T. A. D. 'A buried treasure in the Gospels', *EQ*, 39 (1967), 93–101.

Limburg, J. 'The root rîb and the prophetic lawsuit speeches', *JBL*, 88 (1969), 291–304.

Lindars, B. 'ΔΙΚΑΙΟΣΥΝΗ in Jn 16. 8 and 10' in *Mélanges Bibliques*, eds. A. Descamps and R. P. André de Halleux (Gembloux, n.d.), pp. 275–85.

Lofthouse, W. F. 'The Holy Spirit in the Acts and the Fourth Gospel', *ExpT*, 52 (1940–1), 334–6.

McCasland, S. V. 'The demonic "confessions" of Jesus', *JR*, 24 (1944), 33–6.

McCaughey, J. D. 'The Epistles of Paul: some notes on the translation of δικαιοσύνη and δικαιοῦν in Romans', *ABR*, 9 (1961),18–23.

BIBLIOGRAPHY

Macleod, J. 'The witness of Moses to Christ', *EQ*, 17 (1945), 5–12.
McDormand, T. B. 'Dialogue or witness?', *Christianity Today*, 10 (1965–6), 257.
McEachern, V. E. 'Dual witness and sabbath motif in Luke', *CJT*, 12 (1966), 267–80.
McKenzie, D. A. 'Judicial procedure at the town gate', *VT*, 14 (1964), 100–4.
McPolin, J. 'Mission in the Fourth Gospel', *ITQ*, 36 (1969), 113–22.
Manson, T. W. 'Martyrs and martyrdom', *BJRL*, 39 (1957), 463–84.
Manson, W. 'The ΕΓΩ ΕΙΜΙ of the messianic presence in the New Testament', *JTS*, 48 (1947), 137–45.
Marcel, P. 'Le Témoignage en parole et en actes', *RR*, 9 (1958), 36–47.
Marshall, I. H. 'Martyrdom and the parousia in the Revelation of John', *StudEv*, 4 (1968), 333–9.
Martin, R. P. 'Authority in the light of the apostolate, tradition and the canon', *EQ*, 40 (1968), 66–82.
Marzal, A. 'Mari clauses in "casuistic" and "apodictic" styles', *CBQ*, 33 (1971), 333–64, 492–509.
Masson, C. 'Le témoignage de Jean', *RHPR*, 38 (1950), 120–7.
Meeks, W. A. 'Galilee and Judea in the Fourth Gospel', *JBL*, 85 (1966), 159–69.
Menoud, P. H. 'Jésus et ses témoins', *EeT*, 23 (1960), 7–20.
'Le Plan des Actes des Apôtres', *NTS*, 1 (1954), 44–51.
Michael, J. H. 'The meaning of ἐξηγήσατο in St John 1. 18', *JTS*, 22 (1921), 13–16.
'Paul and Job: a neglected analogy', *ExpT*, 36 (1925), 67–70.
Michaelis, W. 'The trial of St. Paul at Ephesus', *JTS*, 29 (1928), 368–75.
Michel, O. 'Biblischen Bekennen und Bezeugen', *EvTh*, 2 (1935), 231–45.
'Ὁμολογέω', *TDNT*, v, 199–220.
Moss, R. V. 'The witnessing church in the New Testament', *TaL*, 3 (1960), 262–8.
Moule, C. F. D. 'A note on "under the fig tree" in John I. 48, 50', *JTS*, N.S., 5 (1954), 210–11.
'Punishment and retribution – an attempt to delimit their scope in New Testament thought', *SEA*, 30 (1965), 21–36.
Muilenburg, J. 'Literary form in the Fourth Gospel', *JBL*, 51 (1932), 40–53.
Napier, B. D. 'Community under Law', *Int*, 7 (1953), 404–17.
Nineham, D. E. 'Eye-witness testimony and the gospel tradition', *JTS*, N.S., 9 (1958), 13–25; 10 (1959), 243–52; 11 (1960), 253–64.

252

Osborne, H. 'Συνείδησις', *JTS*, 32 (1930–1), 167–79.

Piper, O. A. 'The origin of the gospel pattern', *JBL*, 78 (1959), 115–24.

Ploeg, J. van der. 'Studies in biblical law', *CBQ*, 12 (1950), 248–59, 416–27; 13 (1951), 28–43, 164–71, 296–307.

Pollard, T. E. 'Martyrdom and resurrection in the New Testament', *BJRL*, 55 (1972), 240–51.

Pond, E. 'The evidence of testimony', *BS*, 102 (1945), 179–93.

Pope, R. M. 'Studies in Pauline vocabulary; of boldness of speech', *ExpT*, 21 (1909–10), 236–8.

Potter, R. D. 'Topography and archaeology in the Fourth Gospel', *TU*, 73 (1959), 329–37.

Preiss, T. 'The inner witness of the Holy Spirit', *Int*, 7 (1953), 259–80.

Rétif, A. 'Témoignage et prédication missionaire dans les Actes des Apôtres', *NRT*, 73 (1951), 152–65.

Riddle, D. W. 'From Apocalypse to martyrology', *ATR*, 9 (1927), 260–80.

Riesenfeld, H. 'The meaning of the verb ἀρνεῖσθαι', *CN*, 11 (1947), 207–19.

Riga, P. 'Signs of glory – the use of "semeion" in St. John's Gospel', *Int*, 17 (1963), 402–24.

Robinson, D. W. B. 'To submit to the judgement of the saints', *TB*, 10 (1962), 1–8.

Robinson, H. W. 'The Council of Yahweh', *JTS*, 45 (1944), 151–7

Robinson, J. A. T. 'The most primitive christology of all?' *JTS*, N.S., 7 (1956), 177–89.

Ruland, V. 'Sign and sacrament', *Int*, 18 (1964), 450–62.

Ryan, W. F. J. 'The church as the servant of God in Acts', *Sc*, 15 (1963), 110–15.

Schlier, H. 'παρρησία', *TDNT*, v, 871–86.

Schrenk, G. 'ἐκδικέω', *TDNT*, ii, 442–6.

Simon, U. 'The poor man's ewe-lamb – an example of a juridical parable', *Bib*, 48 (1967), 207–42.

Smith, S. 'The threshing floor at the city gate', *PEQ* (1946), 4–14.

Snaith, N. H. 'The meaning of "The Paraclete"', *ExpT*, 57 (1945), 47–50.

Tenney, M. C. 'The meaning of "witness" in John', *BS*, 132 (1975), 229–41.

Thrall, M. E. 'The Pauline use of Συνείδησις', *NTS*, 14 (1967–8), 118–26.

Torrance, T. F. 'The mission of the church', *SJT*, 19 (1966), 129–43. 'A study in New Testament communication', *SJT*, 3 (1950), 298–313.

Trites, A. A. 'The importance of legal scenes and language in the Book of Acts', *NovT*, 16 (1974), 278–84.

'The idea of witness in the Synoptic Gospels – some juridical considerations', *Themelios*, 5 (1968), 18–26.

'*Martys* and martyrdom in the Apocalypse: a semantic study', *NovT*, 15 (1973), 72–80.

'The woman taken in adultery', *BS*, 131 (1974), 137–46.

'Two witness motifs in Acts 1: 8 and the Book of Acts', *Themelios*, 7 (1970), 17–22.

Unnik, W. C. van. 'The "Book of Acts" – the confirmation of the gospel', *NovT*, 4 (1960), 26–59.

'The purpose of St. John's Gospel, *StudEv*, 1 (1959), 382–411.

Vanhoye, A. 'Notre Foi, oeuvre divine d'après le quatrième évangile', *NRT*, 86 (1964), 337–54.

Vick, E. W. H. 'Faith and evidence', *AUSS*, 5 (1967), 181–99.

Vincent, P. L. H. 'La Palestine dans les papyrys ptolémaïques de Gerza', *RB*, 29 (1920), 182–3.

Waldow, H. E. von. 'The message of Deutero–Isaiah', *Int*, 22 (1968), 259–87.

Ward, R. B. 'Partiality in the assembly: James 2: 2–4', *HTR*, 62 (1969), 87–97.

Ward-Perkins, J. B. 'Memoria, martyr's tomb and martyr's church', *JTS*, N.S., 17 (1966), 20–37.

Weads, D. W. 'The Johannine double meaning', *RQ*, 13 (1970), 106–20.

Westermann, W. L. 'Slave transfer: deed or sale with affidavit of vendor', *Aeg*, 13 (1933), 229–31.

Williams, F. E. 'Is almsgiving the point of the "unjust steward"?', *JBL*, 73 (1964), 293–7.

INDEX OF REFERENCES

I. OLD TESTAMENT

II. APOCRYPHA AND PSEUDEPIGRAPHA

III. NEW TESTAMENT

IV. DEAD SEA SCROLLS

V. RABBINICAL LITERATURE

INDEX OF REFERENCES

VI. CLASSICAL AND HELLENISTIC AUTHORS AND EXTRA-CANONICAL CHRISTIAN WRITINGS

VII. MISCELLANEOUS

INDEX OF MODERN AUTHORS

INDEX OF GREEK WORDS